Ambedkar in Retrospect

Ambedkar in Retrospect

Essays on Economics, Politics and Society

EDITED BY
SUKHADEO THORAT
ARYAMA

INDIAN INSTITUTE OF DALIT STUDIES, NEW DELHI

RAWAT PUBLICATIONS
Jaipur • New Delhi • Bangalore • Guwahati • Kolkata

ISBN 978-81-316-0047-4

Published in association with
Indian Institute of Dalit Studies
Q 3, Green Park Extension, New Delhi 110 016
Phone: 011-41643981/82 Fax: 011-41643982
E-mail: iids@dalitstudies.org
Website: www.dalitstudies.org

Published by
Prem Rawat for **Rawat Publications**
Satyam Apts., Sector 3, Jawahar Nagar, Jaipur 302 004 (India)
Phone: 0141 265 1748 / 7006 Fax: 0141 265 1748
E-mail: info@rawatbooks.com
Website: www.rawatbooks.com

New Delhi Office
4858/24, Ansari Road, Daryaganj, New Delhi 110 002
Phone: 011-23263290

Also at *Bangalore, Guwahati* and *Kolkata*

Typeset by Rawat Computers, Jaipur
Printed at Chaman Enterprises, New Delhi

Contents

Acknowledgements

The compilation of various articles for this volume was a time-consuming and tedious process. Needless to add that this difficult task was made relatively easier by the help we received from a number of individuals. In the initial stages Dr. Umakant has helped in innumerable ways. We thank him for his efforts in bringing out this volume. Pramod and Narendra of IIDS typed the manuscript carefully and cheerfully. We also thank them for bringing their felicity with computers at our disposal. This book witnessed a much delayed and tortuous birth due to a variety of reasons. Considering this the remarkable patience and continued support extended to us by Pranit Rawat of Rawat Publications assumes added significance. We would like to express our gratitude to him and thank him profusely for the unflinching support he extended during the publication of this volume. Finally, the usual disclaimer applies.

Sukhadeo Thorat
Aryama

INTRODUCTION
Ambedkar in Retrospect

SUKHADEO THORAT AND ARYAMA

How to reform the Hindu social order and resolve the problems of those who suffered extreme deprivation due to the specific organization of Hindu social order is the problematic with which Ambedkar was preoccupied and devoted most of his intellectual, social and political efforts during the period between early 1920s to mid-1950s. Although Ambedkar began his intellectual quest with the existential and epistemological issues related to Hindu social order in general and the problems of former untouchables in particular, in later years, he directed his efforts towards multiple issues related to nation-building and socio-economic reconstruction of modern India. Ambedkar eventually ends up with a unique and distinctive perspective about the restructuring of Indian society, economy and polity. His views are not merely an assorted mix of disparate elements. In his writings, an alternative socio-economic and political framework emerges, wherein the pragmatic and the visionary aspects of his thinking meet on even grounds.

Ambedkar stood apart from his eminent contemporaries in three respects. First, he had the distinction of being a great scholar, social revolutionary and statesman—a combination that one rarely comes across. An intellectual giant and prolific writer, he had imbibed knowledge that was truly encyclopaedic. His erudition covered such diverse fields as law, constitution, economics, sociology, anthropology politics, and comparative religion. The range of topics, width of vision, depth and sophistication of analysis, rationality of outlook and essential humanity of the arguments that he came up with made him different from his illustrious contemporaries. Secondly, Ambedkar hardly ever wrote for literary purpose alone. In his scholarly pursuits as in his political activities, he was driven by a desire to comprehend the vital issues of his time and to find solutions to the problems of Indian society. With this motivation, he intervened, at times decisively in shaping the social, economic and political development of the nation during its formative stage. There was hardly any issue that arose between the early 1920s and the mid-1950s to which Ambedkar did not apply his razor-sharp analysis, whether it was the question of minorities, reorganization of states, partition, constitution or the political and economic framework for an independent India.

The third distinctive aspect of Ambedkar lies with the nature and kind of questions he delved into. What is probably most important in a thinker and intellectual is not so much the answers they provide but the questions they raise. Ambedkar raised questions that were simultaneously relevant and uncomfortable. Relevant as they were critical for the nation-in-making and uncomfortable as very few were willing to acknowledge the existence of those issues, let alone taking them up as central, so that they can be addressed, if not resolved. Ambedkar raised certain pressing issues that no one was willing to take up or deal with. However, once they were raised by Ambedkar in his characteristic style, he made it sure that they are not ignored and trampled over by the dominant players and parties that occupied and populated the rubric of all-pervasive anti-colonial nationalist aspirations. Ambedkar had strenuous relationship with his illustrious contemporaries. Part of this can be attributed to the issues he raised and his insistence about their centrality.

Ambedkar also lived in a period that was marked by events, which ultimately shaped the social, political and economic character of India as nation and he played a vital role in shaping the Indian nation. Ambedkar began his social and political activities around early 1920s. The period between 1920 and 1950 is marked by some crucial developments. During this period, India got political independence, partition took place, the issue of reorganization of states was addressed, and India got its Constitution, which laid down the political and economic framework and ultimately the policy framework, including the equal opportunity policy for lower castes. Ambedkar contributed in each of these events, especially through his academic writings. It is also necessary to mention that these events that shaped the nation-building process were shaped by the interplay of several perspectives on the making of nation and articulating a vision and programmes for the national development. It is pertinent to mention them here because it is during this period that important political and social organizations emerged. Through close interaction with various ideological strands Ambedkar's alternative ideological paradigm developed and took a concrete shape.

Gandhiji arrived on the political scene in the early 1920 and with this also emerged 'Gandhism' as an ideology, which in turn had a powerful influence on the question of social reform and political change in India, especially through the Congress. The Communist Party was established in 1920 in Kanpur and with this a formal Indian Communist Movement in India began, attendant with 'communism' as an ideology. Similarly, the strands of democratic socialist thoughts and associations associated with various variants of socialism also emerged during this period. The most prominent among them was Rammanohar Lohiya group. The Arya Samaj Movement, though started earlier, became very active in 1930s, particularly in northern India. At the other ideological extreme was RSS, formed in 1925 in Maharashtra, the state where Ambedkar came from. This is also the period during which non-Brahmanism movement was quite active in Madras with similar initiatives in Maharashtra. Last but not the least, this is also the period of an active Dalit Movement initiated and led by Ambedkar.

It is necessary to recognize that all these movements revolved around the issue of reforming Hindu society in general and untouchables in particular on their agenda in one way or other. Therefore, Ambedkar came in constant contact with most of them and fairly close with two of the ideological strands, namely, Gandhism and Marxism and latter with democratic socialism. The interaction and experience was facilitated by the fact that the centre stage of these movements was western India – more particularly the Maharashtra state and within Maharashtra, city of Bombay – the state and city where Ambedkar came from. Ambedkar not only interacted with Gandhians, Marxists, the socialists, Hindu Mahasabha and backward caste movements but in the initial years, he was also associated with some of them. Through interactions and experiences that grew out of these, Ambedkar's alternative ideological position took a concrete shape in the latter years.

As a background to the papers in the volume, therefore, we thought it appropriate to present the position of Ambedkar on the central issues with which Ambedkar was preoccupied and the issues, which continue to confront the Indian society and its polity and economy and thereby provide a framework for the readers.

First, we trace the encounter of Ambedkar with the alternative ideological paradigms on the issue of restructuring of Hindu social order and the economic and political framework for India that they entailed. We concentrated on two of them, namely, Gandhism and Marxism with which he came in close contact in order to highlight the similarities and differences between Ambedkar and other contesting ideological positions. Secondly, we examine as to how the limitations of these two ideological approaches (in Ambedkar's view) in explaining as well as solving the problems of Indian society induce Ambedkar to search for an alternative perspective, which later on came to be known as 'Ambedkarism'.[1]

Gandhism and Ambedkar

Ambedkar and Gandhiji began social and political activities for eradication of untouchability almost in same period, i.e., in the early 1920s and in fact also worked together for a short period of time. However, soon, Ambedkar could not find much common ground for cooperation and collaboration and initiated activities through his own separate and distinct platform. It is, therefore, necessary to state the differences in the positions of Gandhiji and Ambedkar on the question of restructuring of Hindu society as many ills and evils of our society that troubled them, continue to have significant influence and powerful/guiding force even today. The only common ground for Gandhiji and Ambedkar is their concern for the problem of untouchability, as they both worked for its eradication. In fact, their role in this respect was complementary in some respect, in so far as that Gandhiji's taking the issue of untouchability brought it on national scene and led to its national recognition, if not its rectification/solution.

Notwithstanding this common concern the explanation and solution offered by Gandhiji and Ambedkar with respect to untouchability differs significantly. In this context, at least three important differences about Gandhiji's position need to be reiterated/ understood. More often than not Gandhiji's views on untouchability and caste are interpreted in a manner which contravene the writings of Gandhiji himself.

Firstly, Gandhiji opposed the practice of untouchability but believed that untouchability has no serious connection with Hindu social organization, namely, the caste system. Secondly, till 1922, Gandhiji supported caste system. Ambedkar quotes Gandhiji on this issue:

> I believe that if Hindu society has been able to stand because it is founded on the caste system. Caste has a readymade means for spreading primary education, caste has a political basis. Caste can perform judicial function. I believe that interdining or intermarriages are not necessary for promoting national unity. The caste system cannot be said to be bad because it does not allow interdining or intermarriage between different castes. To destroy caste system and adopt Western European social system means that Hindus must give up principle of hereditary occupation which is the soul of caste system. The caste system is a natural order of society. This being my views I am opposed to all those who are out to destroy the caste system.[2]

However, in 1925, Gandhiji became critical of caste system and observed:

> I gave support to caste system because it stands for restraint. But at present caste does not mean restraint, it means limitations. Restraint is glorious and helps to achieve freedom. But limitation is like a

> chain. It binds. There is nothing commendable in castes as they exist today. They are contrary to the tenets of the shastras. The number of castes is infinite and there is bar against intermarriage. This is not a condition of elevation. It is a state of fall.[3]

Gandhiji suggested an alternative to the caste system:

> The best remedy is that small castes should fuse themselves into a big caste. There should be four such big castes so that we may reproduce the old system of four varnas.[4]

The varna system suggested by Gandhiji is, however, different from that of Arya Samaj or Geeta. The varna system of Geeta and Arya Samaj simply labels the people in four varnas depending on the basis of occupation but there is freedom for individual to move from one varna to another, if the occupation of the individual changes. So, the process of learning (or the taking of occupation of other varnas) is open and free. Gandhiji's concept of the varna is different, in the sense that it makes the learning process open to all varnas, but it does not allow them to use acquired skill and knowledge for earning a living through an occupation that is other than the occupation assigned by the varna system. The principle of hereditary occupation is the basis of new varna system of Gandhiji. So, Gandhiji's concept of varna is close to the traditional concept of caste system. It only makes small concession to the traditional caste system in so far as it allows every varna access to education or learning, but it restricts the use of knowledge for taking the occupation of other varnas than your own. Consequently, the untouchables may have access to education and skill learning/formation but they should continue to carry their traditional or hereditary occupation. Thus, in Ambedkar's view, the alternative concept of varna, as prescribed by Gandhiji, is different from that of traditional varna/caste system in only some respect in so far as it makes learning open to everyone.

Thirdly, Gandhiji denies any connection of caste system with the ideology of Hindu religion. As we shall see later, Ambedkar differs with Gandhiji on each of these points, namely, interconnection of untouchability with caste system and of the relationship of untouchability and caste system with Hindu religious ideology and Gandhiji's modified varna system as an ideal form of social organization. Therefore, there has been a much less common ground on the question of restructuring of Hindu social order between Gandhiji and Ambedkar.

On economic issues also there is difference between Ambedkar and Gandhiji. Gandhiji advocated the concept of 'trusteeship' based on private property, and harmonious class-relations.[5] Ambedkar, on the other hand, favoured economy based on common ownership of property, at least with respect to ownership of agricultural land and key and basic industries were to remain within the jurisdiction of the public sector. Additionally he was in favour of scientific development and promotion of rationality and a nationalized insurance cover for every citizen of India.

Ambedkar and Indian Marxists

Besides Gandhiji, Ambedkar came in close contact with Indian Communists, particularly during early 1930s and the caste and class paradigm of Ambedkar was formed during 1930s in course of engagement and confrontation with Indian Marxists. In 1930s Ambedkar worked quite closely with Marxists in Bombay through his own political platform, namely, Independent Labour Party; however, he developed differences and as a result differed on the issue of interrelationship between class and caste, at least on three main points. Before we identify those points it must be mentioned at the outset that Ambedkar's ideas on the economic system were mainly inspired by the Marxist framework and Buddha's teachings. In the lecture on Buddha and Karl Marx, Ambedkar observed:

> What remains of the Karl Marx is a residue of fire, small but still very important. The residue in my view consists of four items:
>
> (1) That function of philosophy is to reconstruct the world and not to waste its time in explaining the origin of the world.
>
> (2) That there is a conflict of interest between class and class.
>
> (3) That private ownership of property brings power to one class and sorrow to another through exploitation.

(4) That it is necessary for the good of society that the sorrow be removed by the abolition of private property.[6]

Thus, Ambedkar recognized that there is a conflict between classes and private ownership of property is the root cause of deprivation and exploitation of the poor masses and that it can be removed by economic reorganization of society on socialistic pattern. Ambedkar thus agreed with ends that Marxism aspired for, i.e., the socialist objectives. However, he differed with Marx on the means of realizing the objectives and purposes enshrined/entwined with socialism. He advocated democratic means and believed that though democratic means are slow but far more enduring, stable and permanent. This was the first major difference with the Indian Marxists who argued for abrupt uprooting of the entrenched order.

The second difference was on the question of interlinkage between caste and class. Communists took no note of caste problem during the social reform movement of Ambedkar as they assumed that the explanations of all social problems could be provided in terms of class analysis alone. Ambedkar strongly insisted on the recognition of caste and untouchability as a crucial social reality that required an analysis and understanding, independent and separate from the economic-centred class analysis. He differed with the communists on class-caste paradigm on two main grounds. Ambedkar believed that the caste system involves exploitation and hence argued for undertaking reform of Hindu society as a precondition for both political and social reforms. On the first question Ambedkar asked as to whether socialists could ignore the problem arising out of the prevalent Hindu social order. Ambedkar observed:

> They propound that man is an economic creature, and his life is governed by economic facts, that property is the only source of power. They, therefore, preach that political reform by equalization of property must have precedence over every other kind of reform.[7]

Ambedkar argued that economic power is not the only source and basis of power. The social and religious status of an individual can also be a source of power and therefore it has to be dealt with. On second issue Ambedkar emphasized the necessity of undertaking reform of Hindu social order as a precondition for both political and socialist reforms. Ambedkar raises the question, in an unequivocal and terse manner, characteristic of his mode of thinking:

> Can you have economic reform without first bringing about a reform of the social order?... it is not enough for Marxist to say that I believe in perfect equality in the treatment of various classes. To say that such a belief is enough is to disclose a complete lack of understanding of what is involved in socialism. If socialism is a practical programme and is not merely an ideal, distant and far off, the question for socialist is not whether he believes in equality. The question for him is that whether he minds one class ill-treating and suppressing another as a matter of system, as a matter of principle and thus allow tyranny and oppression to continue to divide one class from another.[8]

In the opinion of Ambedkar, Dalits will not join in revolution for equalization of property, unless they know that after the revolution is achieved they will be treated equally and that there will be no discrimination of caste and creed. Ambedkar argued:

> Mere assurance of Marxists is not good enough – the assurance must be the assurance proceeding from much deeper foundation, namely, the mental attitude of compatriots towards one another in their spirit of personal equality and fraternity. Can it be said that the proletariat of India, poor as it is, recognize no distinction except that of rich and poor? Can it be said that the poor in India recognize no distinctions of caste or creed, high and low? If the fact is that they do, what unity of front can be expected from such proletariat in its action against the rich? How can there be a revolution if the proletariat cannot present a united front.[9]

Ambedkar further argued that to excite the proletariat to bring about an economic revolution, Karl Marx told them:

> "You have nothing to lose except your chains". But the artful ways in which the social and religious rights are distributed among the different castes, whereby some have more and some have less, make

> the slogan of Karl Marx quite useless to excite the Hindus against the caste system. Castes form a graded system of sovereignties, high and low, which are jealous of their status and which know that if a general dissolution came, some of them stand to lose more of their prestige and power than others do. You cannot, therefore, have a general mobilization of the Hindus, to use a military expression, for an attack on the caste system.[10]

Therefore, in view of Ambedkar, the socialists must recognise that the problem of social reform is fundamental for the participation of Dalits in the socialistic revolution. Ambedkar put the case for social reform as follows:

> But the base is not the building. On the basis of the economic relations a building is erected of religious, social and political institutions. This building has just as much truth (reality) as the base. If we want to change the base, then first the building that has been constructed on it has to be knocked down. In the same way, if we want to change the economic relations of society, then first the existing social, political and other institutions will have to be destroyed.[11]

As early as 1936 Ambedkar argued:

> The social order prevalent in India is a matter which socialist must deal with, that unless he does so he cannot achieve his revolution and that if he does achieve it as a result of good fortune he will have to grapple with it if he wishes to realize his ideal, is a proposition which in my opinion is incontrovertible. He will be compelled to take account of caste after revolution if he does not take account of it before revolution. This is only another way of saying that, turn in any direction you like, caste is the monster that crosses your path. You cannot have political reform, you cannot have economic reform, unless you kill this monster.[12]

The Indian Marxists did not show much concern about the problem of caste during the most part of Ambedkar's movement (between the 1920s through 1950s) nor did they provide theoretical explanation for the caste-class paradigm in Indian context. The primacy of class in the materialistic interpretation of history was a touchstone, a fundamental tenet for Indian Marxists. Taking caste seriously, as it were, was a departure from the fundamental tenet and canon of Marxism. It seems to them, caste has only residual value and their energies were exclusively devoted to class analysis. They were not inclined to probe the possible links between class and caste and how they might maintain irreducibility, while reinforcing each other.

There was no theoretical attempt that sought to analyze the interrelation between institution like caste and class as well as enquire about the 'material basis for caste' that allowed caste to maintain its hold in the Indian context for centuries. The shifting and continuous material basis of caste not only perpetuated an exploitative system but also planted its root deep in the Indian setting. So much so that caste turned into one of the mode of being synonymous with tradition in India. Problematizing the interrelationship between class and caste holds possibilities that are lost from the theoretical horizons, when we insist only on the primacy of class or caste as the ultimate factors of analysis. Indeed, there are other important pragmatic and practical considerations that can be served only by analyzing their interconnection and intersection. Ambedkar underscored this requirement much earlier than the theoretical debates that have emerged in recent decades.

The blindness and loss in face of the question of caste exhibited by Indian Marxists during Ambedkar's movement was not in tune with the insights that were available within Marxism itself. It appears that the limitations of insisting on primacy of economic determination as the sole factor in structuring social life and its reproduction came to Engels much earlier. Writing about the economic determination thesis and its primacy in Marxism, Engels observed:

> ... According to the materialist conception of history, the ultimately determining element in history is the production and reproduction of real life. More than this neither Marx nor I has ever asserted.

> Hence, if somebody twists this into saying that the economic element is the only determining one he transforms that proposition into a meaningless, abstract, senseless phrase. The economic situation is the basis, but the various elements of the super-structure – political forms of the class struggle and its results, constitutions established by the victorious class after a successful battle, etc. judicial forms, and even the reflexes of all these actual struggles in the brains of the participants, political, juristic, philosophical theories, religious views, and their further development into systems of dogmas – also exercise their influence upon the course of the historical struggles and in many cases preponderate in determining their form. There is an interaction of all these elements in which, amidst all the endless host of accidents, the economic movement finally asserts itself as necessary.[13]

Engels further observed:

> Marx and I are ourselves partly to blame for the fact that the younger people sometimes lay more stress on the economic side than is due to it. We had to emphasize the main principle vis-à-vis our adversaries, who denied it, and had not always the time, the place, or the opportunity to give their due to the other elements involved in the interaction. But when it came to presenting a section of history, that is, to making a practical application, it was a different matter and there no error was permissible. Unfortunately, however, it happens only too often that people think they have fully understood a new theory and can apply it without more ado from the moment they have assimilated its main principles, and even those not always correctly. And I cannot exempt many of the more recent 'Marxists' from this reproach, for the most anything rubbish has been produced in this quarter.[14]

However, the Indian Marxists ignored this caution and warning of Engels and its application to the Indian situation and their response during most part of the Ambedkar's social reform movement between early 1920s to mid-1950s provides more than enough evidence required to argue this issue further.

Ambedkar's Alternative

After having recognized the limitations of Gandhism and Marxism in Indian context Ambedkar developed his distinctive approach attuned to the specific situation in India. Ambedkar favoured democratic socialism for economic reorganization of the capitalist economy and choose Buddhism for social reconstruction or reorganization of Hindu society. He thus opposed both capitalism and Hindu social organization based on caste system including Brahmanism and all those elements in Hindu religious philosophy which support directly and indirectly the doctrine of inequality and ritualism, fatalism, blind faith and ignorance. Ambedkar stood against Hindu theory of karma and rebirth, which goes against rational scientific enquiry and temper.

We first discuss the concept of democratic socialism developed by Ambedkar and enquire about the grounds and reasons he singled out for defending democratic socialism. This is necessary because the concept of socialism, as propagated by the democratic socialists, particularly the Indian democratic socialists, is varied in nature and lacks clarity. Ambedkar's opposition to capitalism and its alternative in socialism have grown out of his interpretation of the democratic ideal. In Ambedkar's view, the capitalistic system and the parliamentary form of government, despite their coexistence for a long time, were marked with some painful contradictions. As early as 1943, he observed: "those who are living under the capitalistic form of industrial organization and under the form of political organization called parliamentary democracy must recognize the contradiction of their systems".[15] The first contradiction is between the political and the economic system. Ambedkar contended, "in politics, equality, in economics, inequality. One vote, one man, one value is our political maxim. Our maxim in economics is a negation of our political maxim. The second contradiction was between fabulous wealth and abject poverty coexisting".[16]

Referring to the first, Ambedkar observed that although parliamentary democracy had progressed by expanding the idea of equality of social and economic opportunity. The hope, however, had not been fulfilled, on account of wrong ideology. Speaking about ideology, he said that what had adversely affected parliamentary democracy was the idea of 'freedom of contract'. Freedom of contract had become sanctified and was upheld in the name of liberty. Parliamentary democracy took no notice of economic inequalities and the result of freedom of contract on the parties to the contract was to perpetuate if not deepen inequality, if they were unequal parties to a 'free' contract. In the name of freedom of contract, the strong were given an opportunity to defraud the weak. The result was that the parliamentary system, in claiming to be a protagonist of liberty, had continuously added to the economic wrongs of the poor, the downtrodden and dispossessed classes.

In addition, this ideology did not entertain the possibility that parliamentary democracy might not succeed or that there would be serious discontent, if these were not founded on social and economic democracy. Social and economic democracy is the tissues and fibres to constitute parliamentary democracy. Parliamentary democracy developed a passion only for liberty. But liberty to be real must be accompanied by certain social and economic conditions. First, there had to be social equality. Traditional and entrenched privileges tilted the balance of social action in favour of their possessors. The more equal the social rights of citizens, the more able they will be to utilize their freedom. Therefore, if liberty was to move to its appointed end, it was important that there should be social equality. In the second place, there had to be economic security. Ambedkar wrote:

> A man may be free to enter any vocation he may choose... yet if he is deprived of security in employment he becomes prey of mental and physical servitude, incompatible with the very essence of liberty. The perpetual fear of the morrow, its haunting sense of impending disaster, its fitful search of happiness and beauty, which perpetually eludes, shows that without economic security, liberty is not worth having. Men may well be free and yet remain unable to realize the purpose of freedom.[17]

Parliamentary democracy, Ambedkar wrote, made not even a nodding acquaintance with economic equality. "It failed to realize the significance of equality and did not even endeavour to strike a balance between liberty and equality, with the result that liberty swallowed equality and thus left a progeny of inequalities".[18]

Extending the argument further, Ambedkar observed that in a social economy based on private enterprise and pursuit of personal gain, many people both employed and unemployed had to relinquish their rights in order to earn their living and subject themselves to be governed by a private employer. The assumption in the capitalistic system was that the state should refrain from intervention in private affairs— economic and social— that would result in liberty. Ambedkar observed that "but for whom was liberty? To the landlord to raise rent and reduce wages, and for the capitalist to increase hours of work and reduce the rate of wages? It could not be otherwise. For an economic system employing armies of workers producing goods *en masse* at a regular interval, someone had to make rules so that the worker would work and the wheel of industry would turn. If the state did not do it the private employer would do it, and do it, to his advantage".[19]

To protect the right of the employed as well as unemployed to liberty and to the pursuit of happiness, the most that democratic governments did was to impose arbitrary restraints in the political domain. But, such a remedy was of doubtful value. Given that even under adult suffrage all legislatures and governments are controlled by the more powerful, an appeal to the legislature to intervene was a very precarious safeguard against the invasion of the liberty of the less powerful. As an alternative, he suggested limiting not only the power of government to impose arbitrary restraints but to limit the more powerful individuals as well. Ambedkar favoured limiting and regulating the control that more powerful enjoyed over peoples' economic life.

Therefore, Ambedkar argued that the state had to intervene actively to plan the economic life of people to provide for equitable distribution of wealth. Ambedkar proposed state ownership in agriculture with equitable access to agricultural land and a modified form of state socialism in the field of industry and insurance with the remaining economic activities left with the private sector. The state should be bound to supply the necessary capital for agriculture and industry. Public sector enterprises were to be run most efficiently, with the highest level of productivity possible. Ambedkar was indeed concerned about the efficiency of the public sector institutions and therefore emphasized that the efficiency and not merely welfare should be the rationale for state-run enterprises. He observed, for example, as regards the structure and nature of the Damodar Valley Corporation (in development of which he was involved in 1942-43 as Minister of Labour):

> I am not prepared to accept that the project should be run on non-profitable basis. Nor do I accept that any profit which may accrue after meeting all proper charges shall only be used for reduction of capital expenditure and for betterment of the system. It is impossible to forget the fact that a large part of the misery of the people of the country is entirely due to the inadequate revenue resources of the government. The object of the government business concern is to enable the government to make a profit as any business concern does in order to supplement its resources. I am therefore quite unable to see any justification for ruling out this important purpose from the contribution of Damodar Valley Authority.[20]

Ambedkar saw no alternative to political democracy and therefore firmly believed in it as an appropriate form of political organization, but at the same time he emphasized the need to strengthen the social and economic foundation for a smooth functioning of democracy, which he saw as the tissues and fibres of political democracy by making socialism as part of the constitution. So, his concept of state socialism is 'constitutional state socialism with parliamentary democracy'. He, therefore, advocated a political-economic framework, namely, constitutional state socialism with parliamentary democracy. This combination was necessary to ensure that the social and economic organizations would be more egalitarian and consequently, the political means, i.e., the parliamentary democracy, would become more meaningful to the poor and underprivileged.

Alternative to Hindu Social and Religious Order

Ambedkar recognized and emphasized the need for not only social reforms but also economic restructuring of the Hindu social order, for he believed that exclusive reliance on economic equalization may not change the exploitative social, religious and ideological sub-structure of the caste system altogether, although it may reduce its intensity. So he saw a greater need to have social reform movement. Ambedkar's in-depth analysis of Hindu social and religious order leads to the firm conclusion that roots of untouchability and discrimination lie in social and material sub-structure of the Hindu social and religious order. Ambedkar believed :

> Hindu observed untouchability and caste not because they are inhuman or wrong headed. They observed caste because they are deeply religious. People are not wrong in observing caste. .....In my view... what is wrong is their religion, which has inculcated this notion of caste..... If this is correct then obviously the enemy, you must grapple with, is not the people who observed caste, but the Shashtras, which teach them this religion of caste. Criticizing and radicalizing people... is a futile method of achieving the desired end. The real remedy is to destroy the belief in the sanctity of Shashtras... how do you except to succeed, if you allow the Shashtras to continue to mould the belief and the opinion of the people... Reformers working for removal of untouchability... do not seem to realize that the acts of the people are merely the result of their belief inculcated upon their mind by the Shashtras and the people will not change their conduct until they cease to believe in the sanctity of the Shashtras on which their conduct is founded.[21]

Ambedkar therefore suggested:

> To agitate for and to organize inter-caste dinners and inter-caste marriages is like forced feeding brought about by artificial means. Make every man and woman free from the thralldom to the Shashtras, cleanse their minds of the pernicious notions founded on the Shashtras, and he or she will inter dine and inter marry, without your telling him or her to do so.[22]

In Ambedkar's view the real remedy is to replace the social relations governed by the caste system by the one based on equality, justice and fraternity. It is in this context, Ambedkar favoured the social philosophy of Buddha, which he thought would help to restructure the social, cultural and political relations to promote well-being of majority of people.

Besides the ideological writings, Ambedkar also contributed on various pressing issues that emerged during 1920-1950. On each of the issues and problems, Ambedkar wrote in an authoritative manner. It needs to be recognized that all of his academic writings were driven by a desire to understand the vital issues of his times and to find solutions to the problems of Indian society. His writings thus reflect his vision of India. It is in this sense Ambedkar was deeply involved in designing the destiny of India. Apart from academic writings, as the member of Bombay Legislative Council in early 1920s and 30s, as minister during British period (1942-46), as law minister in independent India, and after independence as a member of parliament (Rajya Sabha), Ambedkar contributed significantly on formulation of policy as well as their implementation.

This volume, therefore besides reflecting and representing the theoretical issues that are implicated in the writings of Ambedkar, also attempts to capture the position of Ambedkar on issues whose relevance is acutely felt even today. Dealt primarily by academicians in a seminar who are engaged in discourse on social, political and economic issues, the volume includes twenty papers on some of the central issues, if not all, on which Ambedkar has devoted his academic efforts. These are: Ambedkar's thoughts on economic development and planning, socialism and democracy, issues related to nationalism, representation and formation of states, Panchayati Raj and political decentralization, caste discrimination and untouchability. Ambedkar's perspective on history, question of Hindu women, education and Ambedkar's solution for social exclusion in Indian society is also taken up by various contributors in this volume. The canvas of Ambedkar's writings is vast, and the issues discussed in this volume are a modest attempt to mirror the breadth and vision of the writings of Ambedkar.

Looking back at Ambedkar is an enriching and rewarding experience. Ambedkar in retrospect is not an attempt to fathom a bygone historical period and personality, whose writing needs to be dusted off and vestiges recovered from the debilitating effects of time and shifting patterns of social forces. Ambedkar is critical and relevant. Notwithstanding the current academic notions of nuances and subtle distinctions and criticality, even today, the dalit social reality is regrettably black and white. To emphasize the critical importance of caste and in painting an authentic picture of problems that beset India, Ambedkar remains unrivalled till date. The issues and problems of dalits were presented as they were and still are in India, in Ambedkar's account. However, his description of dalit reality is not paralysing, despite the horrific and inhuman reality within which dalit lives are confined. Ambedkar provides an enabling, emancipatory and liberating schema, an egalitarian vision and a promise that has remained largely unfulfilled. Ambedkar's critical analysis of Hindu social order and the hold it had over the masses was unmasked layer by layer, through the sophisticated and nuanced analysis that marked his writings. His insight about its operating ideological mechanisms and day-to-day machinations that sustains the Hindu social order emerges in a clear and concrete terms in his accounts. Nuances and subtle distinctions cohere in the systematic treatment that Ambedkar brings to the topics and themes he took up during his lifetime. Ambedkar in retrospect is India at prospect that confronts the substantive predicaments and momentous issues that beset India in the present, closely and critically, while charting out a trajectory of social transformation.

We believe that this overview of Ambedkar's position on the social, political and economic system and vision of Ambedkar on issues that continue to confront us as critical, will help in unfolding the various dimensions related to the contemporary society and its polity and economy and facilitate a better grasp of issues at stake.

In a number of his writings, Ambedkar expressed/shared his anguish about 'the strategy of silence' deployed by the mainstream academics toward his writings. However, he was sanguine about the future generation. Ambedkar noted in introduction to one of his books, *Who Were the Sudras*, "If the Hindus of this generation do not take note of what I have to say, I am sure the future generations will. For I take consolation in the words of poet Bhavabhuti who said:

> 'Time is infinite and earth is vast,
> some day there will be born a man
> who will appreciate
> what I have said'.[23]

Notes

1. Gail Omvedt, *Dalits and the Democratic Revolution: Dr Ambedkar and the Dalit Movement in Colonial India*, Sage Publications, Delhi, 1994, pp. 223-59.
2. B.R. Ambedkar, *What Congress and Gandhi Have Done to the Untouchables,* Thacker, Bombay, 1945, p. 276.
3. Ibid, p. 277.
4. B.R. Ambedkar, "Annihilation of Caste" in Vasant Moon (1979) *Dr. Babasaheb Ambedkar, Writing and Speeches,* Vol. 1, Education Department, Government of Maharashtra, Mumbai, p. 129.
5. B.R. Ambedkar, *What Congress and Gandhi Have Done to the Untouchables,* Thacker, Bombay, 1945, p. 275.
6. B.R. Ambedkar, (1956) 'Buddha and Karl Marx' in Vasant Moon (1987), *Dr. Babasaheb Ambedkar Writing and Speeches*, Vol. 3, Education Department, Government of Maharashtra, Mumbai, p. 441.
7. B.R. Ambedkar, "Annihilation of Caste", p. 107.
8. Ibid., p. 109.
9. Ibid., p. 47.
10. Ibid., p. 46.
11. Gail Omvedt, *Dalits and the Democratic Revolution: Dr Ambedkar and the Dalit Movement in Colonial India*, Sage Publications, Delhi, 1994, p. 228.
12. B.R. Ambedkar, "Annihilation of Caste", p. 47.

13. Lewis Feuer (ed.), *Marx and Engles: Basic Writings on Politics and Philosophy*, Anchor Books, New York, 1959, p. 477.
14. Ibid., p. 478.
15. B.R. Ambedkar, Labour and Parliamentary Democracy Speech, Indian Federation of Labour, Delhi, Bombay, 17th September 1943, p. 106-110.
16. B.R. Ambedkar, State and Minorities: What are their Rights and How to Secure them in the Constitution, in Vasant Moon, *Dr. Babasaheb Ambedkar Writing and Speeches,* Vol. 1, Education Department, Government of Maharashtra , Mumbai, 1979, p. 408.
17. B.R. Ambedkar, Labour and Parliamentary Democracy Speech, p. 110
18. B.R. Ambedkar, State and Minorities: What are their Rights and How to Secure them in the Constitution, p. 428.
19. Ibid., p. 429.
20. Minutes of the First Conference on Damodar River Valley Project, File No. DW-105(1)/45 DWI, Finance Department, Planning Division.
21. B.R. Ambedkar, "Annihilation of Caste", p. 68.
22. Ibid., p. 69.
23. B.R. Ambedkar, *Who were the Shudras*, Thacker, Bombay, 1946, p. 15.

Part One Economic Development and Planning

1 Economic System, Development, and Economic Planning

SUKHADEO THORAT

Babasaheb Ambedkar began his academic career as a professional economist. He obtained his PhD in economics from Columbia University (USA) during 1913-16, and DSc, also in economics, from London School of Economics (UK) during 1917-18. Both the PhD and DSc theses were published in the early 1920s. As an academic economist Ambedkar has made significant contributions to the various fields of economics. In the early period of his academic career (1915-25) the focus of his writings was mainly centred on themes like public finance, monetary and international economics, particularly during the colonial period. In later period the focus shifted to other economic issues. Later period's economic writings covered a wide range of interrelated issues, varying from perspective on economic development and planning, economic systems, to political economy of caste system and others.[1] Besides academic writings, he was also involved in actual process of policy making and economic planning, particularly as a minister (in charge of labour, irrigation and power portfolio) during 1942-46. Ambedkar also expressed his views on several policy issues in Bombay Legislative Assembly and in the Parliament as a member of these bodies, particularly on the issues related to water and power development and labour. In this paper, I propose to discuss Ambedkar's economic thoughts, particularly on economic systems, economic development, planning, agriculture development, and political economy of caste system and issues related to water resources development, labour and others. In doing this I shall follow the writings in sequence of time in which Ambedkar has written and also attempt to capture the changes that had occurred in his economic thinking over a period of time.

On Economic Development

We begin with his views on economic development. Ambedkar's writing on the issue of economic development goes back to 1918, when he participated in an academic debate on the problem of small holdings, through a thought-provoking paper.[2] Although the paper centres on the problem of small holdings, however, in its formulation and solution, the analysis was placed in a much wider theoretical framework of economic development. It began with a discussion on small holdings, went on to an economic analysis of agricultural backwardness and ended with its solution in industrial development. It thus laid down a theoretical and policy framework for general economic development with many policy implications.

The underlying assumption in the academic discussion was that the small and scattered landholdings were economically inefficient. How to consolidate these small, scattered and economically inefficient holdings and, once consolidated, how to maintain the size at an economically viable level? The solution put forward by the academic economists was two-fold, namely, the voluntary exchange of owned land to reduce the parcelling and to increase the size; and, compulsory consolidation by the government of farms of the village, including restricted sale of right of occupancy. The compulsory or voluntary restriction was to be decided on the principle of 'economic holding', which was to be fixed on the basis of acreage of land owned. The lower land ceiling was to be fixed in such a way that it would be "a parcel of land necessary to keep fully engaged and support one family" or a "holding which allows a man the chance of producing sufficient to support himself and his family in reasonable comfort, after paying his necessary expenses". The solution offered was more by way of administrative and legal measures and treated the consolidation of holdings as a practical problem.

Ambedkar approached the issue differently. In his view, this issue was essentially an issue of economic factors underlying the farm size and is not related to legal or administrative measures. He differed from others on two important grounds: one, the definition of economic holding and, two, the economic principles underlying the size of holdings and hence the solutions of their enlargement. While the others viewed an economic holding from the standpoint of consumption rather than of production, Ambedkar maintained that consumption was not the correct standard. True economic relation could subsist only between total output and investment. If output paid for all the investment, no producer would think of closing his farm. One could thus speak of the farm as a paying economic unit in terms of production and not consumption. Production in turn was not governed by land as a factor alone but was the result of the use of combination of land, capital and labour. It was the right or wrong proportion of other factors of production to a unit of land (and not the size of land alone) that rendered a piece of land economic or uneconomic. A small farm might be economic as well as a large farm.

According to Ambedkar, the problem of small holdings was not fundamental but derived from the parent evil of maladjustment in the social economy. The household with a small holding was unable to acquire and use factors of production in the right combination. While there was too little capital (in the form of capital inputs and implements) and land, the supply of labour was in excess. Land and capital being in short supply, they were relatively expensive compared to labour and hence became major constraints. The solution, therefore, was to increase capital in the form of capital goods and implements and reduce the use of labour. The remedy was to siphon off the surplus labour to non-agricultural production. This would at one stroke lessen the pressure and eliminate the premium that weighed heavily on land in India. Besides, the remaining labour would be productively employed and would give a surplus; and since more surplus is akin to having more capital, it could be invested in agriculture. In short, in Ambedkar's view, industrialization of India was the best remedy for its agricultural problems, as it would reduce the surplus labour in agriculture. The cumulative effects of industrialization would lead not only to an increase in labour productivity and capital investment in agriculture but would also cater to the economic necessity of enlarging landholding. Industrialization, by eroding the premium attached to land, would give rise to few instances for sub-division and fragmentation of land. Thus, the problem of agriculture would be curbed by the indirect consequence of industrialization.

To reiterate, the problem of agricultural backwardness (of which the issue of small farms was a part) was essentially due to deficiency of capital in relation to land and labour. Low capital accumulation was due to low capacity to save, which, in turn, was the result of low productivity and income from agriculture. The solution to agricultural development was seen to lie in improvement in the productivity of land and labour, increase in the farm income of the cultivating households and the expansion of the domestic capacity to save for productive investment. The way out was inter-sectoral transfer of labour from agriculture to industry. This was expected to increase productivity and hence the income, both of the labour in agriculture and in industry. The reduced pressure of population would encourage the enlargement of farm size by reducing the premium on land. The availability of implements and more flexible supply of land for cultivation would thus provide the opportunity for optimal use of resources in production.

It may be noted that some of the theoretical formulations on economic development for developing countries, such as the Arthur Lewis model of economic development with unlimited supply of labour, models based on inter-sectoral linkage of labour and capital, developed in the 1950s and 1960s and also the theoretical principles underlying the strategy of planned economic development in India assumed a theoretical framework identical to that conceived by Ambedkar much earlier in 1918.[3]

On Economic Planning: Post-War Economic (Reconstruction) Plan

Ambedkar's entry into the Central Cabinet as minister-in-charge of the labour (and also irrigation and power) portfolio in 1942 coincided with the formulation and implementation of the post-war economic plan for India's reconstruction and economic development. Such a plan became necessary in order to overcome some urgent post-war problems pertaining to the rehabilitation of defence personnel and the conversion of industry from the requirements of war to those of peace. Unlike the war-affected countries of Europe and Asia, in India, the plan did not remain confined to measures for rehabilitation but included plans for economic development also. In fact, this particular plan marks the beginning of systematic economic planning by the central government with an all-India perspective. The policy measures and action plan conceived and implemented during 1942-44 not only had an impact on the type of economic planning that India adopted on gaining independence but many of these plans continued and became a permanent feature of India's planned economic development.

Being a member of the Central Cabinet, Ambedkar was also a member of the Reconstruction Committee of the Council, the highest body set up to decide the objective and policy of the plan. In addition, he was President of the Policy Committee set up to formulate policy and plans for improving the condition of labour, development of irrigation and electric power. He contributed significantly to the formulation of the objectives of the plan, in general, and the formulation of policy for labour, irrigation and electric power development, in particular, leaving his distinct impact on India's post-war economic planning and development.

A perusal of his writings and discussion during 1942-46 provides an opportunity to understand his thinking about economic planning for India. While writing about the objective and approach of post-war reconstruction plan, Ambedkar argued:

> The problem of post-war reconstruction in India is essentially different from the problem of reconstruction in other war-affected countries, because for them the problem of reconstruction is a problem of rehabilitation of industries, which were destroyed in war. The problem of reconstruction in India, on the other hand, is mainly of the industrialization of India as distinguished from the rehabilitation of industry.[4]

Based on the theoretical framework developed in the paper of 1918, he emphasized the need for industrialization for overall economic development as also for the development of the agricultural sector. Poverty in India, according to him, was due entirely to Indian economy being made dependent upon agriculture alone. Agriculture failed to produce sufficient food to feed its people. The roots were to be found, as observed earlier, in the maladjustment of its social economy. Ambedkar further argued:

> India is caught between two sides of pincers, the one side of which is progressive pressure of population and the other is limited availability of land in relation to its needs. The result is that at the end of each decade we are left with negative balance of population and production and a constant squeezing to standard of living and poverty. The population pressure is giving rise to an army of landless and dispersed families as well. It can be stopped when agriculture is made profitable. Nothing can open possibilities of making agriculture profitable except a serious drive in favour of industrialization. For it is industrialization alone which can drain away excess of population into gainful employment other than agriculture.[5]

Inside the government, Ambedkar, therefore, emphasized the need for industrial development in order to gain increased agricultural productivity and income through the reflex effect of the former on the latter. The policy prescriptions suggested on the basis of theoretical formulation conceived in 1918 were restated in 1943 and eventually incorporated in the objective of post-war reconstruction plan. The section on general objectives, which relates to the sectoral dimension, read:

> Agriculture is and will remain India's primary industry but the present imbalanced economy has to be rectified by intensive development of the country's industries so that both agriculture and industry may develop side by side. That will enable the pressure of population on the land to be relieved and will also provide the means required for the provision of better amenities.[6]

The development of infrastructure, such as roads and communication and transport services, irrigation and electric power in the development of which Ambedkar had played a pioneering role, was treated as prerequisites for industrial development. It was believed that this would bring a relatively higher (annual) rate of growth in industrial production and employment and help absorb the surplus labour from agriculture.

Economic Planning, the Labour and Downtrodden

As mentioned above, Ambedkar was personally involved in formulation of the objectives and strategy, and more specifically the labour policy and planning of water and power resources of India's post-war economic plan.

Aware of the limitations of capitalistic economic system under parliamentary democracy in ensuring economic security to the masses, Ambedkar argued for an important place to be given to labour and the depressed classes in the planned economic development of the country. He was particularly of the view that planned economic development should not only develop programmes but also translate them in terms which the common man could understand, namely, peace, housing, clothing, education, good health and above all, the right to work with dignity. The state could not be content with securing merely fair conditions for work for labour but also fair conditions for life. Ambedkar laid great responsibility on the state to provide the poor with facilities for their growth according to their needs. In Ambedkar's opinion, in order to do that, the government could not be laissez-faire in its action but would have to be a government, essentially based on a system of control.

Influenced by Ambedkar's views and also facilitated by the Labour Government in Britain during 1940s, labour was accorded an important place in the objectives of the post-war plan of economic development:

> The declared objective was to raise the standard of living of the people as a whole and to ensure employment for all. To that end the purchasing power of the people was to be increased to bring

> improvement in the efficiency and consequently the productivity of labour on the one hand and simultaneous development and reorganization of agriculture and industries and services on the other.[7]

Labour was to be made more productive (in order to raise productivity in agriculture and industry) through several measures, which included provision of various amenities, free or subsidized services, such as education up to the age of 14, medical relief, water supply, and other public utility services, including electric power. This would improve the health and efficiency of labour too. Other measures in this direction would be attempts to secure a fair wage deal for labour, maternity and sickness benefit, holidays, etc. Ambedkar, being the President of the Policy Committee on labour many of these schemes for Labour, were undertaken by the Labour Department due to his advice.

In Ambedkar's view, however, the Scheduled Castes (SCs) and depressed classes needed to be treated as a separate entity in the planning exercise because of the special problem of discrimination that they suffer from. The special provision was incorporated in the plan objectives. The Plan Document stated:

> One of the objectives of the government would be to take steps to ameliorate the condition of the Scheduled Castes and backward classes. Care must be taken to see that social amenities such as education, public health, water supply, housing, which are meant to be provided under the plan, work especially for the benefit of such classes and that the handicap of ignorance and poverty under which they now labour is offset by special concessions in the shape of educational facilities, grant, scholarships, hostels, improved water supply and similar measures. It would be the special responsibility of the government to see that early measures are taken to remove the handicap of these classes and help them to raise their level to that of their more fortunate fellow citizens. The provision of full employment as well as various measures of social security contemplated under the section of labour would also automatically benefit the backward and the depressed classes.[8]

Besides labour, as we see later, the central government's irrigation and electric power policy of 1942-44 also reflected the view of Ambedkar about the poor and their place in planned development of the water resources of the country. He urged the policy makers to incorporate measures in the irrigation development policy to benefit the poor and oppressed sections of society.

Ambedkar was also in favour of improvement in productive efficiency. But, unlike Jawaharlal Nehru, he was not merely a growth-maximizer (of national income). He did talk about letting the national income grow large enough before adequate standard of living could be provided for all. At the same time, he was much concerned about the distribution of national income to the common man. In 1943, he emphasized:

> We must be prepared for the revaluation of the value. It will not be enough to make industrial development of India as a goal. We shall have to agree that any such industrial development shall be maintained at a socially desirable level. It will not be enough to bend our energies for the production of more wealth in India. We shall have to agree not merely to recognize the basic right of all Indians to share in that wealth as a means for a decent and dignified existence, but devise ways and means to insure him against insecurity.[9]

This view was emphasized in the formulation of the irrigation and hydroelectric policy for India. In October 1943, in his presidential address to the Policy Committee on Electric Power, Ambedkar pointed out the significance and the ultimate objective behind the need for electrical development in India. He said:

> Before I conclude may I make a few observations pointing out the significance and the ultimate objective that lies behind the need for electrical development in India. It is necessary that those who are placed in charge of the subject should have the fullest realisation of the significance of its objectives. If you agree with me in this I will request you to ask yourself a question. Why do we want cheap and abundant electricity in India? The answer is that without cheap and abundant electricity no effort for the industrialization of India can

> succeed. Ask another question. Why is industrialization necessary? And you will have the full significance made clear to you at once, for the answer to the question is; we want industrialization of India as the surest means to rescue the people from the eternal cycle of poverty in which they are caught. Industrialisation of India must; therefore, be grappled with immediately.[10]

He went on to add that India would have to tackle the problem connected with electricity in an earnest, statesman-like manner, thinking in terms of human life and not in terms of competing claims of the central versus the provincial government.

A similar emphasis was to be accorded in planning to the development of irrigation. In his presidential address to the Conference on Multipurpose Development of Damodar Valley, Ambedkar stressed:

> The Centre expects the Provinces to bear in mind the absolute necessity of ensuring that the benefits of the project get ultimately right down to the grass roots, i.e., everyone living in the valley and some of those in the vicinity, all have their share in the prosperity which the project should bring. This, in my view, is essential and for this reason we want the establishment of some agency early enough so that that agency can set about planning at once in a manner in which its essential and ultimate objective can be secured.[11]

On another occasion he observed:

> I hope we shall be guided by the right spirit, leaving aside the sectional points of view, and proceed to our business with a determination to agree upon the best solution and open a way to the inauguration of new water policy regard to our waterways and lay the foundation for a regime of prosperity for the poverty-stricken millions of this country.[12]

On Economic System

The discussion in the preceding sections (which covered the period till the late 1940s) indicates that Ambedkar attributed the key role to industrialization, favoured economic planning, particularly in infrastructure and social service sector, progressive labour laws and planning with a focus on labour and the downtrodden. The theoretical arguments for industrialization were nevertheless developed within the framework of mainstream economics assuming a private economy. Prior to the 1940s, Ambedkar did emphasize industrialization as a progressive agenda but no particular reference was made about its organization under the public sector, except his insistence on state or public ownership and distribution of electric power.

Between the mid-1930s and late 1940s Ambedkar's position changed to an economic radicalism that covered critical analysis of capitalism, the positive role of state, abolition of a feudalistic land tenure system (like Khoti system and Mahar Vatan system in Maharashtra), cultivation by cooperative farms, and production and distribution of electric power under state ownership and control. Again, these measures were put forward assuming the inevitability of capitalist organization (although occasionally he showed a preference for socialism). No serious alternative economic framework, however, was offered during these years of economic radicalism.

The precise statement of alternative radical economic and political framework, which made a departure from the earlier position, came in *State and Minorities*, written as a memorandum for Constituent Assembly in 1947. The economic section of this document calls for 'state socialism' involving nationalization of basic and key industries such as insurance and of agricultural land and its working with collective farms with peasants treated as tenants of the state. For the first time here, Ambedkar provided explanation, why he preferred industrialization and agriculture to lie with the state sector, the need for economic planning, stronger role for the state and special safeguards against social and economic discrimination of socially deprived classes.

Providing a justification for state socialism, Ambedkar stated:

> The main purpose behind it is to put an obligation on the state to plan the economic life of the people on lines which would lead to the highest point of productivity without closing the avenues to private enterprise and also provide for equitable distribution of wealth. The

> plan set out proposes state ownership in agriculture with a collectivized method of cultivation and a modified form of State socialism in the field of industry. It places squarely on the shoulders of the state the obligation to supply capital necessary for agriculture as well as industry ... state socialism is essential for rapid industrialization of India. Private enterprise cannot do it and if it did, it would produce those inequalities of wealth, which private capitalism has produced in Europe and which should be a warning to India.[13]

In the case of agriculture, unlike the 1930s and 1940s during which time Ambedkar argued for land distribution and tenancy rights, in 1947, he now argued:

> Consolidation of holdings and tenancy legislation are worse than useless. They cannot bring about prosperity in agriculture. Neither consolidation nor tenancy legislation can be of any help to the 60 millions of untouchables who are just landless labourers. Neither consolidation nor tenancy legislation can solve their problem. Only collective farms on the lines set out in the proposal can help them.[14]

Ambedkar's criticism of capitalism was mainly drawn from Marx but not the whole of it, although he agreed with the basis of it. While writing about the relevance of Marx in 1956, Ambedkar observed, "What remains of Karl Marx is a residue of fire, small but still very important. The residue, in my view, consists of four items:

- That the function of philosophy is to reconstruct the world and not to waste its time in explaining the origin of the world.
- That there is a conflict of interest between class and class.
- That private ownership of property brings powers to one class and sorrow to another through exploitation.
- That it is necessary for the good of society that sorrow be removed by abolition of private property."[15]

Taking the points from the surviving Marxist creed, Ambedkar clearly built up the case in favour of socialism. He agreed that in a social economy based on private enterprise and personal gain people both unemployed and employed, are required to relinquish their rights in order to earn their living and subject themselves to be governed by a private employer. He observed:

> For the unemployed persons fear of starvation, the fear of losing house, fear of being compelled to take children away from school, the fear of having to be on public charity are the factors too strong to permit a man to stand out for his fundamental rights. The poor are thus compelled to relinquish their fundamental rights for the sake of securing the privilege to work and subsist.[16]

Writing about the safeguards suggested by the constitutionalists, Ambedkar observed:

> Constitutional lawyers assume that the enactment of fundamental rights is enough to safeguard their liberty and that nothing more is called for ... if the State refrain from intervention in private affairs economic and social, the residue is liberty. What is necessary is to make the residue as large as possible and State intervention as less as possible. It is true that where the State refrains from intervention what remains is liberty. ... But to whom and for whom is this liberty. Obviously, this liberty is liberty to the landlord to increase rents, for capitalists to increase hours of work and reduce the rate of wages. This must be so, it cannot be otherwise. For in an economic system employing armies of workers producing goods in mass at a regular interval someone must make rules so that workers will work and the wheels of industry run on. .... In other word what is called liberty from the control of State is another name for the dictatorship of the private employers.[17]

Ambedkar was thus critical of the remedies adopted by liberal democratic governments. What most democratic countries did was to limit the power of the government to impose arbitrary restraints in the political domain and to invoke the ordinary power of legislature to restrain the more powerful individuals from imposing arbitrary restraints on the less powerful in the economic field. In Ambedkar's view:

> The inadequacy and the futility of the plan have been well established. Therefore the successful invocation by the less powerful of the authority of legislature is a doubtful proposition. Having regard to the fact that even under adult suffrage all legislatures and governments are controlled by the more powerful an appeal to the legislature to intervene is a very precarious safeguard against invasion of liberty of the less powerful.[18]

Therefore, Ambedkar favoured an economic system where not only was the power of the government to impose arbitrary restraints limited, but also of the more powerful individual. In other words, to eliminate the possibility of the more powerful imposing arbitrary restraints on the less powerful, he thought that it could be achieved by minimizing the control of the more powerful from the economic life of the people.

The book *State and Minorities* (1947) was, in fact, a memorandum prepared for submission to the Constituent Assembly for acceptance. Indeed, while responding to the resolution related to the aims and objectives of the future Constitution of India moved by Jawaharlal Nehru on 13 December 1946, as a practical strategy, Ambedkar (as a member of the Constituent Assembly) argued for a socialistic economic framework for Indian society. In response to the "Aims and Objectives" resolution, Ambedkar said:

> I must confess that coming as the resolution does from Pandit Jawaharlal Nehru who is reputed to be a socialist, this resolution, although non-controversial is to my mind is very disappointing. I should have expected him to go much further than he has done ... there are certain provisions which speak of justice, economic, social and political. If this resolution has a reality behind it and sincerity of which I have not the least doubt coming as it does from the mover of the Resolution, I should have expected some provision whereby it would have been possible for the State to make economic, social and political justice a reality and I should have from that view expected the Resolution to state in most explicit terms that there may be social and economic justice in the country, that there would be

> nationalization of industry and nationalization of land. I do not understand how it could be possible for any future government which believes in doing justice, socially, economically and politically, unless its economy is a socialistic economy.[19]

Ambedkar continued and observed, "therefore, personally although I have no objection to the enunciation of these propositions, the resolution is to my mind, somewhat disappointing. I am however prepared to leave this subject where it is with the observation I have made". Ambedkar knew that it was little too much for Congress-dominated Constituent Assembly, and Ambedkar therefore, could not push this proposal as much as he wanted to. He, however, had to make adjustment in his position on this occasion as he did on other occasions, such as Poona Pact.

On Political Economy of Caste System

Another sphere where Ambedkar made a significant contribution is the economic analysis of caste system. Ambedkar examined in greater detail economic principles underlining the caste system and the role of social and religious ideologies in the origin, perpetuation and sustenance of the caste system and captured the nature of interaction between economic structure involved in the caste system and the role of Hindu social/religious philosophy in mutually enforcing each other. He also analyzed the economic consequence of the caste system on economic development and income distribution (or equity).

In Ambedkar's view the caste system involves in itself a producer's organization and scheme of distribution. The relevant economic attributes of the caste system, which make it a peculiar system of producer's organization and a scheme of distribution, are: (a) assignment of economic, civil and cultural rights, particularly the property rights for each caste by birth and continuance thereof by heredity; (b) unequal distribution of economic and property rights among the caste groups; (c) hierarchical arrangement of occupations in terms of status and dignity–some occupations being treated superior and the others as inferior with a stigma of purity and impurity; (d) provision for a comprehensive system of social and economic ostracism and penalties to enforce the caste-based economic and social order and; finally, (e) support and justification from the Hindu religious philosophy. Let us elaborate and understand each of these features more closely.

The foremost principle of caste-based fixation of occupation (or property rights) and continuance thereof, by heredity and birth implied that every member must follow the occupation assigned to the caste to which he belonged. It left no scope for change, individual choice and inclination.

The second principle on which the caste system is based is that occupations and economic rights are not only pre-determined by birth but their division (across the castes) is highly unequal. In fact, inequality in distribution of sources of income is the core of the caste system. The burden of this, however, falls too heavily on low-caste untouchables. The way economic rights are arranged leaves no scope for the low castes for economic improvement as they are deprived of rights to occupation, property and education. Their only occupation is to serve the higher castes as labourers.

The last but equally important feature of the Hindu social order is the prescription of a mechanism of social and economic penalties to maintain the system. The instruments of social and economic boycott are the main forms of penalties that are laid down against the violation of the codes of the system.

To put in brief, Ambedkar's economic characterization of caste system is based on three interrelated elements, namely, fixed and hereditary occupation and economic rights by birth, unequal and hierarchical (or graded) division of these economic/property rights across caste groups and provision of strong instrument of social and economic ostracism to sustain the rigid system with ideological support from the Hindu religion.

Economic and Social Consequences

Ambedkar argued that the manner in which the customary rules regarding the occupation, property rights, employment, wages, education, dignity of labour, etc., are devised under the caste system, it could not but produce vast economic inefficiency and income inequalities. Thus, in his view, caste system as a organization for production has produced gross economic inefficiency, economic stagnation and backwardness. Ambedkar analyzed in detail the economic consequences of factors like immobility, restrictions on individual choice and initiative, social status associated with occupation, and the dignity of labour involved under caste system.

Ambedkar recognized that the caste system's basic feature of ascribed occupations for each caste implies exclusion of one caste from undertaking the occupation of another caste. Exclusion and discrimination in occupation, and unemployment of labour, is thus internal to the system and necessary outcome of its economics. It is reasonable to assume that in a market economy the occupational immobility would operate through restrictions in various markets such as labour, land, credit, other inputs and services necessary in any economic activity. Labour market exclusion would, therefore, manifest itself in exclusion in employment from another caste's occupation. Immobility of labour, and capital, under caste-wise division, essentially means occupationally segregated, and imperfectly (though not completely) immobile market situations. This would necessarily imply that occupationally segmented, and imperfectly mobile labour, and capital markets would generate economic outcomes, which will be less than optimum, and this is turn will hamper overall economic growth. In its ultimate outcome, the performance of caste economy would be lower than in competitive economy.

There are other consequences of a caste economy towards which Ambedkar has drawn our attention. The efficiency of labour is adversely affected by a number of customary rules regarding dignity of labour, and social status ascribed to the so-called polluting occupations. The social and individual efficiencies require that the capacities of an individual be developed to the point of competency to choose, and make one's own career. The economic pursuit in caste system, as it exists, is not based on individual choice, sentiment and preference, as it assigns tasks to an individual in advance, and the individuals are selected not on the basis of training or capacities, but social status. Some of these occupations are considered polluting and impure and, therefore, socially degrading. The social stigma of impurity and pollution, in fact, reduces the social status of the person engaged in them, such as in scavenging, and leather-related works. Forced into these occupations on account of their caste origin, people do not derive job satisfaction, and are constantly provoked to aversion, ill-will, and desire to malinger.

In this context, Ambedkar observed:

> There are many occupations in India which on account of the fact that they are regarded as degraded by Hindus provoke those who are engaged in these occupations. There is a constant desire to evade and escape from such occupations which arise solely because of the blighting effect which they produce upon those who follow them owing to the slight and stigma casting on them by the Hindu religion.[20]

He further adds: What efficiency can there be in a system under which neither men's hearts nor their minds are in their work?[21]

One of the negative impacts of restrictions and immobility and the social status and stigma associated with occupation is on unemployment, which has been emphasized by Ambedkar. By putting restrictions on mobility of labour from one occupation to other and thereby not permitting readjustment of employment, caste becomes a direct cause of much of voluntary unemployment for higher-caste persons and involuntary unemployment for low-caste persons. The high-caste Hindu would generally prefer to be voluntarily unemployed for some time than to take up an occupation not assigned to his caste and which is considered an inferior occupation. On the other hand, for the low-caste untouchables, the restrictions to take other caste's occupation also compel them to remain involuntarily unemployed.

This brings us to the income distribution or equity implications of the caste system. The consequences of the caste system in terms of equity are more serious than for economic efficiency and growth. Ambedkar's analysis implies that since the economic rewards under the caste system are determined by job assignment, the result is an income distribution generally skewed along caste line. In fact, the caste system as an economic organization is based on the principle of hierarchy of economic rights and hence economic inequality. Economic inequality (as much as the social-cultural inequality) under the caste system has not emerged as matter of indirect historical consequence but was a direct outcome of its governing principles, the core and centre of which is the doctrine of economic inequality and exploitation. In fact, the legitimate dislike for the caste system is due to the fact that the principle of equality is completely alien to its spirits. Ambedkar argued that the manner in which the customary rules and norms regarding right to property, occupation, employment, wages, education, dignity of labour, and other economic relations are framed and defined, they involved nothing but inequality and immense exploitation of the castes located at the bottom of caste hierarchy.

Synthesis

This brief synthesis of Ambedkar's economic ideas, provides an insight into his thoughts on economic development, planning, role of the state, alternative economic system and political economy of the caste system. This also brings out the evolution in economic thinking of Ambedkar since the early 1920s to the mid 1950s. While Ambedkar's major writings on economic issues in the 1920s bear the mark of general mainstream economic perspective, they also involve identification with the working classes and also includes a harsh critique of colonialism and imperialism. After the 1930s there was a gradual change in his economic thinking and a height of economic radicalism came in the late 1940s in the form of preference for state socialism with parliamentary democracy. By mid-1950s the position of Ambedkar on main economic issues had been crystallized and one could see, in the end, a fairly systematic framework of economic ideas being developed. The discussion clearly indicates that although Ambedkar had written at different point of time in his political career, nevertheless, there is a common approach and thread which runs through his economic writings and thus present an internally coherent economic vision and perspective. Having analyzed his views on several issues in some detail, let me now summarize and place them in perspective.

Firstly, at a more general level, Ambedkar in his economic vision supports modern civilization and scientific development. Responding to the opposition by Gandhiji to the use of machinery and civilization, in 1945, Ambedkar had observed:

> The fact that machinery and modern civilization have produced many evils may be admitted. But these evils are no argument against them. For the evils are not due to machinery and modern civilization. They are due to wrong social organization which has made private property and pursuit of personal gain matters of absolute sanctity. If machinery and civilization have not benefited everybody the remedy is not to condemn machinery and civilization but to alter the organization of society so that the benefits will not be usurped by the few but will accrue to all.[22]

It is this social organization of capitalism based on absolute sanctity of private property and pursuit of personal gain with its detrimental consequences on the propertyless classes that induced Ambedkar to look for the alternative economic and social system. In the end, he favoured socialistic economic framework of a particular type. The overwhelming weight in favour of socialistic economy was based on his understanding of capitalism as detrimental system for the property-less masses. However, he did not argue for socialistic organization of the entire economy, which is observed in communist regimes but identified only certain basic sectors such as agriculture, basic and key industries like insurance, infrastructure like power, irrigation and social services like road, education, health and social security to be the responsibility of the state, leaving the rest of the economic and social activities for the private sector. Further, he insisted that the public sector undertakings should be run efficiently so that they could earn profit for investment in the economy. In this respect, Ambedkar was much ahead of his time in recognizing the need for running the public sector economic activities on the principle of economic efficiency.

Another important aspect of Ambedkar's views on socialism is that he favoured switch over to socialism through democratic means of parliamentary democracy. But, at the same time, he was immensely aware, perhaps more than anybody else, about the limitations of parliamentary form of democratic government in providing stability to the socialistic economy. To overcome the problem of this instability, he suggested an alternative in terms of 'constitutional state socialism'. In his view acceptance of state socialism and its inclusion in the constitution by popular and majority will (and making it un-amendable by any subsequent government) will provide stability to the socialism and at the same time retain parliamentary democracy. This was indeed an innovative method, which was suggested to realize socialism and at the same time retain democratic form of government.

Two important implications of Ambedkar's views on socialism need to be emphasized. One is that the markets based on unequal distribution of private property is not the ultimate solution for removal of the poverty of the people and that the structure of property ownership and relations is important in determining as to how the markets work and whom do they benefit. In this context, the central message of Ambedkar, namely, of fair access to the sources of income, particularly land and capital, is important. Fair distribution of land and capital is a key for removal of the poverty in any form of production organization – cooperative or private. Ultimately, what is important in his view is that the ownership arrangement of production organization should be such that it provides fair access to basic source of income like agricultural, land, capital and employment. The second implication of Ambedkar's views on socialism is his insistence on the running of the state and the public sector undertakings and enterprises on the basis of efficiency and profitability to generate surplus for investment. This position was made quite clear at the time of deciding the economic principle for the working of Damodar Valley Project. Ambedkar had observed:

> I am not prepared to accept that the project should be run on non-profitable basic. Nor do I accept that any profit which may accrue after meeting all power shall only be used for reduction of capital expenditure and for betterment of the system. It is impossible to forget the fact that a large part of misery of the people of the country is entirely due to the inadequate revenue resources of the

> government. The object of the government business concern is to enable the government to make a profit as any business concern does in order to supplement its resources. I am therefore quite unable to see any justification for ruling out this important purpose from the contribution of Damodar Valley Authority.[23]

The other important elements of Ambedkar's economic views are his emphasis on active role and participation of the state in economic and social development through the instrument of planning. He favoured the use of this instrument for planned economic development. Within the broader framework of planning, he also emphasized the need for a focus on the poor and the labouring classes in the economic plan. Further, due to discrimination of the depressed castes inside and outside market, he also favoured special planning for them and the policy of reservation for protecting against discrimination and promoting their effective participation in the economic and social sphere.

With respect to the sectoral priorities, Ambedkar has emphasized industrial development as a solution to the problem of agriculture development. He believed that development of industrial sector is necessary to reduce the surplus labour in agriculture and to create favourable conditions for production. Removal of surplus labour in agriculture through industrialization, in his view, will reduce the pressure on land and bring consolidation of holdings and enhancement of farm size. This will also create conditions for generation of surplus and private investment in agriculture. However, Ambedkar also favoured direct investment in agriculture by state to supplement the private investment so that deficiency of capital formation in agriculture is reduced.

Notes

1. Ambedkar's main academic works in the 1920s include his M.A. dissertation "Administration and Finance of East India Company" submitted to the Columbia University, published in *Dr. Babasaheb Ambedkar: Writing and Speeches*, Vol. 6, "On Economics", Vasant Moon (ed.), Education

Department, Government of Maharashtra (1989); PhD dissertation on the "The Evolution of Provincial Finance in British India", London: King and Son (1925); DSc dissertation, "The Problem of Rupees", London: King and Son (1923); "Small Holding in India and their Remedies", *Journal of Indian Economic Society*, Vol. 1, 1918 and "State and Minorities", Bombay: Thacker (1947).

2. B.R. Ambedkar (1918), "Small Holdings in India and their Remedies", *Journal of Indian Economic Society*, Vol. 1.
3. See Sukhamoy Chakravarty (1987), *Development Planning: The Indian Experience*, Delhi: Oxford University Press. Professor Chakravarty writes: "The underlying causes of structural backwardness were perceived as follows. First, the basic constraint on development was seen as being an acute deficiency of material capital, which prevented the introduction of more productive technologies. Secondly, the limitation on the speed of capital accumulation was seen to lie in the low capacity to save. Thirdly, it was assumed that even if the domestic capacity to save could be raised by means of suitable fiscal and monetary policies, there were structural limitations preventing conversion of savings into productive investment. Fourthly, it was assumed that whereas agriculture was subject to secular diminishing returns, industrialization would allow surplus labour, currently underemployed in agriculture to be more productively employed in industries, which operated according to increasing returns to scale."
4. File No. 1(4), Proceedings of the Reconstruction Committee of the Viceroy's Council – The Policy Statement on Irrigation, Waterways and Power prepared by the Labour Department, 1943, p. 45.
5. Ibid.
6. File No. 1(10), Proceedings of the Four Meetings of Consultative Committee of Economists, 1943, p. 45
7. File No. 1(4), Proceedings of the Reconstruction Committee of the Viceroy's Council – The Policy Statement on Irrigation, Waterways and Power, prepared by the Labour Department, 1943, p. 45.
8. Ibid.
9. Ambedkar (1943), "First Session of the Plenary Labour Conference, Dr. Ambedkar on Social Security", Indian Information, September 15, p. 105.
10. Ambedkar (1945), "Multipurpose Development of the Damodar Valley", August 23, 1945, Indian Information, Delhi, October 10.

11. Ambedkar (1945), Damodar Valley Scheme, Presidential Address, First Calcutta Conference, January 3, 1945, Indian Information, February.
12. Ibid.
13. B.R. Ambedkar (1947), "State and Minorities" in Vasant Moon (1979), *Dr. Babasaheb Ambedkar: Writing and Speeches*, Vol. 1, Education Department, Government of Maharashtra, Mumbai, p. 408.
14. Ibid.
15. B.R. Ambedkar (1956), "Buddha and Karl Marx" in Vasant Moon (1987), *Dr. Babasaheb Ambedkar: Writing and Speeches*, Vol. 3, Education Department, Government of Maharashtra, Mumbai, p. 441.
16. Ambedkar (1947), "State and Minorities" in Vasant Moon (1979), *Dr. Babasaheb Ambedkar: Writing and Speeches*, Vol 1, Education Department, Government of Maharashtra, Mumbai, p. 410.
17. Ibid.
18. Ibid., p. 411.
19. Ambedkar (1946), Comment on Nehru's Resolution on Aims and Objectives, "Dr. Ambedkar: Principle Architect of Constitution of India" in Vasant Moon (1994), *Dr. Babasaheb Ambedkar: Writing and Speeches*, Vol 13, Education Department, Government of Maharashtra, Mumbai, pp. 7-13.
20. Ambedkar (1936), "Annihilation of Caste" in Vasant Moon (1979), *Dr. Babasaheb Ambedkar: Writing and Speeches*, Vol 1, Education Department, Government of Maharashtra, Mumbai, p. 60.
21. Ibid., p. 61.
22. Ambedkar (1990), "What Congress and Gandhi has done to the Untouchables" in Vasant Moon, *Dr. Babasaheb Ambedkar: Writing and Speeches*, Vol. 9, Education Department, Government of Maharashtra, Mumbai, p. 284.
23. Minutes of the First Conference on Damodar River Valley Project, File No. DW-105(1)/45 DWI, Finance Department, Planning Division.

2 On Exchange Rate, Trade Balance and Distribution

G. NANCHARAIAH

Early writings of Babasaheb Ambedkar have been mainly in the academic discipline of economics. The academic contributions, which largely came through research for PhD in economics from Columbia University during 1913-16 and DSc in economics from London School of Economics during 1917-19 were in the field of public finance, monetary and international economics covering colonial period. Further, in the general backdrop of theoretical development in these fields, his research work on public finance and international economics was based on the extensive use of empirical data relating to the early part of the twentieth century. In this paper, an attempt is made to capture the views of Ambedkar on the theme of exchange rate, trade and income distribution. Much of his writings on these themes are contained in the DSc thesis, which he did in London School of Economics, and published as *The Problem of Rupees* in 1925 and *Statement of Evidence to Royal Commission on Indian Currency* in 1926. The discussion in this paper is largely based on these writings.

In the wake of the policy shift toward the liberalization of international trade in India since early 1990, there has been a renewal of interest on the issue of exchange rate and its implications for trade, income distribution and poverty. In this context, Ambedkar's views on exchange rate, trade balance and income distribution merit serious consideration as he worked on these issues with specific reference to Indian economy in early part of the twentieth century. In the backdrop of the theoretical development of that times Ambedkar addressed the issue of fixed versus flexible exchange rate and their implications for trade balance and also income distribution among the business class and the workers.

Through a extensive analysis of data, Ambedkar offered arguments in favour of stable exchange rate regime as he believed that exchange rate stability (as against the flexible one) is a better option from the point of view of both investors and workers. In the remaining part of the paper, we discuss the arguments provided by Ambedkar in favour of stable exchange rate policy for favourable environment for investors, as well as workers.

Liberalization of exchange rate has been viewed as an important measure to improve the export performance and thereby, balance of payments under the new trade policy, which was initiated in 1990 in India. Liberalized exchange rate management system (LERMS) was adopted in March 1992. Earlier, an effective exchange rate was fixed by Reserve Bank of India (RBI) under basket mechanism, where the value of rupee was linked with currencies of five countries depending on the importance of these countries in terms of volume of trade with India. During 1992-93, a dual exchange rate system was introduced. Thereby the exporters in the market could sell 60 per cent of the export earnings and the remaining 40 per cent has to be sold to the RBI. During 1993-94 convertibility of rupee on trade account was introduced under which exporters and importers could sell and buy foreign exchange in the market. Convertibility was then extended to current account. As a result, there was a continuous depreciation in the external value of rupee in terms of dollar, pound sterling and other important currencies. The theory behind this is that currency depreciation promotes exports and discourages imports leading to improvement in the balance of payments. Exchange rate liberalization facilitates traders by reducing transaction costs in acquiring foreign exchange and offers higher rupee price for the dollars earned by exporters.

The liberalization of exchange rate policy during the liberalization period is largely based on the neo-classical theory of exchange rate, which asserts that disequilibrium in the exchange rate market would be automatically corrected depending on demand and supply forces, if exchange rate is allowed to move freely without restrictions. It is also to be noted that after the breakdown of the Bretton Woods system in 1971 many countries shifted to flexible exchange rates, which allowed varying degrees of flexibility. India also adopted managed floating exchange rates from 1971.

However, from 1991, exchange rate was made more flexible and left to the market on current account with a right to intervene in the market, whenever it is warranted. As a result, there has been a continuous depreciation of rupee in terms of dollar and pound sterling in the post-liberalization period. The exchange rate, which was about Rs. 18 for $1 in 1990, increased to about Rs. 43 in August 1998. But export performance did not increase at expected rate and average growth rate of exports, which was about 20 per cent during 1992-96, drastically declined to about 2 per cent during 1996-98, while imports growth rate always remained higher than exports growth rate. Thus, although, there was some improvement in the balance of trade in the early part of the last decade, it deteriorated substantially in the later years. This clearly indicates that there is no guarantee that currency depreciation or devaluation is always accompanied by improvement in the export performance and balance of trade.

Moreover, another consequence of this could be high rate of inflation leading to redistribution of income in favour of the rich with detrimental impact on the income of working classes and the poor. Many developing countries, particularly Latin American and African countries, had this kind of negative experience, although the experiment was successful in some developed countries like the U.K.

Ambedkar examined the relationship between exchange rate and external trade in the book *The Problem of Rupee* analyzing the trend from second half of the nineteenth century to the early part of the century, when the silver and gold standards were in use. Given the use of metal currency the exchange between any two countries would be stable, if they employ the same metal functioning as their standard money. But if the exchange is between two countries having different metals as their currency standards the fixed par of exchange could not be ensured. In that case their exchange would be governed by the relative values of gold and silver and fluctuates as their relative values change. The gold-silver exchange, which was stable before 1873 between England and India, fluctuated widely after that. Sterling-rupee exchange,[1] which was a reflection of gold-silver exchange, was also fluctuating after 1873. One reason was demonetization of silver as standard money medium by the principal countries of the world due to the agitation for uniformity of weights, measures and coinages and the other was great increase in the production of silver compared to gold. There was a continuous fall in exchange rate due to decline in the relative value of silver in terms of gold and it increased the burden of those which had the obligation to pay in terms of gold. Amongst the countries, Ambedkar described, the most heavily charged was the Government of India as it had the obligation to make certain payments to England in terms of gold, but silver being sole legal tender, the revenues of India were in silver.

The burden of these gold payments increased due to growth in their magnitude and also due to fall in the exchange rate during 1875-92. The excess amount required, due to fall in the exchange rate, rose significantly. The Government of India enforced a policy of high taxes and rigid economy to meet this increased burden. The excise duties on imported spirits were not only raised in 1890 but afterwards added to in every province. The yield of the taxes and duties levied increased considerably. This entire additional burden was due to the enhanced cost of meeting the gold payments due to fall in the exchange rate.[2] Despite these measures the government was in financial strains throughout the period of falling exchange rate and could not find money for public works. The government also inaugurated a policy whereby 'extraordinary' public works were to be financed by the public. As Indian public could not raise such finance, India resorted to external borrowings but foreigners were reluctant to invest in the rupee securities due to fall in the value of silver in terms of gold.

But, the fall in the exchange rate had a different effect on trade and industry and it was flourishing, compared to the affairs of the Government of India. Exports increased during 1870-71 and 1891-92 and imports also rose during this period. Not only was trade increasing, but the nature of trade was also changing. India, which was a primary goods exporting country before 1870, started exporting manufactured goods also. There was 43 per cent increase in the exports of manufactured goods during 1879-92. Jute and cotton industries witnessed rapid advance. After 1870 farming also tended to be more market-oriented. During this period, England, which was on gold standard, tended to be at a standstill.[3]

Could such changes in trade be attributed to monetary disturbances such as exchange rate changes? Some argued that falling exchange rate gave bounties to the Indian producer and imposed a penalty on the English producer. That is, the fall in exchange rate stimulated exports, while hindering imports into silver standard countries. And, the fall of exchange rate exposed English exporters to higher degree of competition compared to their rivals in silver standard countries.

There was also a common notion that the bounty arising from export trade, due to fall in exchange rate was a gain to the whole nation.[4] But Ambedkar argued that bounty on exports arose due to fall in exchange, only when the exporter was able to buy more goods and services in India with the silver he obtained for his produce. In other words, his bounty was the difference between the price of his produce and the price of his inputs. Therefore, the bounty, if any, was not a bounty on export trade as such, but was an outcome of disharmony between the general level of prices and the prices of particular goods and services within the county and would have existed, even if the country had no export trade. The bounty was felt because the prices of all goods and services in India did not move uniformly in the same direction. General prices during 1873-93 had fallen in England but wages had not fallen to the same extent. And, in India, prices had risen but wages had not risen to the same extent. The Indian producer got bounty because he did not have to pay higher wage, although the price of his product had risen. The falling exchange rate might have acted as a motivating force to export more. But it did so by bringing about changes in the distribution of wealth in society. In India, where prices were rising, it was the wage earner who suffered. The fall of exchange rate in so far as it was a gain, registered a loss to large section of the Indian people with fixed incomes.[5]

There was a steep fall in the exchange rate, particularly in 1907, 1914 and 1920 and this was explained by the adverse balance of trade by some. But Ambedkar argued that trade deficit occurs, when the value of exports is less than the value of imports and this was due to rise in the domestic prices, that is, fall in the purchasing power of the rupee. He explained it in terms of excess creation of currency under gold exchange standard. From the point of economic stability, he preferred the gold standard to gold exchange standard, as the discretion of the currency-issue was not regulated under gold exchange standard. The progress of trade depends on stability of exchange rate. To maintain exchange rate stability, Ambedkar suggested that since all important countries had moved towards gold standard, the silver standard countries should change over to gold standard or as an alternative, countries following the two metal standards should establish fixed ratio of exchange so as to make the two metals into a common standard of value.[6]

There was a proposal to stabilize exchange rate in India at pre-war ratio of 1s.4d as the whole of Europe was planning to restore pre-war conditions of currency in course of reconstruction. But, the Indian government seems to have opposed this proposal as it wanted to have 2s ratio for Indian currency. The exchange rate prevailing in 1924 was 1s.6d. Ambedkar did not favour the idea of either bringing it back to pre-war level ratio, i.e., 1s.4d or to raising it to the ratio of 2s. Exchange rate between two currencies would be fixed depending on the relative purchasing power of the currencies in their respective countries. The exchange rate between India and England remained at 1s.4d for a long time, but the prices in India and the level of prices in England were very different. Exchange rate cannot be said to be in complete harmony with the whole of prices. Exchange rate affects only such things that enter international trade. It depends on the volume of external trade in proportion to internal trade.

Ambedkar also showed that the index number of sale prices rose from 100 in 1914 to 174 in 1924 and the question of considering the extreme ratio of 2s did not arise. At the same time returning to the ratio of 1s.4d would not mean current price level going down to pre-war prices. If exchange rate was brought down from 1s.6d to 1s.4d, there would be inflation and while the business class would benefit by investing, the working class would face hardship. He also observed that most of the contracts between the investing class and business class were of recent origin. One had therefore to choose between 1s.4d and 1s.6d, preferably more towards 1s.6d.[7] Ambedkar also explained that low exchange rate might encourage export trade. But low exchange rate would cause a rise in prices and therefore this gain was not a gain coming from outside but a gain for one class at the cost of another class. He explained that the class that suffers is the poor labour class which gives the bounty to the richer or the business class. Such transfer of wealth from the poor to the rich can never be in the general interest of the country. Ambedkar argued, "I therefore strongly oppose the higher prices and low exchange rate and a righteous government should not be party to such a clandestine picking of the pockets of the poor class in the country."[8]

It follows from the above analysis that, according to Ambedkar, a fall in the exchange rate would lead to rise in prices, thereby causing redistribution of income in favour of the business class at the cost of the working class, whose wages generally would not rise in proportion to price rise. In the opinion of Ambedkar, given the differential impact of unstable exchange rate, while deciding the exchange rate, the interest of all the classes – investor, business and working class – should be borne in mind so that trade and industry expands but at the same time interest of working classes and poor is not harmed. As growth of trade and industry depends on economic stability, there is a need for controlling exchange rate fluctuations within limits. This view of Ambedkar is largely based on the behaviour of exchange rate, export trend, domestic prices and wage rate of workers.

During 1889-90 there was a sharp fall in the gold-silver or pound sterling-rupee exchange rate (rupee depreciation) between England and India. As a result, there was an increased burden on the Government of India, which had certain obligations to pay in gold to England. As its revenues were not adequate, it had to resort to increased taxation and duties on imports, while controlling government expenditure. Public works also suffered due to paucity of funds. Foreign investment also did not flow due to instability in the silver price.

There were some gains in term of improvement in Indian trade. However, it was not due to any bounty on exports but due to rise in the prices, while wages did not raise to the same extent in India, eroding the purchasing power of workers. Therefore, in Ambedkar's view, this kind of gain, due to export trade, should not be considered as gain to the nation as it was a gain to one class at the cost of another class in society. The intermittent fall in exchange rate during 1900-19 was due to rise in the prices in India on account of excess issue of currency under gold-exchange standard in which currency could be issued without any regulation. Hence, Ambedkar preferred gold exchange standard to have exchange stability and thereby economic stability, growth and favourable price regime for the workers.

Notes

1. Exchange rate was defined as number of units of pound-sterling to be obtained for one unit of Indian currency, in Vasant Moon, *Dr. Babasaheb Ambedkar: Writings and Speeches*, Vol. 6, 1989, Education Department, Government of Maharashtra, p. 397.
2. Ibid., pp. 426-30.
3. Ibid., p. 430.
4. Ibid., p. 435.
5. Ibid., p. 436.
6. Ibid.
7. Ibid., pp. 631-632.
8. Ibid., p. 633.

References

Ambedkar, B.R. (1915), 'Administration and Finance of the East India Company,' MA Thesis, Columbia University, in Vasant Moon (1989), *Dr. Babasaheb Ambedkar: Writings and Speeches*, Vol. 6, 'On Economics', Education Department, Government of Maharashtra, 1989.

— (1925), *The Evolution of Provincial Finance in British India*, King and Son, London.

— (1925), *The Problem of Rupee*, King and Son, London.

— (1926), 'Statement of Evidence to Royal Commission on Indian Currency', in Vasant Moon (1989), *Dr. Babasaheb Ambedkar: Writings and Speeches*, Vol. 6, 'On Economics', Education Department, Government of Maharashtra, 1989.

— (1925), 'The Present Problem in Indian Currency I and II', in Vasant Moon (1989), *Dr. Babasaheb Ambedkar: Writings and Speeches*, Vol. 6, 'On Economics', Education Department, Government of Maharashtra, 1989.

— (1993 published first time), 'Ancient Indian Commerce', in Vasant Moon (1989), *Dr. Babasaheb Ambedkar: Writings and Speeches*, Vol. 12, 'Unpublished Writings', Education Department, Government of Maharashtra, 1993.

3 Remedies against Discrimination and Inequalities

SUKHADEO THORAT AND ARYAMA

Caste System and Inequalities

Historically, the caste system has formed the regulatory base for the social, cultural and economic life of the people in India. Ambedkar devoted considerable intellectual efforts to understand the nature of caste system, its effect on the standard of living of groups, particularly located at the bottom of caste hierarchy in order to suggest possible remedies against the discrimination induced deprivation in Indian society. In this paper, we discuss the Ambedkar's interpretation of caste system, its economic consequences and the remedies suggested against the discrimination and deprivation, especially for low-caste untouchables.

Ambedkar recognized that in its essential form, caste as a system of social and economic governance or organization (of production and distribution) is based on certain customary rules and norms, which are unique and distinct. In general, the caste-based society and economy is one in which property rights (or occupations) are hereditary, compulsory and endogamous. The organizational scheme of the caste system is based on the division of people in social groups (or castes) in which civil, cultural, religious and economic rights of each individual caste are pre-determined or ascribed by birth and made hereditary.

Moreover, endogamy remains the central feature of caste system. The assignment of civil, cultural and economic rights, however, is unequal and hierarchical. The system also provides for a regulatory mechanism to enforce the social and economic organization through the instruments of social ostracism (or system of social and economic penalties), and reinforces it further with justifications from the philosophical elements in the Hindu religion (Ambedkar, 1916, 1936 and 1987). It is these features, which make the institution of caste rigid and stubborn, resisting change.

These features imply that the Hindu social order is based on three interrelated principles, namely, pre-determination of social, religious and economic rights of each caste based on birth; the unequal and hierarchical (graded) division of these rights among the castes; and provision of strong social, religious and economic ostracism supported by social and religious ideology to maintain the Hindu social order. In Ambedkar's view, the doctrine of inequality is the core and the heart of the Hindu social order. What is important is that the philosophical elements in Hinduism also directly and indirectly supports the system. This leaves no difference between legal philosophy (and law) and moral philosophy (morality) in Hinduism. What is legal also becomes moral. There being no distinction between the legal and the moral, morality becomes social and binding force on all (Ambedkar, 1987).

The notion of 'human rights' under the Hindu social system takes a specific meaning. It becomes clear that unlike other human societies, the Hindu social order in its classical form does not recognize the individual and his distinctiveness as the centre of the social purpose. The unit of the Hindu society is not the individual. Even, the family is not regarded as a unit of society, except for the purposes of marriages and inheritance (Ambedkar, 1987). The caste system is also governed by the principle of rank and gradation, in so far as the rights increase in ascending order from untouchable to Brahmin. It is a hierarchically interlinked system. In this framework castes are artfully interlinked with each other in such a manner that the rights and privileges of higher castes become the disabilities for the lower castes, particularly the untouchables. In this sense, in Ambedkar's view, the caste in a single number cannot exist. Caste can exist only in plural number. There cannot be such a thing as caste as a singular phenomenon. So castes need to be conceived as a 'system' of societal governance, which are interlinked in unequal measures of social, cultural, religious, economic relations with each other.

Isolation and exclusion (of untouchables) – social and physical – is also a unique feature of the Hindu social order. Ambedkar observed:

> Classes or social groups are common to all societies, but as long as the classes or social groups do not practice isolation and exclusiveness, they are only non-social in their relations towards one another. Isolation and exclusiveness makes them anti-social and inimical to one another.[1]

Remedies against Discrimination and Inequalities

The caste system's fundamental characteristic of fixed civil, cultural and economic rights for each caste, with restriction for change implies 'forced exclusion' of one caste from the rights of the other castes. Exclusion and discrimination in civil, cultural, and particularly, in economic spheres, such as occupation and labour employment is, therefore, internal to the system and a necessary outcome of its basic features. Since the civil, cultural and economic rights of each caste are fixed and compulsory, the institution of caste necessarily involves forced exclusion of one caste from rights of another. It is necessary to recognize that though an unequal and hierarchical assignment of economic rights obviously restricts the freedom of occupation and development, and leads to inter-caste inequalities, but it may not necessarily lead to deprivation and poverty among them, if every caste person has access to reasonable sources/resources of livelihood in his assigned occupation. However, in the case of lower castes, particularly the untouchables, exclusion leads to deprivations and poverty in so far as they are denied of all sources of livelihood, except in manual labour (they are assigned occupations considered to be polluting and inferior), and service to castes above them. Therefore, their exclusion has multiple dimensions and is simultaneously comprehensive and results in severe deprivation for them as a social group. Besides, the untouchables also suffer from social and residential separation, and isolation, due to the practice of untouchability. The concept of purity/pollution brings in an additional dimension to their discrimination and exclusion, and in more respects than one, further segregates them from the human capability and capacity-building processes.

The notion of caste-based exclusion and discrimination, thus, necessarily involves a failure of entitlement, not only to the economic rights, but also to civil, cultural and political rights. It involves what has been described as living-mode exclusion, exclusion in political participation, and exclusion and disadvantage in social and economic opportunities.[2] This form of exclusion could take following forms:

1. The exclusion and denial of equal opportunity in economic spheres would necessarily operate through market and non-market transactions and exchange. Firstly, such exclusion may be practised through the denial in labour markets in hiring for jobs, in capital markets through the denial of access to capital, in agriculture (land) markets through the denial of the right to sell and purchase/lease in land, in input markets through the denial in sale and purchase of factor inputs, and in consumer markets through the denial in sale and purchase of commodities and consumer goods. Secondly, the exclusion or discrimination may also occur due to the lack of access to social and public goods supplied by the government or public or private institutions in education, housing, health, and in common property resources like water bodies and grazing land/other land of common use.
2. In civil and cultural spheres, the untouchables may face discrimination and exclusion in the use of public services like roads, temples, water bodies, and institutions delivering services like education and health, and other public services.
3. In political spheres, the untouchables can face discrimination in the use of political rights, and also in participation in decision-making process.
4. Due to the physical (or residential) segregation and social exclusion on account of the notion of untouchability, they can suffer from a general societal exclusion.

Ambedkar also devoted considerable intellectual efforts to suggest remedies against the exclusion and discrimination-induced deprivation, particularly of untouchables, and the structural inequalities in Indian society. In order to get insights into the evolution of Ambedkar's approach, it is necessary to go back to the formative stage of the present policies for which systematic intellectual efforts were made by Ambedkar since the early 1920s. Ambedkar articulated a set of remedies against caste discrimination and inequalities, beginning from 1919 and deepened and enriched his set of remedies through his systematic efforts throughout the 1930s, 1940s and 1950s.

Systematic articulation of arguments in favour of remedies against caste discrimination was spelled out in Ambedkar's first statement, submitted in January 1919 to Southborough Committee, at the time of reform in the Government of India Act, 1919. About ten years later, in May 1928, when the second attempt was made to revise the 1919 Act, during early 1930, through a series of round Table Conferences, Ambedkar submitted two statements, one to the Simon Commission in May 1928 and another, two years later in 1930, at the First Round Table Conference. The final statement came in 1947 in the "State and Minorities: What are their rights and how to secure them in the Constitution of free India" at the time of framing of India's Constitution. These statements indeed provide insights into the evolution of Ambedkar's thinking on the problems of Indian society and remedies to solve the problems of untouchables in particular and of deprived sections in general. In their intellectual exercise these documents are basic to the understanding of the malady of Hindu society and the remedies proposed by Ambedkar against denial of equal opportunity to untouchables (Ambedkar, 1919, 1928, 1930 and 1946).

From these writings in the 1920s through 1940s it becomes clear that Ambedkar grounded the case for remedies against discrimination of untouchables on the historical and current denial of basic human rights and rights to development to the untouchables. In the first systematic written statement, in 1919, Ambedkar argued:

> Not only the untouchability arrested the growth of personality of untouchables but also comes in the way of their 'material well-being'. It deprived them of certain civil rights. The untouchable is not even a citizen. Citizenship is bundle of rights such as personal liberty, personal security, right to hold private

> property, equality before law, liberty of conscience, freedom of opinion, and speech, right of assembly, right of representation in country's Government, and right to hold office under the state. The untouchability of untouchables puts these rights far beyond their reach.[3]

Substantiating the claim before the Simon Commission, Ambedkar argued, about ten years later in 1928 at the time of reform in Government of India Act: "Depressed classes cannot be employed in the army, navy, and police because such employment is opposed to the religious notion of majority. They cannot be admitted in schools, because their entry is opposed to the religious notion of majority. They cannot avail themselves of government dispensaries, because doctors will not let them cause pollution to their persons or to their dispensaries. They cannot live cleaner and better life, because to live above their prescribed station is opposed to the religious notion of majority."[4]

Ambedkar adds:

> So rigorous is the enforcement of the social code against the Depressed Classes that any attempt on the part of Depressed Classes to exercise their elementary rights of citizenship only ends in provoking the majority to practice the worst forms of social tyranny known to history.[5]

Repeating the same argument in the plenary session of the First Round Table Conference on November 1930, Ambedkar argued:

> What is worse that this servility and bar to human intercourse, due to their untouchability, involves not merely the possibility of discrimination in public life, but actually work out as a positive denial of all equality of opportunity and the denial of those most elementary of civic rights on which all human existent depend.[6]

And finally, seventeen years later, in 1947, while justifying the need for safeguards against discrimination of the scheduled castes in the constitution of independent India, Ambedkar argued: "Unequal treatment has been the inescapable fate of the untouchables in India"[7] and added that "in country like India where it is possible for discrimination to be practiced on a vast scale and in a relentless manner fundamental rights have no real meaning for untouchables".[8]

A close look at the four memorandums prepared and presented by Ambedkar, in fact, captures his interpretation about the problems of untouchables. In his view, the problems of untouchables are rooted in denial of basic human rights to them, which are essential for the growth of human being. Therefore, Ambedkar grounded the justification for remedies against caste discrimination of untouchables on the denial of citizenship and other rights.

We also see broadening of solution, since Ambedkar first articulated his formal position in 1919, which later on took a definite shape in 1946. Ambedkar suggested multiple remedies, to be used in combination, to ensure equal opportunity and fair access, participation and representation of the untouchables in social, political and economic processes in the society. In a sequence, these include (overturning the customary rules of caste system based on inequality) first, the provision of equal rights to all, legal safeguards against violation of rights in terms of punitive measures, measures to ensure equal access and participation (through reservation policy) in civil, political and economic spheres, and in addition, a definite strategy by the state for the development and empowerment of untouchables to compensate for denial of equal opportunities in the past.

Let us now discuss the logic and reasons behind each of these measures.

Remedies against Present Discrimination

Equal rights

Guarantee of the equality before law and possession of equal rights common with other citizens of India in all public spheres was suggested as an initial pre-condition. This requires an abolition of customary laws governing institution of untouchability and the caste system.

Legal safeguards against violation of rights

Guaranteeing equal rights, however, is not enough, unless adequate legal safeguards and protection accompany them, when the rights are violated. Ambedkar argued that equality of opportunities is impossible under the Indian social situation, which does not recognize equality, and attempts by untouchables to secure equal rights are opposed by high castes. Those in the government, particularly the executive and civil service, also oppose the equality of opportunity. Therefore, remedy is not only that untouchable has equal rights that every community have, but that there is a mechanism which provides legal ways and means by which the untouchables are protected in the exercise of rights, which consists of legal penalties against infringement of the rights.

Ambedkar suggested the legal safeguards against the practice of caste discrimination both for private and public sector. He writes:

> Discrimination against citizens by government officers in public administration or by private employers in factories and commercial concerns on the grounds of race or creed or social status should be treated as offences.[9]

The private sector is defined in a manner so as to include not only employment but also commercial concerns, which include transactions in various markets. In the context of punitive measures associated with social boycott, Ambedkar clarified that spheres under the private sectors be included under 'commercial concerns'. Private sphere includes renting and use of houses (housing market) and land (agriculture land market and lease market), hiring of workers (employment market), undertaking business with another person (capital, product and consumer markets), to render and receive any service (transactions and services carried through market and non-market channels), and things which are commonly done in the ordinary course of business.[10]

Looking at it from market economy perspective, the spheres that are included in the definition of private sector for legal safeguards include transactions in various markets and non-market channels such as all input goods and their markets (that is, agricultural land markets, labour market, capital market), product and consumer markets, private housing markets, educational institutions and exchange undertaken in other services necessary for any business activity and other provisions related with social and public goods.

Strategies for fair share, participation and representation

The anti-discrimination measures in the form of 'equality before law' and 'legal safeguards against violation' have their limitations. The laws only prevent members in the society from taking steps that puts minorities in disadvantageous situations in the market and other spheres. Despite laws, due to practice of discrimination and opposition by high castes, the untouchables, however, may not enjoy fair access and participation in economic, social and political processes. In this context, Ambedkar contended, "in a country like India where it is possible for discrimination to practice on vast scale and in relentless manner fundamental rights can have no meaning."[11] Therefore, in addition to legal safeguards against discrimination, there is a need to have protection against discrimination to provide fair access and participation in legislature, executive, government services, educational institutions and other spheres.

Therefore, Ambedkar suggested measures to ensure fair access and participation in various spheres, which include legislative bodies, executive, public services, educational institutions and all public spheres, by representation in proportion to population. Besides these legal safeguards, Ambedkar suggested pro-active measures on the part of government to provide equal access and participation in various public spheres. Why there is a need for pro-active measures in the form of reservation? The legal measures have their limitations in ensuring fair participation to discriminated groups, therefore, the legal safeguards need to be supplemented by methods like reservations that facilitates, equal share, representation and participation to discriminated groups in various spheres.

Remedies against Structural Inequalities Associated with Past (or Historical) Exclusion

From the above discussion, it is clear that Ambedkar recognized the need of a three-fold strategy: first, provision of equal rights, (overturning the customary framework of caste system based on the principles of inequality and denial of equal rights particularly to untouchables); second, provision of legal safeguards against the violation of these rights in term of laws; and third, the pro-active measures against discrimination for fair share and participation in legislature, executive, public services, educational institutions and other public spheres for discriminated groups of untouchables (in the form of reservation policy).

However, Ambedkar also recognized that the present poverty, deprivation and marginalization of untouchables were deep rooted and hence a solution of present deprivation could not be effective, if one does not take into account the effects of historical denials on present capabilities to gainfully engage with available opportunities. As stated earlier, the legal measures, in terms of equal laws and legal safeguards for fair representation and participation in public spheres (in the form of reservation policy), cannot overcome the poverty and deprivation caused by exclusion and isolation in the past, which is reflected in abject lack of resources (agriculture land and non-land assets), education, employment, and also lack of basic civil, cultural rights for development, which is required to make use of the provision of equal opportunity in a meaningful way. Remedies against discrimination are indeed necessary, but these anti-discriminatory measures serve as safeguards against discrimination in the present and are ineffective, when it comes to overcoming the cumulative deprivation caused by historical exclusion and isolation. Therefore, certain policies are required to compensate the discriminated groups of untouchables for historical denial of ownership of resources, access to education, employment, and social needs.

Ambedkar also recognized this limitation of anti-discrimination policies of legal and fair participation. In his view, the real solution lies in removing the structural inequalities caused by past exclusion and isolation in more fundamental ways and recommended the policies of 'structural equalization'. In his systematic and comprehensive elaboration on this issue, Ambedkar, thus, suggested dual remedies: firstly, a set of policies/remedies relating to the safeguards against discrimination in the present or current discrimination discussed above (that is, equality before law, legal safeguards against discrimination and strategy for participation and representation) and secondly, strategies to overcome deep-rooted deprivation caused by historical exclusion and isolation of untouchables. Emphasizing the solution against structural inequalities, Ambedkar observed:

> There can be no doubt that in view of the circumstances, the uplift of the Depressed Classes will remain a pious hope unless the task is placed in the forefront of all governmental activities and unless equalisation of opportunities is realised in practice by a definite policy and determined efforts on the part of government.[12]

For this purpose, Ambedkar suggested three measures. The first among these is to entrust the state with the responsibility to develop policies and programmes for educational and economic development of the scheduled castes (SCs). Such a policy is suggested specifically with respect to educational and economic development. The denial of right to education, with property and business rights, has led to high illiteracy, landlessness and lack of ownership of capital assets or business. Therefore, Ambedkar put singular responsibility on the state for the development of education and enhancement of ownership of capital assets in terms of agricultural land and non-land assets. In *State and Minorities,* in the section on the "Special Responsibilities of the Government", Ambedkar suggested few remedies. For example, in the economic sphere, Ambedkar put responsibility on the state for providing access to agricultural land and capital to SCs and others. He suggested for more radical remedy in the form of 'state socialism' for protection against economic exploitation. Ambedkar observed:

> The main purpose behind the clause is to put an obligation on the state to plan the economic life of the people on the lines which would lead to highest point of productivity without closing every

> avenue to the private sector and provide for the equitable distribution of wealth. The plan set out in the clause proposes state ownership in agriculture with collectivised method of cultivation and a modified form of State Socialism in the field of industry. It places squarely on the shoulders of the state the obligation to supply capital necessary for agriculture as well as for industry. It also proposes state owned insurance system.[13]

Ambedkar also suggested a statuary obligation to maintain a separate administrative division to deal with their problems, that is "to watch the interests of the Depressed Classes and promoting their welfare" and argued for representation of untouchables in the process of preparation and formulation of the general policy of the government so that they can influence the decision-making process with their presence at all levels. In this respect, Ambedkar observed:

> Just as it is necessary that the Depressed Classes should have the power to influence governmental action by seats in the Legislature, so also it is desirable that the Depressed Classes should have the opportunity to frame the general policy of the government. This they can do only if they can find a seat in the Cabinet.[14]

Thus, the participation of the depressed classes to influence the state policies in its various arms, such as legislature, executive and public services, was considered essential and necessary by Ambedkar. For Ambedkar, merely representing the 'interests' of Dalits was not enough. He believed that the interests of discriminated groups could be meaningfully ensured by their own participation in decision-making process at all levels. He also recommended participation of Dalits in the democratic polity at all levels from legislation to execution of policies and measures, which will regulate the working of modern Indian society and its institutions. In this manner, in the conceptual scheme and vision of Ambedkar, representation and participation were fused together. His arguments for reservation in the Indian conditions are an innovative and original formulation to bring together the requirement of representation and participation of marginalized groups through an elaborate system of rights. For ensuring participatory democracy and equal opportunity, rights embodied in the constitution were emphasized by Ambedkar. He was aware that if a society practises discrimination, then the impetus for change can only be located in the state, outside and autonomous of society and its practices. As historically society has practised discrimination and isolated a certain group of individuals through hierarchical arrangement, Ambedkar recommended fair terms for their inclusion in the democratic polity, economy and social and cultural life. Bearing in mind the discriminatory attitude of society, he advocated an elaborate system of safeguards to ensure an inclusive, equal and participatory polity through rights embodied in constitution. The fact that historical discrimination was still pervasive and prevalent in Indian society, Ambedkar argued for intervention in the way society reproduces itself to arrest the retrogressive practices and ideas on which much of the social order was based, presenting itself as 'natural'.

It is also necessary to emphasize that Ambedkar suggested constitutional obligations on the state to undertake developmental measures, just not leaving state's effort to the voluntary initiative of the legislature and the government. In a statement/scheme submitted to the Round Table Conference in 1930 Ambedkar observed:

> In and for each Province in India it shall be the duty and obligation of the Legislature and the Executive or any other Authority established by law to make adequate provision for the education, sanitation, recruitment in public services and other matters of social and political advancement of Depressed Classes.[15]

In a similar manner, Ambedkar also suggested safeguards against the failure of administrative authority to implement the statutory and other provisions for advancement of depressed classes.

Concluding Observations

This journey through the formative stage of evolution of policy for the remedies against structural inequalities associated with institution of caste system and untouchability in general and discrimination and deprivation of untouchables in particular from 1919 to 1946, provides the insights into the Ambedkar's interpretation of caste system and its consequences. Ambedkar articulated the remedies against the consequences of caste and untouchability based exclusion and discrimination in Indian society in general and the untouchables in particular, in successive stages from 1919 till 1947, which ultimately culminated in the present policy at the time of framing of Indian Constitution in 1950.

Ambedkar suggested two sets of remedies: a set of remedies against continuing (present) discrimination, and another set of remedies against the historical deprivation due to denial of economic, civil and cultural rights in the past and structural inequalities in Indian society.

Three safeguards are suggested against the continuing practice of untouchability and caste discrimination in the present. Safeguards against the present discrimination include provision of equal rights, legal safeguards in the form of preventive laws against the violation of the legal rights and pro-active measures for fair share and participation in legislature, executive, public services, educational institutions and other public spheres for discriminated groups of untouchables (in the form of reservation policy).

Given the limitations of these measures (which are used as safeguards against discrimination in the present) as solution to the problems of deprivation due to historical exclusion, Ambedkar also suggested more fundamental measures for addressing the issue of 'structural inequalities' and suggested developmental measures for equalization, through 'state socialism' specifically in the economic spheres.

In Ambedkar's view equal rights would provide the legal framework, overturning the unequal customary legal framework of the institution of caste system and untouchability. Legal safeguards in the form of punitive laws will not only provide protection against violation of laws but also against discrimination in public and private spheres, and the pro-active measures will provide for fair share, participation and representation through reservation in public spheres as a safeguard against present discrimination. The strategy against structural inequalities as compensatory measures for past denial of economic and education rights would help empower the discriminated groups and reduce inequalities between them and rest of the sections in Indian society.

Notes

1. Ambedkar, B.R. (first published 1987), "The Hindu Social Order: Its Essential Features" in Vasant Moon (ed.), *Dr. Babasaheb Ambedkar: Writing and Speeches*", Vol. 3, Department of Education, Government of Maharashtra, Mumbai, pp. 95-115.
2. Human Development Report: Cultural Liberty in Today's Diverse World (2004), Oxford University Press, New Delhi, p. 32.
3. In this respect, Ambedkar suggests: "Discrimination against citizen by government officers in Public Administration or by private employers in factories and commercial concerns on the grounds of race or creed, or social status shall be treated as an offence. The jurisdiction to try such cases shall be vested in a tribunal to be created for the purpose", "State and Minorities" (1947) in Vasant Moon (ed.) *Dr. Babasaheb Ambedkar: Writing and Speeches,* Vol. 1, Department of Education, Government of Maharashtra, Mumbai, 1979, p. 256 and p. 261.
4. Ambedkar, B.R. (1928), "Statement Concerning the Safeguards of the Depressed Classes as a minority in the Bombay Presidency and the changes in the composition of and the guarantees from the Bombay Legislative Council necessary to ensure the same under Provincial Autonomy" submitted by Depressed Class Institute of Bombay, in Vasant Moon (ed.) (1982), *Dr. Babasaheb Ambedkar: Writings and Speeches* – In the Bombay Legislature, with the Simon Commission and at the Round Table Conference – 1927 to 1939, Vol. 2, Education Department, Government of Maharashtra.
5. Ibid., p. 445.
6. Ambedkar, B.R. (1930), Proceeding of Round Table Conference: (1) Plenary Session-Fifth Sitting-20th November 1930, Need for Political Power for Depressed Classes.(2) In Sub-Committee No. III (Minorities) Second Sitting-31st December 1930, Government of India, in Vasant Moon (ed.) (1982), *Dr. Babasaheb Ambedkar: Writings and Speeches* – In the Bombay Legislature, with the Simon Commission and at the Round Table

Conference – 1927 to 1939, Vol. 2, Education Department, Government of Maharashtra, p. 504.

7. Ambedkar, B.R., State and Minorities: What are their Rights and How to Secure Them in the Constitution, Scheduled Caste Federation, Bombay, 1946, pp. 406-407.
8. Ibid.
9. Ibid., p. 396.
10. Ibid., p. 399.
11. Ibid., p. 408.
12. Ambedkar, B.R. (1930), op. cit., pp. 553-54.
13. Ambedkar, B.R. (1946), op. cit., p. 408.
14. Ambedkar, B.R. and Rao Bahadur R. Srinivasan (1930), "A Scheme of Political Safeguards for the Protection of the Depressed Classes in the Future Constitution of Self-Governing India" – Appendix to Report of Sub-Committee No. III (Minorities), in Vasant Moon (ed.) (1982), *Dr. Babasaheb Ambedkar: Writings and Speeches* – In the Bombay Legislature, with the Simon Commission and at the Round Table Conference – 1927 to 1939, Vol. 2, Education Department, Government of Maharashtra, p. 554.
15. Ambedkar, B.R. (1930), op. cit.

References

Ambedkar, B.R. (1917) "Castes in India: Their Mechanism, Genesis and Development", *Indian Antiquary*, May 1917, Vol. XLI.

— (1936) "Annihilation of Caste" in Vasant Moon (ed.) *Dr. Babasaheb Ambedkar: Writings and Speeches*, Vol. 1, Education Department, Government of Maharashtra, Mumbai.

— (1946) *State and Minorities: What are Their Rights and How to Secure Them in the Constitution*, Scheduled Caste Federation, Bombay.

— (1956) "Buddha and Karl Marx" in Vasant Moon (ed.) *Dr. Babasaheb Ambedkar: Writing and Speeches,* Vol. 3, Education Department, Government of Maharashtra, Mumbai.

— (1989) "On Economics". In Vasant Moon (ed.), *Dr. Babasaheb Ambedkar: Writings and Speeches*, Vol. 6, Education Department, Government of Maharashtra, Mumbai.

— (1987), "The Hindu Social Order: Its Essential Features" in Vasant Moon (ed.): *Dr. Babasaheb Ambedkar: Writings and Speeches*, Vol. 3, Department. of Education, Government of Maharashtra, Mumbai.

— and Rao Bahadur R. Srinivasan (1930) "A Scheme of Political Safeguards for the Protection of the Depressed Classes in the Future Constitution of Self-Governing India" –Appendix to Report of Sub Committee No.III(Minorities),in Vasant Moon (ed.) (1982), *Dr. Babasaheb Ambedkar: Writings and Speeches*, in the Bombay Legislature, with the Simon Commission and at the Round Table Conference – 1927 to 1939, Vol. 2, Education Department, Government of Maharashtra, Mumbai.

— (1919) "Evidence before the Southborough's Committee on Franchise" January, 1919 in Vasant Moon (ed.) (1979) "Evidence Before the Southborough's Committee on Franchise" January, 1919" in *Dr. Babasaheb Ambedkar: Writings and Speeches*, Vol. 1, Education Department, Government of Maharashtra, Mumbai.

— (1928) Statement concerning the safeguards of the Depressed Classes as a minority in the Bombay Presidency and the changes in the composition of and the guarantees from the Bombay Legislative Council necessary to ensure the same under Provincial Autonomy submitted by Depressed Class Institute of Bombay, in Vasant Moon (ed.) (1982), *Dr. Babasaheb Ambedkar: Writings and Speeches*. In the Bombay Legislature, with the Simon Commission and at the Round Table Conference – 1927 to 1939, Vol. 2, Education Department, Government of Maharashtra, Mumbai.

— (1930) Proceeding of Round Table Conference: (1) Plenary Session-Fifth Sitting-20th November 1930, Need for Political Power for Depressed Classes. (2) In Sub-Committee No. III (Minorities) Second Sitting-31st December 1930, Government of India, in Vasant Moon (ed.) (1982), *Dr. Babasaheb Ambedkar: Writings and Speeches*. In the Bombay Legislature, with the Simon Commission and at the Round Table Conference - 1927 to 1939, Vol. 2, Education Department, Government of Maharashtra, Mumbai.

Banerjee, Biswjit (1991) "Job Discrimination and Untouchability" in Nancy Birdsall and Richar Sabot (eds.), *Unfair Advantage: Labour Market Discrimination in Developing Countries*", The World Bank, Washington D.C.

Deshpande, Ashwini (1999) "Recasting Economic Inequality", Carolina Population Centre, University of North Carolina at Chapel Hill (USA).

Haan, De Arjan (1997) 'Poverty and Social Exclusion: A Comparison of Debates on Deprivation', Working Paper No. 2, Poverty Research Unit at Sussex. Brighton: University of Sussex.

Lal, Deepak (1984) *Hindu Equilibrium: Cultural Stability and Economic Stagnation*, Vol. I, Clarendon Press, Oxford.

Thorat, S.K. (1999) "Caste and Labour Market Discrimination" (with R.S. Deshpande), *Indian Journal of Labour Economics*, Conference Issue, November.

— (2002) "Oppression and Denial: Dalit Discrimination in the 1990s", *Economic and Political Weekly*, February 9.

— (1996) "Ambedkar on Economics of Hindu Social Order: Understanding Its Orthodoxy and Legacy" in Walter Fernandez (ed.), *The Emerging Dalit Identity*, Indian Social Institute, Delhi.

— (2003) (with Prakash Louis) "Caste, Ethnicity and Religion: An Overview of Exclusion/Discrimination and Deprivation", Concept Paper for DFID, Delhi May 2003.

— (2003) 'Caste, Exclusion/Discrimination and Deprivation: The Situation of Dalits in India', Concept Paper for DFID, Delhi, May 2003.

— (2005) (with Maha Mallick) 'Persistence Poverty: Why Scheduled Caste and Scheduled Tribes Stay Chronically Poor?' Working Paper, IIPA, Research Centre for Chronic Poverty, London.

— (2005) (with S., Venket) 'Human Poverty and Disadvantage Groups', Working Paper, UNDP, Delhi,

United Nations (2004) *United Nation Development Report – Culture and Liberty – 2004*, New York.

William, Darity Jr. (ed.) (1995) *Economics and Discrimination*, Vol. I, Edward Elgar Publishing.

William, Darity, Jr. & Steven Shulman (1989), *Question of Discrimination – Racial Inequality in the U.S. Labour Market*, Wesleyan University Press, Middletown, Connecticut.

William, Darity, Jr., (1997) "Reparations" in Samuel L. Myers, Jr. (ed.), *Civil Rights and Race Relations in the Post Reagan-Bush Era*, Praeger, London.

4 Labour Policy

BHALCHANDRA MUNGEKAR

Annihilation of caste[1] was the mission of Dr. Ambedkar's life. He, therefore, fought it at all the levels – economic, social, political, and the foremost, intellectual. And yet, it would be erroneous to view Dr. Ambedkar only as a crusader against the caste system. As a champion of liberty, equality and fraternity, he identified himself with the sufferings of all the downtrodden in the Indian society and struggled for securing them justice.

In this paper an attempt is made to throw light on Dr. Ambedkar's perspective on the labour problem. Part I of the paper deals with his views about the ideological position that, according to him, the labouring classes in a capitalist society ought to take. Part II outlines some of his views and suggestions for maintaining harmonious industrial relations. In Part III, a brief account of the measures for labour welfare that Dr. Ambedkar undertook, during his tenure as the Labour Member in the Viceroy's Executive Council, is presented. In the fourth and last part, an attempt has been made to bring out the relevance of Dr. Ambedkar's perspective on the contemporary labour problem in India.

I

In order to understand the background of Dr. Ambedkar's perspective on the labour problem, it is necessary first to delineate his views on the nature of the parliamentary democracy in the capitalist economy.

Labour and the Parliamentary Democracy

Dr. Ambedkar held that coexistence of parliamentary democracy and capitalist economy involves inherent contradictions. He argued:

> Those who are living under the capitalistic form of industrial organization and under the form of political organization called Parliamentary Democracy must recognize the contradictions of their system. The first contradiction is between fabulous wealth and abject poverty, not in its simple form, but in its aggravated form, in which we see it, wealth to those who do not work and poverty for those who do.[2]

In other words, there is a clear-cut division of the capitalist society into 'rich' and 'poor' which only gives rise to the second contradiction, i.e., equality in politics and inequality in economics.[3] Thus, according to Dr. Ambedkar, "what has vitiated Parliamentary Democracy is the failure to realize that political democracy cannot succeed where there is no social and economic democracy. Social and economic democracies are the tissues and the fibres of a political democracy. The tougher the tissue and the fibre, the greater will be the strength of the body. Democracy is another name for equality".[4] It therefore follows that inequality in economics renders equality in politics ineffective and meaningless. This led Dr. Ambedkar to argue that though "Parliamentary Democracy developed a passion for liberty, it never made even a nodding acquaintance with equality. It failed to realize the significance of equality, and did not even endeavour to strike a balance between liberty and equality, with the result that liberty swallowed equality and left a progeny of inequalities".[5]

According to Dr. Ambedkar, yet another reason for the disfiguring of the parliamentary democracy is the nature of 'freedom of contract' in the capitalist economy, because it is a contract between two parties that are unequal. Thus, Dr. Ambedkar maintained:

> What has ruined Parliamentary Democracy is the idea of freedom of contract. The idea became sanctified and was upheld in the name of

> liberty. Parliamentary Democracy took no notice of economic inequalities and did not care to examine the result of freedom of contract on the parties to the contract, should they happen to be unequal. Parliamentary Democracy ignores the implications of freedom of contract that allows the strong to defraud the weak. The result is that Parliamentary Democracy in standing out as protagonist of liberty has continuously added to the economic wrongs of the poor, the downtrodden and the disinherited class.[6]

Dr. Ambedkar then turned to the most pertinent issue. He attributed the miseries and the deprivations of the labouring and the downtrodden classes to themselves. He criticized the labouring classes for having "shown a most appalling indifference to the effect of the economic factor in the making of men's life".[7] According to him, these classes have "failed to give economic facts the imperative force they have in determining the term of associated life".[8] Thus, having argued that "man does not live by bread alone", he wished that the "labouring classes thought of bread first and everything else afterwards".[9]

According to Dr. Ambedkar, another besetting sin of the labouring classes is that they are easily led away by an appeal to nationalism. They unfortunately overlook the fact that "the free independent nation state which emerges from a successful nationalism and which rears on their sacrifices turns out to be the energy of the working class under the hegemony of their masters".[10] Dr. Ambedkar held that "this is the worst kind of exploitation that labour has allowed itself to be subjected to".[11]

But, perhaps, the biggest crime that the labouring classes have committed against themselves, Dr. Ambedkar maintained, is that "they developed no ambition to capture government", and they "are not even convinced of the necessity of controlling government as a necessary means of safeguarding their interests".[12] This, he considered, is the biggest and the most lamentable of all the tragedies which beset mankind. This, however, does not mean that he was against trade unions. He agreed that trade unions do useful job, but held that it was not enough. He argued that trade unions should not be considered a panacea for all the ills of the labour, because according to him, howsoever powerful the trade unions may be, they "are not strong enough to compel capitalists to run capitalism better". Therefore, he suggested that the "control of Government must be the target for labour to aim at. Unless Trade Unionism aims at controlling government, trade unions will do very little good to the workers and will be a source of perpetual squabbles among trade union leaders".[13]

Thus, in order to turn the Parliamentary Democracy to their own benefit, Dr. Ambedkar advised the labouring classes to organize themselves into a political party, viz., The Labour Party.[14] Since, according to him, "there were two classes in the world – the 'haves' and the 'have-nots', the 'rich' and the 'poor', the 'exploiters' and the 'exploited' – he exhorted the peasants and the workers to think over the causes of their poverty and told them that they lay in the richness of the exploiters".[15] Therefore, he concluded, "the only way for them (the labouring classes) was to organise a labour front without any regard to caste, or creed, and to elect the legislatures those who were their real representatives. If they did so, they would have shelter, clothing, and they who produced food and wealth of the nation would not die from hunger".[16]

In this context, Dr. Ambedkar spelt out two specific issues. Firstly, he emphasized that the Labour Party must dissociate itself from communal or capitalistic political parties.[17] Secondly, the Labour Party must acquire knowledge so as to equip itself with fitness to govern. In this context, he maintained that the Labour government cannot be a government of *laissez faire* but "must essentially be based on a system of control; and a system of control needs a far greater degree of knowledge and training than a *laissez faire* government does".[18]

Thus, Dr. Ambedkar passionately desired the labouring classes to rise to the status of the governing class.

II

The Bombay Presidency Government introduced in 1938 an Industrial Disputes Bill dealing with various aspects of industrial relations. The provisions of the Bill were so comprehensive that it sought to replace the Bombay Trade Disputes Conciliation Act, 1934. For instance, the Bill sought to differentiate between registered, recognized, qualified and representative unions; it provided for the appointment of Conciliation Officers; it defined, for the first time, legality or otherwise of a strike/lockout, and so on.[19] Dr. Ambedkar was then representing the Independent Labour Party (in Bombay Legislative Assembly). He actively participated in the discussions over the Bill. The views he expressed on this occasion are of such fundamental nature that they transcend the provisions of the Bill, and clearly bring out his vision of industrial relations in a much wider perspective.

Strike: A Right to Freedom

First of all, it would be pertinent to underscore Dr. Ambedkar's views on strikes. According to him, a strike is an expression of the 'right to freedom'. This is because a worker cannot be made to work against his will. Thus, according to Dr. Ambedkar, a strike is "simply another name for the right to freedom of one's services on any terms that one wants to obtain".[20] Arguing as a staunch believer in democracy, he went a step further and argued that if the "right to freedom is a divine right" then the "right to strike is also a divine right".[21]

In this context, he further argued that "a strike is nothing more than a breach of contract of service" and therefore it is "only civil wrong". In most certain terms Dr. Ambedkar made it clear that a strike "is not a crime".[22] Therefore, he argued that "whenever a man breaks a contract of service all that the aggrieved party (i.e., employer) is entitled to is damages; he can never seek specific relief, and a court can never give relief whereby it can compel a man to perform the contract of service which he has entered upon".[23]

Thus, according to Dr. Ambedkar, "to penalise a strike" amounts to "making the worker slave" as "slavery is nothing else but involuntary servitude" which is "contrary to ethics" and also "contrary to jurisprudence".[24] He therefore opposed the provision of the Bill prescribing a fine or imprisonment, or both, to an employee joining this strike or making others to participate in it, even if a strike is declared illegal due to non-fulfilment to certain conditions.[25] Dr. Ambedkar opposed penalizing a strike even in a public utility service though he agreed that such a strike causes inconveniences to the public. He argued that "no doubt such a strike is inconvenient and interferes in our ordinary comforts, but it is monstrous to claim that if any body of men refuses to minister to our comfort, if any to claim that body as criminals especially when the strikers feel that these comforts and conveniences can only be satisfied by their own degradation and misery".[26] He granted that if at all a strike was to be declared illegal, it should relate to only those "services on which the sustenance of life of the community depends".[27] However, even in such cases, he ruled out criminal prosecutions of the strikers. He even opposed the use of police force against the striking workers on the pretext that the strike results in a breach of peace.

Recognition to Unions

'Recognition to unions' is one of the most important issues influencing industrial relations. It becomes all the more crucial when the employer prefers to negotiate, and rightly so, only with the representative union, and simultaneously there are more than one unions in the occupation or in the industry claiming to represent the workers. It is in this context that the legal provision for recognizing a 'representative' union assumes paramount importance.

Now, the Bill under consideration provided for two categories of unions. The first category of union was required to have not less than 20 per cent of the workers as its members and thus could be recognized by the employer as a representative union. The second category of union could become representative only if it could command more than 50 per cent of the total workers as its members.[28] Further, the latter was to lose its recognition as a representative union as and when its membership declined to less than 50 per cent. Now, Dr. Ambedkar called the first category of union as a 'slave' union and the second as a 'free' union. He thus argued that the condition of registering more than 50 per cent of the total workers in an industry as member was practically impossible to fulfil. He therefore alleged that by laying down such a difficult condition, the government intended to give freedom to the employers to bring into existence the unions of their own choice. Consequently, according to Dr. Ambedkar, the only kind of union that would represent labour while negotiating with the employer or in the conciliation proceedings would be "none other than the slave union recognised by the masters. Such provisions in the long run would only hamper the growth of free trade union movement in the country".[29]

One Industry, One Union

Multiplicity of unions in an industry has been considered one of the major shortcomings of the trade union movement in India. This is mainly because, it divided the strength and unity of the workers and benefits only the employer. This reinforces the view of considering 'one industry, one union' desirable. Apparently, this line of argument seems to be irrefutable.

However, Dr. Ambedkar examined the issues of 'one industry, one union' from a different perspective. He argued that no doubt, a trade union has to pursue economic issues such as wages, hours of work, and other working conditions, etc., which are called 'purely trade union objects'. Trade unions also have/need to pursue certain social objects, viz., old age pensions, employment benefits to the members, providing pension for their widows, and so on. But, in addition to these pursuits, Dr. Ambedkar held, a trade union also has a political purpose.[30] In this context, a problem would certainly arise when all the workers in an occupation or an industry are unable to agree upon all the three purposes. Further, of all the three purposes mentioned above, an agreement on political purpose is virtually impossible to achieve. Under those conditions, there are bound to be more than one union in one occupation or industry, whatever the desirability of having one union in one industry.[31] Taking into consideration these crucial dimensions, Dr. Ambedkar opposed the provision of the Bill empowering the Registrar not to "register more than one union in any local area in respect of any industry or occupation, as the case may be".[32] He, therefore, submitted that the provision of the Bill intended to compel the people not to have any union at all, and thus it was "fraught with a great mischief".[33]

Wages: The First Claim on Profits

Grievances of workers over the levels of wages have been the most prominent cause of industrial conflicts in India.[34] It is because the workers always feel that the wages paid to them are lower than the ones they ought to receive. Contrary is the perception of an employer. Dr. Ambedkar justified the feelings of the workers and maintained that the workers' wages should be made "the first charge on the profits of the industry".[35] Disapproving the claim of the employer that the industry belongs to him (i.e., capital), he argued that as a matter of fact "the owner of the industry gets his earning not entirely by his capital, but also by the sweat of another man"[36], i.e., worker. He therefore suggested that every employer must be compelled to disclose the details of the management, including his budget. This would enable the workers to scrutinize "whether the balance that is left to be divisible among the labourers is fair or whether the employer has taken a undue and underserved portion of the total profits".[37] He hoped that such a procedure, among other things, would reduce labour troubles, make the negotiations more effective and fruitful, and ultimately help secure more industrial peace.

Need for Uniformity in Labour Legislation

Dr. Ambedkar advocated the uniformity of labour legislation in India. In fact, the Government of India Act of 1935 made it more imperative than before. The Act had created a federal contribution and includes 'labour' in the Concurrent Legislative List. Thus, in the absence of the central legislation, each province can make a particular law suited to itself and it may not only be different from the laws made by the neighbouring states, but its provincial considerations may also dominate over the considerations of national importance. Therefore, on becoming the Labour Member in the Viceroy's Executive Council in 1942, Dr. Ambedkar took the initiative in promoting the uniformity in labour legislations in India.[38]

Joint Labour Conference

According to Dr. Ambedkar, peace in industry, among other things, depends upon two things, viz., existence of mechanism that could settle quickly the industrial disputes, and removal of any such conditions in industry "that deteriorate the morale of the people engaged in it and cause industrial unrest".[39] Now, one of the requirements would be constant dialogue and discussions among the three parties that are responsible for the maintenance of industrial peace, viz., the employees, the employer, and the government. With these objectives in view, Dr. Ambedkar, as the Labour Member, took the initiative in establishing two permanent national level organizations in India, viz., a Tripartite Labour Conference, and a Standing Advisory Committee.[40] Both these organizations have gone a long way in shaping the industrial relations and also the trade union movement in India in general. It is, therefore, rightly acknowledged that "the beginning of industrial relations dynamics can be traced back to the inception of the Indian Labour Conference as far back as in 1942 by Dr. Ambedkar, when the policy of bringing together the three parties, namely, the government, management and labour on a common platform as a consultative tripartite forum for all matters of labour policy and industrial relations was accepted".[41]

III

As it was mentioned in the beginning, throughout his life, Dr. Ambedkar championed the cause of the Depressed Classes. Since labour has obviously been the exploited and deprived section of the society, he always remained committed to the welfare of labour. His ideological position towards labour on the structure of industrial relations, or on the institutional arrangement he visualized for maintaining industrial peace – all clearly speaks for his wider concern toward the workers.

It is therefore natural that the welfare of labour got a prominent place in the election manifesto of the Independent Labour Party that he founded in 1936. Thus, among other things, the manifesto promised to implement measures such as the provision of a minimum standard of living to the workers compatible with civilized life. Similarly, for the benefit of the industrial workers, the party would endeavour to "introduce legislation to control the employment, dismissal and promotion of employers in factories, to fix minimum hours of work, to make provision for the payment of adequate wages, for leave with pay, and as many amenities of life as possible, and to provide payment to the workers of bonus, pension or other provisions on retirement from active work, on account of old age or other incapacity. The party would also introduce a scheme of social insurance, which would provide protection to the workers against sickness, unemployment and accident. The party would endeavour to provide cheap and sanitary dwellings for the workers".[42]

During his tenure as the Labour Member in the Viceroy's Executive Council (VEC) (1942-46), Dr. Ambedkar took initiative in introducing a series of welfare measures for the industrial workers. In this context, what is gratifying to observe, and in fact creditable to Dr. Ambedkar, was that even while serving in the VEC, he did not compromise his concern towards the welfare of the industrial workers.

In 1943, Dr. Ambedkar introduced in the Central Assembly the War Injuries (Compensation Insurance) Bill. It sought (i) to give compensation to workmen who may become victims of war injuries, (ii) to make employers liable for such compensation, and (iii) to compel employers to insure against liabilities upon them.[43]

Dr. Ambedkar took keen interest in accelerating the provision of housing for industrial workers. The seventh meeting of the Standing Labour Committee presided by him resolved to appoint a sub-committee to work out the details of the housing scheme for industrial workers.[44] The terms of reference of the sub-committee were to recommend, whether a Building Fund for the housing of workers was necessary and the manner in which it can be raised, to decide the basis on which the workers can be required to pay rent to prescribe minimum standards for workers' houses, and so on. The sub-committee composed of representatives of the Central Government, of the provinces, of the Indian states, and those of employers and employees including the representatives of municipalities and municipal workers.[45]

Welfare of Women Workers

Women constituted one of the most disadvantaged sections of the Indian society. Therefore, since beginning, Dr. Ambedkar was sympathetic to their cause and championed their interests. Thus, as the

Labour Member, he unfailingly proposed some welfare measures to improve the lot of women industrial workers.

In 1943, he introduced an amendment to the Mines Maternity Benefit Act, 1941. According to the original provisions of the Act, a woman worker was entitled to eight weeks' maternity leave, of which she may avail voluntarily four weeks before delivery, or work during the period and get full wages, but after delivery, it was compulsory for her to take leave and rest. Now, the difficulty arose as to whether she would be entitled to pre-delivery, four weeks' leave even when the mine was closed by the owner on a particular day. Dr. Ambedkar's amendment removed the uncertainty and maintained that "for everyday during the four weeks preceding delivery the women would be entitled to maternity benefit".[46]

In 1945, he once again sought to amend the Mines Maternity Benefit Act. This time the purpose of the amendment was to extend the maternity benefit to pregnant women working in mines, below the ground. Thus, firstly, no woman was allowed to work underground for ten weeks before confinement, and was supposed to rest compulsorily for four weeks after confinement. Secondly, only such women were qualified to this benefit who would work underground for 90 days during the period of six months.[47]

State's Obligation towards Labour

As regards the fulfilment of the state's obligation towards labour welfare, Dr. Ambedkar dealt with some important issues. The first related to the urgency of labour welfare legislation. In this context, it was argued that the British people waited for a century to get the Labour Code and hence, we should not be in hurry to bring about the legislation. To this Dr. Ambedkar's reply was characteristic and, therefore, needs to be expressed in his own words. Dr. Ambedkar maintained:

> Labour may well say that the fact that the British took 100 years to have a proper code of labour legislation is no argument that we should also in India take 100 years. History is not to be studied merely with a view to know how well to imitate the mistakes of

other countries. We study history with a view to know the errors people have made and how they could be avoided. History is not always an example. More often it is a warning.[48]

To those who gave Russia's example and argued that the working class there was forced to accept low living standards in order to enable industries to grow, Dr. Ambedkar's reply was profound. Dr. Ambedkar contended:

> Labour is bound to say that the example of Russia is entirely out of place in a discussion about labour standards in a country in which industry is run as a private enterprise working in pursuit of private and personal gain. In Russia, industry is a State enterprise and the profits of industry go to fill the Treasury of the State and not to swell the private fortunes of individuals. Where the profits of industry belong to the State, the subjects of the State may well be asked to undergo, during an interim period, reduction in wages and other standards of life in order that the State industries may be stabilised. No worker would mind such a sacrifice knowing that, in the end, the industry would belong to the State and that he would be able to share in the prosperity of the State. How can the workers be asked to agree to reduce standards of life in an economy in which the profits which are to result from such reduced standards are to go to private individuals.[49]

Finally, to the argument that the state as well as private employers does not have the capacity to bear the cost of labour welfare programmes, Dr. Ambedkar's answer is of historical significance. Reacting sharply to this contention, Dr. Ambedkar observed:

> Labour may well ask statesmen to say how many houseless persons could have been decently housed, how many naked persons could have been properly clothed, how many hungry men and women could have been given full nourishment, how many uneducated persons could have been educated, how many sick persons could have been restored to health, if the money spent on war had been

> spent on public welfare? Labour may ask moneyed classes a very pertinent question saying, if you do not mind paying taxes to meet expenditure on war, why do you object to raising funds when their purpose is to raise labour standards?[50]

The view of Dr. Ambedkar expressed above show his total and unflinching commitment to labour welfare.

IV

The foregoing discussion succinctly demonstrates that Dr. Ambedkar's perspective on labour problem was much wider in scope as well as in content. He argued that the labouring classes should grasp/seize the inherent contradictions between the norms of parliamentary democracy based on equality, on one hand, and the capitalist economy breeding economic inequality, on the other. Ambedkar was not prepared to reconcile with the fact that the capitalist economy gives wealth to those who do not work and poverty to those who work. He, therefore, advised the labouring classes to pay maximum attention to economic factors as they decisively influence human affairs, though he did not entirely agree to Marx's materialistic interpretation of history. He warned the working classes to dissociate themselves from communal and capitalist political parties. He provoked them to transcend the limits of day-to-day trade union activities (trade unionism) and nurture the ambition of rising to the level of the ruling class. With this aim, he founded in 1936 the Independent Labour Party as the representative of the labouring classes in India.

Secondly, so far the scenario of industrial relations is concerned, he considered strike as a right to freedom. According to him, strike is only a civil wrong, and hence a worker joining it must not be punished with imprisonment. Further, he was against any provisions of industrial relations legislation that would flourish the unions 'sponsored' or 'approved' by the employers as such unions cannot fight genuinely for workers' rights. He championed free and fearless trade union movement in the country. Therefore, he wanted labour legislations of such nature that would contribute to a healthy trade union movement and not to create obstacles in its growth.

Thirdly, Dr. Ambedkar was all along sympathetic towards the pathetic conditions of the working classes in general. He therefore defended and supported comprehensive social security measures that would better the living conditions of the sweating sections of the society. The relevance of Dr. Ambedkar's labour perspective is unquestionable. The fact that a sizeable section of the Indian population persistently fall below the poverty line, most of them are working in the unorganized sector of the economy, that trade union movement in general could not rise above the day-to-day issues confronting the workers and hence could not develop an ambition to size political power, that to make the matter worse, the tendency among the workers to be swayed by parochial, regional, sectarian and, at present, communal considerations, all this clearly vindicates, Dr. Ambedkar's prophetic understanding of the socio-economic genesis of the labour problem in India.

Notes

1. This is the title of one of Dr. Ambedkar's outstanding contributions to the analysis of the caste system in India. See, Government of Maharashtra, *Dr. Babasaheb Ambedkar: Writings and Speeches*, Vol. 1, 1979, pp. 23-96. Hereafter, *Writings and Speeches*.
2. *Writings and Speeches*, Vol. 10, p.104.
3. Ibid.
4. Ibid., p.108.

   As the Chairman of the Drafting Committee of the Indian Constitution, Dr. Ambedkar had also warned the rulers of the post-Independence India about the contradictions between equality in political life, and inequality in social and economic life of the country. The extent of inequalities in social and economic life of the country and the threat that they have come to pose not only to the political stability but also to the very integration of the country today is a clear testimony to Dr. Ambedkar's warning. In this context, see his last speech in the Constituent Assembly on November 25, 1949.
5. Ibid., pp. 108-09.

6. Ibid., p. 108.
7. Ibid.
8. Ibid., p. 110.
9. Ibid., p. 109.
10. Ibid., p. 111.

    Here, Dr. Ambedkar was obviously referring to the freedom movement of India in which the workers and all the toiling masses fully participated. In this context, one would recall Dr. Ambedkar's comment on the Indian National Congress when he said that "the Congress was a combination of the exploiters and the exploited; it might be necessary for the purpose of achieving of political freedom, but was worse for the purposes of social construction", see, Keer, Dhananjay, *Dr. Ambedkar: Life and Mission*, Popular Prakashan, Mumbai, 1971, p. 286.
11. Ibid., p. 111.
12. Ibid., p. 110.
13. Ibid.
14. Dr. Ambedkar had himself founded in 1936 such a party and named it the Independent Labour Party. The term 'Labour' in the title represented all the socio-economically exploited and downtrodden sections of the Indian society.
15. Keer, op. cit., p. 301.
16. Ibid.
17. Dr. Ambedkar referred to the Hindu Mahasabha and the Congress as the communal and capitalistic political organisations respectively. Though this reference related to the pre-Independence period, the post-Independence scenario is not at all different. In fact, recently, the *Hindutva* forces have become much stronger and aggressive, and therefore Dr. Ambedkar's warning to the working classes becomes more relevant than before.
18. Dr. Ambedkar championed a planned economy with democracy as a system of government, and he described the set up as the "Parliamentary Democracy with State Socialism". See, "the States and Minorities" in *Writings and Speeches*, Vol. 1, 1979, pp. 387-449.
19. See, *Writings and Speeches*, Vol.3, pp. 201-32.
20. Ibid., p. 208.
21. Ibid.

22. Ibid., p. 207.
23. Ibid., p. 205.
24. Ibid., p. 207.
25. For conditions, see Ibid., pp. 203-04. Since the Bill provided for penalizing a strike, Dr. Ambedkar described it as "The Workers Civil Liberties Suspension Act", Ibid., p. 210.
26. Ibid., p. 215.
27. Ibid.

    These services referred to those relating to the public safety and life of the community such as supply of water, light and sanitation, supply and distribution of food and so on. But, he described them as 'social security services' and not 'public utility services', though the distinction between them is thin. In fact, Dr. Ambedkar was opposed to the provisions of the Bill as they were being extended to 'every trade and industry'. Ibid., p. 215.
28. Ibid., pp. 218-19.
29. Ibid., p. 223.

    However, Dr. Ambedkar himself does not seem to have provided a sound and satisfactory criterion for granting recognition to a union as a 'representative' union.
30. Ibid., p. 225.
31. The whole history of the trade union movement in India is a testimony to this view. In this context, Dr. Ambedkar mentioned an interesting and pertinent illustration which related to the workers belonging to the untouchables community. He argued that these workers "may become members of a certain union, but they may also insist that the union ought to promote certain social objects and social purposes for the benefit of the community from which they are drawn. They desire that certain other facilities may be provided and the workers of the other classes do not agree with them. How then is a union to be formed?" (Ibid., p. 225).

    Furthermore, there is a growing tendency among the SC/ST employees in Bombay to form their separate groups particularly for the implementation of reservation meant for them.
32. Ibid.
33. Today, nearly 40 per cent of the total industrial disputes in India are caused due to wages and other related economic factors.
34. Ibid.

35. Ibid., p. 231.
36. Ibid.
37. Ibid.
38. *Writings and Speeches*, Vol. 10, 1991, "The Promotion of Uniformity in Labour legislation in India" was the first among three items of agenda of the first Tripartite Labour Conference in India held in New Delhi on August 7, 1942. As a Labour Member, Dr. Ambedkar presided over the Conference. See Ibid., pp. 13-14.
39. Ibid., p. 15.
40. For details, see Ibid., pp. 13-15.
41. Kudchedkar, L.S., "Aspects of Personnel Management and Industrial Relations" 1979, p. 134 quoted in *Dynamics of Industrial Relations in India* by G.B. Mamoria and S. Mamoria, Himalaya Publishing House, Mumbai, 1991, p. 309.
42. Jadhav, Narendra, *Dr. Ambedkar: Arthik Vichar and Tatvajnan,* Sugava Prakashan, Pune, 1992, p.114. For the manifesto of the Independent Labour Party, see, Jadhav, Ibid.
43. *Writings and Speeches*, Vol. 10, p. 69.
44. Ibid., p. 291.
45. Ibid.
46. Ibid., p. 88.
47. Ibid., p. 264.
48. Ibid., pp. 295-96.
49. Ibid., p. 296.
50. Ibid., p. 297.

5 Water and Power Policy

SUKHADEO THORAT

Ambedkar is widely known for his contribution towards a number of spheres. His social and political efforts for the socially deprived classes, his role in the framing of India's Constitution and his scholarly ideas on the vital issues of his times helped decisively in shaping the social, political and economic character of India at a crucial period of its history. Equally important, but less known, was his contribution to the making of India's developmental policies. As a Cabinet Member, during 1942-46, he was instrumental in laying the foundation of India's water and electric power policy. In the early 1940s, which were a crucial period in the evolution and adoption of economic planning in India, he initiated and gave a definite shape to the policy and planning of its water and electrical power development. Thus, no less important but less well known among Ambedkar's contributions to the nation are his direct participation and role in the development of water and power resources in the country. In this paper, I have tried to present the thinking and role of Ambedkar in water and power development in the country as minister-in-charge during 1942-46.

An independent Department of Labour had been created in November 1937, which was earlier a part of a combined Department of Industry and Labour. Subjects like irrigation, electricity and other areas related to public works were also transferred to the newly created Department of Labour. The policy formulation and planning for the development of irrigation and electric power, including hydroelectric power, thus became the major concern of the Labour Department, when Ambedkar took it over in July 1942.

During the 1942-46, when Ambedkar took charge of Labour, Irrigation and Electricity Department, it was a crucial period for the evolution and adoption of the concept of economic planning at an all-India level. The post-war economic plan for the reconstruction and economic development for India was then taking shape. The government took a very ambitious initiative to develop a framework within which positive policies were centrally formulated. It was to be an action plan. The policy regarding water resources and electric power development was conceived, initiated and was given a definite shape as part of this post-war economic plan.

The Labour Department began all-India planning for the development of irrigation, waterways and navigation virtually from scratch. It was the first time that the Centre began to consider planning as a fundamental subject for water and power on a comprehensive all-India scale and against an all-India background. A central policy with regard to water resources and hydroelectric power development was accordingly evolved and given a definite shape. Among the consequences of these efforts were:

(a) the emergence of a definite all-India policy with regard to the development of water and electric power resources in the country;
(b) the creation of an administrative apparatus and technical bodies at the Centre to assist the states in the development of irrigation and electric power resources, such as the present-day Central Water Commission and Central Electricity Authority;
(c) the adoption of the concept of River Valley Authority or Corporation to overcome constitutional problems regarding the jurisdiction of Central and State Governments and to develop irrigation and hydroelectric power from inter-state rivers;
(d) the introduction of the concept of regional and multipurpose development of river valley basin for the first time in India; and
(e) the initiation of some important present-day river valley projects, major and minor, which include the Damodar River Valley, Sone River Valley, Orissa River Schemes including the Mahanadi, the Chambal River Scheme and the schemes for the rivers of the Deccan.

Ambedkar, being at the helm of affairs of the Labour Department, was instrumental in initiating these steps. With his deep knowledge in the area of economics, politics and constitutional law, he helped the Central Government and his own department in the articulation of water and power policy.

What follows is an attempt to understand the views and contributions made by Ambedkar during 1942-46 to this aspect of India's development. The achievements were in terms of policy formulation, creation of an administrative apparatus and technical bodies at the Centre that provided an alternative solution to central-state problems, and setting in motion several present-day major and medium river valley projects.

Post-War Economic Plan (1942-46) and Water Policy

The roots of the new water policy at the centre are to be found in the Post-War Reconstruction Plan of Government of India during 1942-46. World War II left in its wake destruction and instability of indescribable proportions, which the post-war world needed to repair. In many countries, which had seen battle, the problem of reconstruction was mainly of replacement of war-devastated physical infrastructure and industrial plants. In India, the needs were more long-term oriented than of immediate repair. The immediate concern of the Central Government was rehabilitation and resettlement of defense personnel and workers employed in war-related industries and conversion of industry from war to peace. The situation here was significantly different from that of the European and other Asian countries.

The objective and scope of the Indian plan of economic reconstruction therefore had to be different. It was argued that in its long-term perspective, restructuring in India should necessarily include the building of new physical infrastructure and industries as distinguished from rehabilitation of industries destroyed in the war that Europe had to attend to. In so far as the Indian plan provided measures for rehabilitation of defense service personnel displaced from war industry and the steps for conversion of industry from war to peace, it was a reconstruction plan. But, in its long-term objective, as we shall see later, it was a plan for economic development of India.

The seriousness, with which the government's plan for the economic restructuring of India was conceived, initiated and published, evoked lively interest and positive reaction from various political parties and groups.[1] Alternative plans were prepared and submitted to the Central Government. These included the Bombay Plan by J.R.D. Tata and others[2], the People's Plan and the Congress Plan prepared by the National Planning Committee with which Jawaharlal Nehru and eminent scientists such as Meghnad Saha were associated. The alternative plans were put forward as statements of objectives and strategies to be kept in mind in developing a perspective on economic planning in India, and the general lines on which planning should proceed. While differing in their objectives and strategies, all the alternative plans uniformly assumed that a national government was in store for the Indian nation. The underlying assumption was that on the termination of the war or shortly thereafter, a national government would come into existence at the Centre which would be vested with full freedom in economic matters.[3]

The government plans were conceived with continuity in view for at least fifteen to twenty-five years. This was facilitated by the fact that several eminent Indian economists, like V.K.R.V. Rao, D.R. Gadgil, C.N. Vakil and P.S. Lokanathan, were associated with the formulation of post-war reconstruction plan, who also became closely associated with economic planning during the 1950s and 1960s.[4] As we shall see later, the policy measures and plans undertaken during 1942-46 under the Reconstruction and Economic Development Plan laid down the very base of the water and power policy of post-independence India.

To make the Reconstruction and Economic Development Plan comprehensive and well balanced, the government had set up five committees to formulate policy and action plans.[5] At the apex was the Reconstruction Committee of the Council, popularly known as the RCC, to decide the general plan objectives and thrust. Its members comprised all members of the Central Cabinet, with the Viceroy as the chairman. Each committee had a 'Policy Committee' headed by the minister concerned and was composed of representatives of the central and provincial governments, and some representatives of trade, industry and commerce. Each Policy Committee had in turn an 'Official Committee', headed by the secretary to the department and composed of secretaries of related departments. Policy decisions arrived at by these two committees were submitted to the RCC for approval. The general consensus was that for planning to be effective, it should be on an all-India scale even for provincial subjects, such as irrigation and electric power.

The Reconstruction and Development Plan had a two-fold aim, namely, (a) to raise people's standard of living as a whole and ensure jobs for all, and (b) to ensure that produced wealth was distributed more equitably, without which people's conditions could not be improved and their purchasing power could not be enhanced. Purchasing power was to be increased by improving the efficiency, and consequently productivity, of labour and at the same time developing and reorganizing agriculture, industries and services. The Plan Document stated that agriculture was and would remain India's primary industry but the present imbalance in economy had to be rectified by an intensive development of the country's industries, so that both agriculture and industry could be developed side by side.

To realize this two-fold objective, planning was to be both short-term and long-term. The short-term plan, termed as the Rehabilitation or Reconstruction Plan, naturally coalesced into the long-term policy of development. It included measures for:

(a) the resettlement and re-employment of defense service personnel and of labour displaced from the war industry, military works, etc.;
(b) the conversion of industry from war to peace; and
(c) the removal or adjustment of controls to suit peace conditions.

The long-term planning and projects came under the heading of 'Economic Development'. It was to be an all-India plan, drawn on general lines for fifteen to twenty-five years or more, with a more detailed phased out plan for five years. Sectors coming under long-term planning were those involving large capital expenditure, and creating the infrastructure for development. These included:

(a) improvement in agriculture with the development of irrigation, anti-erosion measures, land reclamation and other measures;
(b) development of electric power, including hydroelectric, as the basis of industrial and agricultural development, and with it pump irrigation and rural industry;
(c) development of industry with special reference to the production of capital and consumer goods, and also the maintenance and development of small-scale and cottage industries; and
(d) comprehensive development of road communications and transport services, especially in rural areas.

The plan called for a balanced development of the agricultural and industrial sector. Both needed development of irrigation and power. Both irrigation and power therefore received high priority in the long-term objective of the plan.

Overseeing this important aspect of development was Ambedkar being a member of the Central Cabinet; he was also a member of the RCC, President of the Policy Committee for Irrigation and Power and was also associated with its Official Committee. The task of the Policy Committee and its Official Committee was to study the problems affecting the development of irrigation and hydroelectric power and suggest practical ways of solving them. By virtue of his position in all the three bodies, Ambedkar significantly helped in formulating the policy and action plan for the optimal development of water and power resources in India.

Though the RCC was the ultimate approving authority for the plan, the ministries concerned were supposed to do the ground work. At the department level, the Policy Committee and Official Committee, of which Ambedkar was President, were required to prepare four statements, namely:

(a) a statement regarding the broad policy of post-war reconstruction and economic development;
(b) a detailed statement of policy on subjects within the department's jurisdiction, namely, labour, irrigation and power;
(c) an action plan; and

(d) policy stand on certain basic questions such as (i) the question of state versus private ownership of irrigation and hydroelectric projects and others; (ii) role of the state and the Centre in the development of irrigation and power; and (iii) areas for Central Government intervention or participation in these two subjects, which were under the jurisdiction of the states.

The Labour Department's work was particularly difficult because, by the Act of 1935, both irrigation and electricity had been brought fully under the jurisdiction of the provincial governments, the Central Government's role being confined to mediation in inter-provincial disputes. This made an all-India outlook difficult. The RCC, therefore, made it clear that if the best results are to be obtained from irrigation, electrical and industrial development, there must be either one all-India plan agreed to by all concerned, or a collection of related plans, which amount to much the same thing. Drawing upon examples from the rest of the world, the Plan Document stated that for the purpose of economic development, they have to come together and formulate a common policy in the general interest of the country as a whole.

Policy Statement on Irrigation and Power

For drawing up a detailed Policy Statement on Irrigation and Power Development, the Labour Department had two options. One was to prepare a draft Policy Statement for circulation among the provinces for feedback, based on which a final Policy Statement based on consensus was to be prepared. The other option was to go ahead and prepare an all-India Policy Statement for the consideration of the RCC. Though, initially, opinion veered towards the first option, the second option prevailed, the principal consideration being that this Policy Statement would serve as a guide to the provinces to form their reaction. The Policy Statement was thus prepared by the Labour Department, which indicated the Central Government's approach on the development of (a) irrigation, waterways and drainage, (b) inland water transport, and (c) development of electric power.

Irrigation, Waterways and Drainage

Development of irrigation, waterways and hydroelectric power, the Policy Statement said, was basic to the industrial and agricultural development of the country. Food supply and people's prosperity directly depended upon wider irrigation, soil conservation and flood control. To increase food supplies and to make more land cultivable, major and medium schemes of irrigation were needed. Greater use of pumps was also to be made, the available supply of water in the existing canal systems increased, and measures taken against waterlogging.[6] The Policy Statement noted that:

1. The planning and execution of the work under this head rested primarily with the provinces and the states. The Central Government would nevertheless offer all possible help by arranging for priority supply of necessary materials and by providing technical assistance.
2. Wherever possible, the Central Government would also be prepared to consider provincial and state projects on a regional basis. In certain deserving cases, financial assistance also could be considered.
3. The Central Government would address a detailed questionnaire to the provinces and states about the projects they proposed and would have these proposals scrutinized by its engineering experts. A Consulting Engineer would be appointed for waterways and another for irrigation to work as a Development Officer.
4. The Central Board of Irrigation would be reorganized to function more effectively, not merely as a clearing house of ideas on irrigation, drainage and allied subjects but also as a board of referees on all pertinent matters.

Inland Water Transport

The use of inland water transport declined during the last century, partly because of competition from the railways and partly due to the deterioration of waterways, sometimes as a direct result of increased irrigation works. Inland water transport was revived during the wartime, because of the congestion on the railways. The main obstacle to significant development of this mode of transport, the Policy Statement said, was the condition of the waterways themselves. Inland waterways being a provincial subject, the role of the Centre would largely be one of coordination and initiative, wherever it was required.

The Policy Statement proposed the following measures to develop inland water transport:

(a) measures to improve the navigability of rivers and other existing waterways;
(b) possible use of irrigation canals for inland traffic;
(c) construction of new artificial waterways;
(d) increased use of steamers, tugs and power-driven barges;
(e) development of country craft; and
(f) meeting the competition from other forms of transport as well as coordination of all means of transport.

Development of Electric Power

All factors in the system that retarded the healthy growth of electric power needed attention. The Policy Statement considered the production and distribution of electricity in India as a state or quasi-state enterprise.

1. In furtherance of this policy the government secured the allotment of manufacturing capacity for additional heavy power equipment for several key electricity development undertakings in the country. A Central Technical Power Board was also to be set up to work for the whole of India.
2. The policy of furthering the agricultural use of electricity was also accepted, e.g., by the manufacture of fertilizers, etc.
3. To enhance large-scale development of electric power throughout India personnel were to be trained abroad to provide expert commercial, administrative and technical staff for electrical undertakings.

New Water Policy: Three New Dimensions

The Policy Statement prepared by the Labour Department advocated for greater participation or partnership by the Central Government in the development of irrigation and hydroelectric power of the provinces than that was permitted under the 1935 Act. While the Centre made it clear that it did not wish to interfere with the freedom of the provinces to draw up and execute their own plans. It also declared that 'more positive participation by the Centre was necessary' in those irrigation and hydroelectric projects, which involved more than one state and which required regional development of the entire river valley basin for the benefit of several provinces and states.

The Act of 1935 virtually debarred the Central Government from assuming executive authority over provincial subjects and from intervening in inter-provincial matters. Section 135 of the Act provided for the appointment of an Inter-Provincial Council for the investigation and discussion of such matters and for making recommendations. It was, however, a purely advisory body, with no executive power.[7]

In these circumstances the task before the Labour Department was three-fold, as under:

(a) to develop a new instrument of executive authority for the regional control and management of projects on rivers flowing through more than one state;
(b) to evolve a definite development approach of water and hydroelectric power resources of inter-state rivers; and
(c) to evolve an administrative set-up with a pool of technical experts to develop a national irrigation policy and render technical and other services to the provinces. In evolving a policy framework the provinces and the states had to be consulted. Accordingly, after a detailed discussion and consultation, the department addressed the so-called 'three famous letters' to the provinces on 'three issues'. The letters forcefully articulated the irrigation and electric policy of the Centre and resulted in the national water and electric policy, which continued in the independence period.

The policy framework had three components, namely:

(a) adoption of a concept of River Valley Authority or Corporation for the management and control of projects on inter-state rivers;
(b) adoption of the concept of regional and multipurpose development of River Valley Basin as a whole; and
(c) establishment of administrative and technical expert bodies at the Centre. The Central Waterways, Navigation and Irrigation Commission, set up for this purpose, was the precursor of the present-day Central Water Commission, the Central Technical Power Board, and that of the Central Electricity Authority.

River Valley Authority

After long deliberation, the Labour Department concluded that the most appropriate mechanism to implement inter-State projects was an independent authority or a corporation, which would derive its authority through an agreement between the provinces/states concerned and the Centre. The matter was explained in a letter sent in December 1944 to all provinces.

In cogency of argument and for its persuasive power the letter of the Labour Department is something of a classic. It pointed out succinctly that

> developing the water and power resources of the country was a priority item with the Department, but a special difficulty was posed by those rivers whose waters passed through many Provinces and States. The river basins presented many and varied problems but the problem of preventing the larger rivers from inflicting devastating floods and their waters to the benefit of all was a major one. The matter concerned not only the several Provinces and States through which these rivers passed but was closely connected with the development of India as a whole. A consolidated development scheme called for multi-purpose river management schemes on a regional basis and assistance in the river projects that concerned more than one Province. While in theory the Provinces and States concerned could by agreement come together and get down to rapid development, the reality could be different. A Province finding its material and manpower resources fully occupied with projects seen

> by its administration to be of more benefit to its own people, might relegate to the background a project that would bring about regional development benefiting several Provinces and States. The Centre entrusted with the development of the entire nation, might then find it desirable to ensure that such projects which benefited more than a State were not impeded by difficulties in arriving at an agreement. Given the constitutional difficulties the Centre might in many cases be in a better position to promote an agreement between the Provinces and the States than the latter themselves. The most suitable manner of implementing an agreement would be by setting up of a corporation to administer the affairs of rivers to which power would be given by agreement between the Centre and the States concerned.[8]

The structure or the functions and responsibilities of the proposed authority were not spelt out in detail at this time. This opportunity was provided by the Government of the United Provinces in the case of river Sone and by the Government of Bengal in the case of river Damodar.

With the right inputs, river Sone, it was felt, would provide excellent development opportunities to the region. To push through the programme, an inter-state conference was held in Delhi in March 1945. Emphasizing the importance of the schemes to the economic development of U.P., Bihar, some Central Indian states and the Central Province, Ambedkar stated in the conference that if the Sone's potentialities were to be fully exploited, it was necessary to have a regional rather than a local approach to the problem. Ultimately, therefore, there had to be an agreement to set up an appropriate organization to which all the parties concerned would give, by agreement, certain powers relating to its field of operations, principal among which would be bulk supply of electricity and water for irrigation and navigation.[9] In case a decision was taken to set up a Sone Valley Authority:

(a) Such Authority must be given, by the provinces and the states, power over the waters of the Sone and its tributaries.

(b) The provinces and the states must agree that such Authority should have the sole right to generate electricity (except for nursery schemes) in the area covered by the Authority.
(c) The provinces and the states must agree not to abstract water without the approval of the Authority.
(d) The provinces and the states in which dam sites would be situated would have to agree to the submergence of lands on such forms as might be arranged.[10]

Further, the Authority or the corporation would be set up by central legislation but the provinces and the states concerned would have to give, by agreement or contract, such executive authority as vested in them, for the erection of dams and other aspects related with the water of the rivers. The Authority to be constituted also needed to be given some of the powers and responsibilities of the partner provinces and states, and a measure of technical independence, if it was to achieve efficient development of hydroelectric power and irrigation.

The next big opportunity for consolidation of the new water policy came in the way of the Labour Department when, in August 1944, the Government of West Bengal forwarded a copy of the report of the Damodar Flood Enquiry Committee to the Government of India for consideration. As a follow-up, R.C. Casey, Governor of Bengal, wrote to the Viceroy shortly thereafter suggesting that the water problem of West Bengal needed extensive study for solution. The Damodar Committee had stated that it will be an advantage in the solution of flood control and soil conservation problems, if forests and rivers of India are made the concern of the Central Government.

The response of the Labour Department to this proposal was, once again, positive. Replying on October 8, 1944, it said that having regard to the multipurpose potentialities in any major scheme relating to the Damodar, the quickest and most efficient way of meeting the various problems would be through the agency of a duly constituted Regional Authority which would control the entire valley of the river and on which the Central Government and the governments of Bengal and Bihar were adequately represented.[11] In reply to the Governor, the Labour Department said that for the regional approach to the development of these rivers, there must be an agreement between the provinces and states concerned and the Centre will do whatever is possible to promote such agreement. In some cases it might be found advisable that the executive authority should be vested in a corporation or other body. In such cases, the Centre might be prepared to become a partner with the province in the enterprise, the letter stated.

The Government of West Bengal, in a constructive approach, promptly agreed to take steps to consider setting up the Authority. It also suggested and hoped that the Government of India will similarly set up such Regional Authorities in connection with other large rivers flowing through other provinces and ultimately having an outlet in Bengal. As we shall see later on, the Labour Department had prepared two alternative models for the establishment of Damodar Valley Authority for consideration by the Second Inter-Provincial Conference held in Calcutta in February 1945.

The result of the untiring effort of the Labour Department was that an agreement was finally reached between the Central Government and the governments of Bihar and West Bengal (the governments participating in the Damodar Valley Project) to form an Authority. This was given legal force, when the Constituent Assembly Legislature enacted in 1948 the Damodar Valley Corporation Act to provide for the establishment and regulation of a semi-autonomous corporation for the development of the valley.

The Damodar Valley Corporation was the first of its kind. With its establishment, the issue of management and control of irrigation and power projects on inter-state rivers was finally resolved.

Multipurpose and Regional Development of River Valley Basins

Multipurpose development of river basins recognizes the interrelation of resource elements in a single basin. The need for integrated river basin development arises from the relationship between the availability of water and its possible uses in various sectors.

Multipurpose development is a concept of recent origin. When dealing with 'interference with water supplies' the relevant provision of the Act of 1935 referred to 'water from any natural source of supply'. There was no mention of river valley basin or catchments. It is only since 1930 that emphasis has increasingly been placed on engineering practices, on the hydrological unity of a river basin and on treating the basin as the unit of development of its water resources. It goes to the credit of the Irrigation and Power Department, under the leadership of Ambedkar, that for the first time in India, in 1945-47 basin-wise plans of multipurpose development for the Damodar Valley and Mahanadi Valley were put forward. In 1948, when the Constituent Assembly of India enacted the Damodar Valley Corporation Act for the establishment of Damodar Valley in the provinces of Bihar and West Bengal, it defined 'Damodar Valley' as including 'the basin of the Damodar river and tributaries'. The Electricity (Supply) Act, also passed in 1948, made it the responsibility of the Central Electricity Authority to examine whether any river works proposed by State Electricity Boards would prejudice the best ultimate development of the river and its tributaries for power generation, consistent with the requirements of irrigation, navigation and flood contort. The stage was thus set for emphasis on optimum multipurpose river valley development, for which the ground work was done by Ambedkar and his department during 1944-46 in connection with the river valley projects on Damodar, Mahanadi, Sone and other rivers.

The multipurpose development of water resources on the basis of river valley basin was suggested for the Damodar Valley Project by the Labour Department. In response to the proposal of the Government of Bengal, the Labour Department, in its letter of October 8,1944, expressed its considered view:

> that although the Bengal Committee have touched on the hydro-electric and irrigation aspects of the problems, their principal recommendations were conceived primarily as a flood control measure within the limits of the Province of Bengal. Such approach to the problem is *prima facie* inadequate. The Government of India feels that the Provincial Government will look at it from the coordinated economic development of the entire Damodar Valley and not only from the point of view of the requirement of West Bengal. Further, the multipurpose potentialities of Damodar Valley Scheme

> including irrigation (for agriculture), navigation, power and water supply to industry, prevention of erosion and of disafforestation and possibilities of afforestation should be solidly considered.[12]

In the Calcutta Conference of January 3, 1944, Ambedkar argued that:

> the project of damming the Damodar should have as its purpose not merely stopping the flood but also include the generation of electricity and supply of water for irrigation, navigation and industrial use. There has not been enough realisation that our policy for waterways must be multipurpose policy so as to include all possible uses of water.[13]

Similarly, the Labour Department also treated the Sone Valley Project as a multipurpose river management scheme covering not only the potentialities for irrigation by canals and perennial hydel power for the area but also for increased irrigational utilization of such power for pumping from the tubewells or from the river and increased fertility by the dewatering in waterlogged area. Provision of cheap power for industrial development, improved supply of water for navigation on the Ganga and improved flood control were other important considerations.[14] Emphasis was also laid on integrated development approach of water and power resources, economic and social planning and development of the river valley basin. The Labour Department observed that though such matters as the plans for industrialization, social well-being, reforestation, relocation of population, roads and schools, provision of extra irrigation, whether by gravity or by pumping, cooperative development, fertilizer and farm demonstration programmes and the setting up of provincial and municipal planning board must necessarily be for the provinces and the states concerned, the River Valley Authority will have a clear interest in such developments and will be required to assist with the coordination and development of plans. There must be fullest cooperation between Authority and the provinces/states, local bodies and with the people in the areas to be developed, if the Authority is to be able to achieve the maximum good of which it is capable.

Thus, the Labour Department not only recommended multi-purpose development of water resources but also wanted its planned development and utilization (for the regional and overall socio-economic development of the entire river basin) to be carried out in close coordination with the provincial and state governments and local bodies.

Technical Expert Bodies

Keeping in view the magnitude of projects it was keenly felt around this time that the technical expert bodies then available at the Centre were not adequate. The Irrigation Adviser with the Government of India was concerned mainly with small emergency irrigation projects under the 'Grow More Food' campaign. The Central Board of Irrigation, on the other hand, essentially consisted of the chief engineers of provinces; functioning mainly through sub-committees working part time, it had no continuing influence on provincial and states' policy.[15]

To make good the lacuna of a full-fledged Irrigation Commission, the Labour Department wrote to all Provincial/State Governments in December 1944, eliciting their views on the proposed Commission. It argued that

> there is a real need for an expert body capable of advising both the Government of India and State Governments when so required. The Government of India feels that it is advisable that they should set up a Central Waterways and Irrigation Commission at the Centre.[16]

While conceding that many of the problems which formed part of the proposed duties and responsibilities of the Commission fell within the provincial legislative and executive spheres, the Labour Department made it clear that there was no intention to usurp or in any way encroach upon the duties and responsibilities of the provinces. The Commission was intended to be a purely fact-finding and advisory body. Composed of expert members with competent and sufficient staff able to devote themselves whole time to the study of India's waterways and irrigation problems, it would collect information, which would be available to study and help in treating waterways problems as a whole and to advise where required. The result was that a resolution to set up the Central Waterways Irrigation and Navigation Commission was approved by Ambedkar in March 1944 and subsequently by the Viceroy on April 4, 1945.

An identical technical body was recommended in the first meeting of the Policy Committee, held on October 25, 1943, for 'public work and electric power'. The proposed Central Technical Power Board was to be a strong technical organization designed to collect data, conduct surveys and prepare schemes for electrical development in consultation with Provincial/State Governments. It was to act as a central planning organization to advise the Central, Provincial and State Governments in regard to the universally accepted policy of encouraging, planning and pressing forward the widespread development of electricity supply throughout the country. The Board was established in November 1944 as a central planning organization, with the concurrence of the Provincial Governments.[17] With the creation of these two strong technical organizations at the Centre, the stage was set for an all-India water and hydroelectric power policy. In its dedicated work of laying down the basic elements of the nation's present-day water and power policy, the Labour Department had been notching one success after another. In a systematic manner, it developed the concept of an Authority or Corporation to overcome the constitutional difficulties in the development of water resources of inter-state rivers, adopted the multipurpose development approach on the basis of river valley basin and created two technical expert bodies at the Centre, the entire exercise having been accomplished in the short span of four years (1942-46). As we shall see in the next section, Ambedkar being in charge of the Labour Department was instrumental in providing an appropriate leadership and direction to the whole policy and planning process.

Ambedkar's Role in Shaping Water Policy

Ambedkar, being at the helm of affairs of the Labour Department, had played pivotal role in the development of water and power policy, and particularly in evolving the concept of multi-purpose development of water resources and the concept of River Valley Authority. His contribution in bringing multipurpose dimension to water resource development was particularly significant.

In the earlier approach to water resource development, excess water was considered to be a major problem, and the remedy suggested was oriented toward one goal, namely, to control floods. Ambedkar differed with those who believed in a single purpose approach. He observed that if conservation of water was mandatory from the point of view of public good, then, obviously, the plan of embankments was a wrong plan. It was a means which does not subserve the end, namely, conservation of water, and must, therefore, be abandoned. The appropriate method, according to him, was that followed and adopted by some developed countries, that is, to dam rivers at various points to conserve water permanently in reservoirs and put it to multipurpose use. Such reservoirs, besides irrigation, could be used for generating electric power and navigation.

Ambedkar particularly emphasized the use of rivers for navigational purpose. In the Conference on Orissa Rivers, he observed:

> Navigation in India has had a very chequered history. During the rule of the East India Company, provision for international navigation occupied a very prominent part in the public works budget of the Company' Shop government. Many of the navigation canals we have in India today... are remnants of that policy. Railway came later and for a time the policy was to have both railways and canal navigation. By 1875 there arose a great controversy in which the issue was railways versus canals. The battle for canals was fought bravely by late Sir Arthur Cotton. ... Unfortunately, supporters of railways won.[18]

He added:

> I am not quite happy about this victory of railways over canals. Much more annoying is the opinion of supporters of railways that canals

> must go because they do not pay without knowing that if the canals do not pay it is not because they cannot pay but because their capacity to pay has been terribly mutilated by leaving them uncompleted. I am sure that internal navigation cannot be neglected in the way in which it has been in the past. We ought to borrow a leaf from Germany and Russia in this matter and not only revive reconstruction of our old canals but make new ones also and not to sacrifice them to the exigencies of railways.[19]

The storage scheme that Ambedkar visualized would not only give irrigation and electricity but also provide a long line of internal navigation. He believed that the multipurpose use of water would convert the forces of evil into powers of good. This perspective he subsequently emphasized for projects on Damodar, Mahanadi, Sone and other inter-state rivers. Ambedkar asserted:

> The Damodar project must be multipurpose project.... it should not only deal with the problem caused by floods it should also provide for irrigation, electricity and navigation.... There has not been enough realization that our policy for water resource development must be multipurpose policy so as to include all possible uses of water.[20]

The Damodar Valley Project was to be the first in a series. He reiterated his belief in multipurpose projects in the second conference on the Damodar Valley Project. He stressed that

> the issue before us is whether we should be content with damming the river for the purpose of stopping the flood only or whether we should make it a multipurpose project so as to cover generation of electricity and supply of water for irrigation and navigation also ... the consensus of the opinion should be that we go for the latter.[21]

Similarly, the Sone Valley Project was treated as a multipurpose river management scheme. Ambedkar stressed the multipurpose use of water even more emphatically in the case of the Mahanadi river. Referring to the water problem, he stated:

> Orissa must ... adopt the method which the U.S.A. adopted in dealing with the problem of its rivers that method was to dam rivers at various points to conserve water permanently in reservoirs. Such a storage scheme as applied to the rivers of Orissa will have the special feature namely that it will not only give irrigation and electricity but also provide a long line of internal navigation. My comment is that this should be regarded as the only method and treated as an immediate programme rather than as an ultimate aim.[23]

In the conference on Orissa's rivers, he urged the participants to adopt the regional approach:

> For a balanced appreciation of the situation it is necessary to carry out comprehensive surveys and investigations with a view to ascertain the possibilities of irrigation, navigation, power development and their facilities in delta as well as in the drainage as a whole. Investigations so far carried out have been mostly limited to the delta.[24]

The second aspect, which he emphasized, was the creation of instrument of River Valley Authority to deal with the problem of inter-state rivers. He stated that the project on inter-state rivers could be a success only if it was treated as a regional project. It could not succeed with local treatment. The systematic steps towards the introduction of the concept of River Valley Authority (or projects on inter-state rivers) and creation of two technical expert bodies at the Centre, namely, the Central Waterways, Irrigation and Navigation Commission and the Central Technical Power Board were attempts to provide technical advice for the multipurpose development of water resources on regional basis. He made this clear in the first Calcutta Conference :

> As a preliminary step for securing the best use of water resources of the country the Government of India have created a central organisation, called the Central Technical Power Board, and are contemplating to create another to be called the Central Waterways,

> Irrigation and Navigation Commission. The objects which have led to the setting up of these two organisations are to advise the Provinces on how their water resources can be best utilized and how a project can be made to serve purposes other than irrigation.[25]

A similar association was highlighted in the conference on the Sone river. Ambedkar emphasized on the occasion that if Sone's possibilities were to be fully exploited, it was necessary to make a regional rather than a local approach to the problem. He urged all parties to realize that this meant that ultimately there must be an agreement to set up an appropriate organization to which they would give certain powers relating to the subjects which would be handled by this organization, the principal of which would be to supply the bulk of electricity and water for irrigation and navigation.[26]

Ambedkar expounded the nature of the new water policy in the First Calcutta Conference. He said:

> It is not far from true to say that so far there has been an absence of positive all-India policy for development of water resources. There has not been enough realisation that our policy for waterways must be multipurpose policy so as to include the provision for irrigation, electrification and navigation. Government of India is very much alive to the disadvantage arising from the present state of affairs and wishes to take steps to evolve a policy, which will utilize the water resource of the country to the best advantage of everybody, and to put our water resources to the purpose, which they are made to serve in other countries.[27]

Multipurpose use of water resources for the regional development of the entire river valley basin was the key element of the new water policy. The adoption of the concept of River Valley Authority (to overcome the jurisdictional problem on inter-state rivers) and the creation of two technical expert bodies at the Centre were means to achieve this objective.

Ambedkar thus left the stamp of his scientific and rational outlook, profound scholarship and humanity on emerging India's water policy. On both fronts, namely, irrigation and power, the achievements realized were truly remarkable. Ambedkar thus laid the foundation of what Jawaharlal Nehru later described as 'temples of modern India'.

In recognizing his contribution to the development of Damodar Valley Project, H.C. Hart wrote about the enterprise:

> They could take account of the rain that falls and of conformation of the valley and how they might fit together, but the other elements, namely, to get the will of the inhabitants in the valley, to get the government of Bihar and Bengal to agree to multi-purpose development of the Damodar, make them accept the concept of River Valley Authority to administer the work of building the Dam, and finally share the costs of development were in the best sense political questions. For thirty months the planning of the Damodar fell in the hand of politicians – the man who in the political sense decided that Damodar would be developed was the Minister of Labour, Dr. Ambedkar. He successfully overcome the obstacles with great skill and contributed to a plan as bold politically as it was hydraulically. Slowly in quite negotiation and in conferences after conferences, vital political interests were discussed and somehow fitted together.[28]

Recognizing this significant contribution of Ambedkar and the team he led in Labour Ministry, C.M. Bhabha, a Cabinet Member, who took over from him in July 1946, said:

> We had moved overnight from the rut of antiquated ideas to the modern conception of waterway development and taken their first step towards a comprehensive planning of resource development in river valley... I attached a particular importance to the first conference on Damodar because the torch lighted here for the first time has been since passed on to the Mahanadi, the Kosi and Sone river valley development schemes ... we owe a debt of gratitude to all those who sponsored and piloted the concept of multipurpose and regional development.[29]

Notes

1. Minutes of the 11th meeting, September 11, 1944, Reconstruction Committee of the Council, File No. 1 (4) P 1945, Finance Department, Planning Branch.
2. Sir Purshotamdas Thakurdas, J.R.D. Tata and others (January, 1944), *A Plan of Economic Development for India, People Plan* by B.N. Banerjee, G.D. Parikh and V.M. Tarkunde, March, 1946.
3. Ibid.
4. Proceedings of the First and Second Meetings of the Consultative Committee of Economists held at New Delhi on the 24th and 25th October, 1941 and 6th and 7th March, 1942, File No. ILD P 145, Finance Department, Planning Branch.
5. Letter to all Provincial Governments regarding Acceleration of Reconstruction Planning, Government of India, Defence Department, New Delhi, January 13, 1944, File No. DWI-1(25)- CWINC/47.
6. Post-War Development Policy, Draft Report, Reconstruction Committee of the Council, 1944, File No. 1(4) P 1945, Finance Department, Planning Branch, p. 35.
7. N.D. Gulati (1972), *Development of Inter-State River Laws and Practice in India*, New Delhi, Allied, p. 80.
8. A Letter of Secretary, Labour Department to Government of Bengal, October 8, 1944, File No. 75 D/359/44, Finance Department, Planning Division.
9. Proceedings of the Meeting held on the 10th March, 1945 to discuss certain proposals regarding the development of Sone Valley, File No. DW/IRI/336/9, Labour Department, p. 45.
10. Proposal for a Corporation to handle Sone Valley Authority, File DW/IRI/336/9, p. 45, Finance Department, Planning Division, p. 45.
11. A letter of Secretary, Labour Department to Government of Bengal, October 8, 1944, File No. 75 D/359/44, Finance Department, Planning Division.
12. A letter of Secretary, Labour Department to Government of Bengal, October 8, 1944, File No. 75 D/359/44, Finance Department, Planning Division.
13. B.R. Ambedkar, 'Damodar Valley Scheme', Address at the First Calcutta Conference, January 3, 1944.

14. Letter to the Secretary, Labour Department to the Secretary to Government of U.P., C.P., and Bihar(Public Works Department), Department of Labour, Government of India, December 1944, File NO. DW/IRI/336/98/45.
15. Labour Department, 'Setting up of the Central Waterways Irrigation and Navigation Commission on Permanent Basis', File No. DWI-(25) CWINC/47.
16. A Letter to all Provincial Governments putting to them the proposal to create a Central Waterways and Irrigation Commission and asking whether Provincial Governments welcome this proposal; Letter by Secretary, Labour, December 1944, File No. 6(1) P/5, Finance Department, Planning Division.
17. Government of India, Reconstruction Committee of the Council, Record of the first and second meeting of Policy Committee, No. 3-C(Public Work and Electric Power) held at New Delhi in October 1943 and February 1945, File No. 6(6), P/45, Finance Department, Planning Division.
18. B.R. Ambedkar, 'Multipurpose Plan for Development of Orissa's Rivers', Presidential Address at the Conference held in Cuttack on November 8, 1945.
19. B.R. Ambedkar, 'Damodar Valley Scheme', Address at the First Calcutta Conference, January 3, 1944.
20. Ibid.
21. B.R. Ambedkar, 'Multi-Purpose Development of Damodar Valley', Second Calcutta Conference, August 23, 1945.
22. Proceedings of a meeting held on March 10, 1945 to discuss certain proposals regarding the development of Sone Valley, File No. DW/IRI/336/P 45, Finance Department, Planning Branch.
23. B.R. Ambedkar, 'Multipurpose Plan for Development of Orissa's Rivers', Presidential Address at the Conference held in Cuttack on November 8, 1945.
24. Ibid.
25. B.R. Ambedkar, First Calcutta Conference on Damodar, January 3, 1945, p. 223.
26. B.R. Ambedkar, Proceedings of the meeting on Sone Valley Project held on March 10, 1945.

27. B.R. Ambedkar, Second Calcutta Conference on Damodar, January 3, 1945, p. 97.
28. H.C. Hart, New Rivers of India.
29. C.H. Bhabha, 'Damodar Valley Scheme Ripe for Implementation', *Indian Information*, February 1, 1947, pp. 69-73.

Part Two

Socialism and Democracy

6 Quest for Democratic Socialism

BHALCHANDRA MUNGEKAR

Throughout his life Ambedkar struggled to find ways and means – intellectual, organizational and in terms of programmes – relevant to establishing an egalitarian society based on liberty, equality, fraternity and social justice. His crusade against the caste system and untouchability is well recorded in modern India's socio-political history. What is amazing, however, is his multi-pronged attack on the inequitable Indian social order, which is intrinsically based on the institution of caste. Naturally, for arriving at solutions to these complex issues, he had to engage himself in a comprehensive intellectual exercise. A social thinker of towering ability, Ambedkar remained a practising politician for nearly half of his later life with unrelenting commitment to finding solutions to India's innumerable problems.

In this essay an attempt is made to throw light on Ambedkar's quest for democratic socialism. This is for two reasons. First, the failure of socialism as demonstrated by the disintegration of the Soviet Union and the collapse of the socialist states in Eastern Europe is seen by many as the triumph of democracy based on capitalist economy. As a logical corollary to this belief, one comes across an unqualified and unquestionable faith in the superiority of the institution of market, which is sought to be held as the panacea for all the economic problems facing the contemporary world, including of course, developing countries like India. Second, and equally important, Ambedkar has given adequate and serious consideration to the problems of democracy and socialism and also arrived at some definite solution. This solution we propose to describe as democratic socialism.

The essay is divided into six sections. In section I, we briefly present the fundamentals of democratic socialism as a social system, followed by the model of democratic socialism as visualized by Ambedkar. In section II, we take up, in somewhat greater detail, the issues of liberty, equality and fraternity, as they constitute the basic value framework of democratic social order. Section III concentrates on the caste system, which negates the very essence and spirit of democracy. In section IV, we explain Ambedkar's insistence on democratic/constitutional means of social change as also his ideological position with regard to Marxism and communism. Section V deals with the challenges that democratic socialism faces in the changed international context, while taking into account the developments taking place in India. The concluding section VI presents final remarks.

I
Ambedkar's Model of Democratic Socialism

Democratic socialism is not a unified, structurally well-defined or integrated theory. There are various interpretations of or approaches to it. Olof Palme, President of the Social Democratic Workers' Party of Sweden once remarked: "There are 71 definitions of socialism. If I were to give the 72nd, it would not make things easier. There is no generally accepted definition" (1980: 12). Further, according to the Socialist International, "Socialism is an international movement which does not demand a rigid uniformity of approach. Whether socialists build their faith on Marxist or other methods of analysing society, whether they are inspired by religious or humanitarian principles, they all strive for the same goal: a system of social justice, better living, freedom and world peace" (ibid: pp. 11-12).

The above statements clearly bring out that democratic socialism stresses plurality in approaches to social reconstruction as its goal: plurality of sources of inspiration as well as that of methods of achieving the desired social changes. Overall, however, democratic socialism subscribes to the following:

- Freedom of an individual is sacrosanct and no tampering with it for any reason whatsoever.
- Equality, fraternity and social justice are the other goals to be simultaneously achieved.
- Co-existence of public and private property.
- Opposition to totalitarian planning.
- Governance of the society through the institution of parliamentary democracy.
- Opposition to dictatorship in any form for any reason whatsoever.
- Social change through 'reforms' and peaceful means and recourse to any drastic or revolutionary means are generally unwarranted. Democratic socialism thus shuns violence.

On behalf of the All India Scheduled Castes Federation, Ambedkar, as its chairman, submitted to the Constituent Assembly of India some proposals (in the form of a Draft Constitution) seeking to safeguard the various interests of the Scheduled Castes and Scheduled Tribes in post-independence India. Among these proposals was the reorganization of India's economy as 'state socialism', which, in its wider perspective, may be described as 'democratic socialism'.

According to Ambedkar, modern political democracy is based on the following premises:

- The individual is an end in himself.
- The individual has certain inalienable rights, which must be guaranteed to him by the constitution.
- The individual shall not be required to relinquish any of his constitutional rights as a condition precedent to the receipt of the privilege.
- The state shall not delegate powers to private persons to govern others (GoM, 1979: 409).

In order to translate these premises into reality, Ambedkar recommended the reorganization of the Indian economy along the following lines:

1. Ownership and running of the key industries by the state.
2. Insurance industry to be the monopoly of the state. The state to make obligatory to every citizen to take an insurance policy commensurate with his income. This would, on the one hand, offer security to the individual, and on the other would give resources to the state for planning and undertaking economic development.
3. Agriculture to be a state industry. The state to acquire ownership of all land so that there would be no landlord, no tenant and no agricultural labourer. The erstwhile landlords to be paid appropriate compensation.
4. Farming to be collective. The land acquired by the state to be let out to the residents of the village without distinction of caste, gender or religion, in size of standard farms, the state to provide all the necessary inputs, and after making due payments to the state in lieu of the services rendered by it as well as the revenue, the remaining produce to be shared among the tenants as prescribed by the government (ibid: pp. 396-97).

Ambedkar wanted this scheme to be introduced in the country within ten years from the commencement of the India's Constitution. It was to form an integral part of it, a basic feature of it. Ambedkar did not want to leave such a fundamental scheme to the discretion of the ruling party. A political party inimical to state socialism coming to power might suspend state socialism by amending the Constitution. By making state socialism an integral part of the Constitution, Ambedkar wanted to establish state socialism, retain parliamentary democracy and avoid dictatorship (ibid: 411-12).

Ambedkar was sure that though the private sector might secure rapid industrialization, it would produce inequalities of wealth of the kind seen in the western capitalist world. He wanted the state to plan the economic life of people on lines which would lead to the highest point of productivity but did not favour closing avenues to private enterprise, provided the equitable distribution of wealth was ensured (ibid: 396).

Thus, the following emerge as the main features of Ambedkar's model of democratic socialism:

- Basic freedoms to the individual vis-à-vis the state to be guaranteed by the Constitution.
- Nationalization of the means of production such as land and key enterprises.
- Recognition of the role of private industries.
- Economic planning.
- No discrimination among citizens on the basis of caste, gender or religion.
- Democratic/constitutional means for social change/transformation.

II
Liberty, Equality and Fraternity as the Value System of Democratic Socialism

Ambedkar's approach to state socialism was an outcome of his commitment to the value system on which modern democracy is founded, namely, liberty equality and fraternity.

Liberty

The nature of economic organization of society has a crucial bearing on individual liberty. Individual freedoms in different spheres – social, economic, political, cultural and so on – are also organically interlinked, because the presence or absence of right to freedom in one sphere results in the presence or absence of freedom in the other spheres. As Milton Friedman (1962) argues, "Economic arrangements play a dual role in the promotion of a free society. On the other hand, freedom in economic arrangements is itself a component of freedom. Broadly understood so, economic freedom is an end in itself. In the second place, economic freedom is also an indispensable means toward the achievement of political freedom" (ibid: 8). Thus, viewed as a means to the end of political freedom, economic arrangements are important because of their effect on concentration or dispersion of power" (ibid: 9).

The political and economic doctrine, known as liberalism, believes that individual liberty is best secured in a society characterized by the private ownership of means of production, which, in turn, is the hallmark of capitalism. The doctrine of liberalism continued to adhere to 'free' and 'competitive market mechanism' vis-à-vis central planning as an alternative to organizing the economic life of society. A major reason for the preference of the liberals for free market economy or competitive capitalism over central planning stems from the supposed superiority of the former vis-à-vis the latter in 'efficient' economic organization of society (i.e., production, distribution, exchange, etc.). According to them, this efficiency (and everything that goes with the word 'efficiency') is ensured through the freedom to the individual economic agents, who adjust the exchange decision to the changing economic phenomena within and outside the country, which in turn are known through the information system. Thus, it is argued that in a market economy the decisions of all economic agents, be they individuals or institutions, and be it the sphere of production, consumption, distribution or exchange, ensure maximum advantage to a given economic activity or transaction. This guarantees not only 'equilibrium' but also maximum social advantage. This, however, does not mean that the advocates of 'market economy' are unaware of the constraints on securing overall economic efficiency. They are aware and hence are not averse to some kind of state regulation or planning. But, they would want these regulations to strengthen competition and not as a substitute. For instance, Hayek (1944), the worst critic of socialism, argued:

> although competition can bear some admixture of regulation, it can not be combined with planning to any extent we like without ceasing to operate as an effective guide to production (because) both competition and central direction become poor and inefficient tools if they are incomplete, they are alternative principles used to solve the same problem, and a mixture of the two means neither will really work and the result will be worse than if either system had been consistently relied upon. Or to express differently, planning and competition can be combined only by planning *for* competition, but not by planning against competition (p. 31, emphasis added).

This is not all. Hayek's advocacy of free market economy comes from a more profound, ideological and philosophical reason, namely, the doctrine of individual liberty. Socialist economy, based on central planning, obviously involves the intervention of the state in economic management, which results in the encroachments of individual economic freedom. And, since economic freedom in itself is an extremely important part of total freedom (p. 9), its encroachment results in the erosion of political freedom. Thus, economic freedom is a necessary condition not only of political freedom, but of total individual freedom. The advocates of free market economy therefore argue that socialism based on collectivism involves too much state intervention in economic activity, and hence excessive reliance on bureaucracy. This negates individual freedom and, in turn, democracy. Thus democracy and socialism are just juxtaposed as substitutes. For instance:

> democracy extends the sphere of individual freedom, socialism restricts it. Democracy attaches all possible values to each man. Socialism makes each man a mere agent, a mere number. Democracy and socialism have nothing in common but one word, equality. But notice the difference: while democracy seeks equality in liberty, socialism seeks equality in restraint and servitude (p. 18).

Hayek cites Max Eastman with approval:

> It seems obvious to me now ... that the institution of private property is one of the main things that have given man that limited amount of freedom and equalness that Marx hopes to render infinite by abolishing this institution. Strangely enough Marx was first to see this. He is one who informed us, looking backwards that the evolution of private capitalism with its faith in market had been a precondition for the evolution of all our democratic freedoms. It never occurred to him, looking forward, that if this was so, these other freedoms might disappear with the abolition of the free market (p. 78).

While advocating the superiority of a free market economy over socialist economy in respect of guaranteeing freedom, Friedman (1962) argued thus:

> one feature of a free society is surely the freedom of individuals to advocate and propagandize openly for a radical change in the structure of the society. So long as the advocacy is restricted to persuasion and does not include force or other forms of coercion, it is a mark of political freedom of a capitalist society that men can openly advocate and work for socialism. Equally, political freedom in a socialist society would require that men be free to advocate the introduction of capitalism. How would the freedom to advocate capitalism be preserved and protected in a socialist society? (p. 16)

Ambedkar approached the issue of economic structure and its profound impact on liberty from a perspective different from that of Hayek and Friedman. According to Ambedkar, in a private enterprise system based on the private ownership of means of production, which operates solely for individual profit motive, the employers command a dominating position and the resourceless workers have to surrender to their dictates. In a private enterprise system a number of people (wage earners of all kinds), "have to subject themselves to be governed by the private employers", and as a result "have to relinquish their constitutional rights in order to get their living." Thus, the private enterprise system "undermines, if it does not actually violate, the last two premises on which democracy rests" (GoM, 1979: 404). Ambedkar recognized the importance of the fundamental rights of an individual whom, as we have seen above, he considered an end in himself. But he went a step further. He did not want the enactment of the fundamental rights in an ornamental sense (which is of course important), but was eager to see that these rights are really enjoyed by the people. Thus, if the fundamental rights were not to remain notional in nature and hence worthless in practice, an appropriate economic institutional arrangement had to be created where the individual would be able to practise his rights. Consider, for instance, a situation where a person is confronted with a choice between getting any privilege, say a job and enjoying a fundamental right of joining a trade union to exercise his right to freedom of speech. He would certainly prefer the former. According to Ambedkar, it had to be so and could not be otherwise. For, he held that

> the fear of starvation, the fear of losing a house, the fear of losing savings if any, the fear of being compelled to take children away from school, the fear of having to be a burden on public charity, are factors too strong to permit a man to stand out for his fundamental rights. The unemployed are thus compelled to relinquish their fundamental rights for the sake of securing the privilege to work and to subsist (ibid: 409-10).

According to Ambedkar, state socialism could bring us out of this predicament. But, what about state intervention in the economy without which state socialism could not be established, and its impact on individual liberty?

We have seen above that according to the libertarian view, the intervention of state in the social and economic affairs of society results in the encroachment of individual liberty and more the intervention, the greater the encroachment. Conceding the fact that "where the state refrains from intervention what remains is liberty" (ibid: 410), Ambedkar posed a fundamental and somewhat polemical question, "To whom and for whom is this liberty?" He argued that (in a society based on private enterprise)

> this liberty is the liberty to the landlords to increase rents, for capitalists to increase hours of work and to reduce rate of wages. This must be so and cannot be otherwise. For an economic system employing armies of workers, producing goods *en masse* at regular intervals, someone must make rules, so that workers must run and the wheels must run on. If the State does not do it then the private employer will do it, life otherwise will become impossible. In other words, what is called liberty from the control of State is another name for the dictatorship of private employers (ibid: 41).

It may be argued that the capitalist system gives the individual the right to 'freedom of contract'. This is a major triumph of a capitalist society over all the pre-capitalist social formations. But there was no reason to be complacent. For Ambedkar the more pertinent question was: what is the result of freedom of contract on the parties to contract, should they happen to be unequal? In an inegalitarian society based on the private ownership of means of production, though the idea of freedom of contract became sanctified and was upheld in the name of liberty it "gave the strong the opportunity to defraud the weak" (GoM, 1991: 108).

Equality

Ambedkar was at pains to notice the grave existing contradiction between the political system known as parliamentary democracy and capitalist form of industrial organization. According to him, economic inequalities are inherent in the capitalist economy, which make political equality assured by democracy worthless. This lands us in the unavoidable situation of equality in politics and inequality in economics. Thus, according to Ambedkar, the failure to recognize that political democracy cannot succeed where there is no social and economic democracy has vitiated parliamentary democracy. Ambedkar maintained therefore that though "parliamentary democracy developed a passion for liberty, it never made a nodding acquaintance with equality. It failed to realize the significance of equality and did not even endeavour to strike a balance between liberty and equality, with the result that liberty swallowed equality and left a progeny of inequalities" (ibid: 108-9). Further, inequalities in the ownership of the means of production, which is the hallmark of capitalist economy, inevitably results in unequal distribution of income and hence that of opportunities. Worse still, "unequal opportunities at one point of time generate unequal opportunities over time" (Okun, 1975: 77).

To illustrate, economists, in fact all social scientists, nowadays talk of 'investment in human capital' which, it is held, considerably accounts for the interpersonal and inter-country differences in productivity and levels of income. It is also recognized that formal education in various disciplines is an effective tool of increasing productive capacity of an individual and thus constitutes an 'investment in human capital'. Now, in a country like India, nearly 60 per cent of the school-going children drop out after the fifth standard, not to talk of the lakhs of children who do not visit school at all. What chance do these millions of children stand in the labour market in the distribution of jobs? They are pushed into the low-paid menial jobs in the informal and unorganized sectors of the economy.

What then is the relevance of the constitutional provision of 'free and compulsory education to the children below the age of 14' as prescribed by the Directive Principles of the State Policy in India to those who are unable to attend school due to poverty? What is the worth of the industrial wage and relations legislation to those who are made to work in the unorganized informal sectors to which the laws are not generally applicable? The examples can be multiplied. What is germane is that modern political democracy does not distinguish among the citizens so far as the right to equal opportunity is concerned. That remains notional in nature. In practice, inequalities abound. What is worse, inequality in one sphere of social life gets transmitted to all the other spheres, and the result is a structure of inequality.

Fraternity

Liberty and inequality are two fundamentals of a democratic society, and yet they are by themselves not adequate. According to Ambedkar, and rightly so, a genuine democratic society necessitates the fulfilment of the third fundamental: fraternity.

Now, other constraints apart, a market economy, based on private ownership of means of production, fragments the whole society into antagonistic classes. In such a society, the interests of the employers and those of workers run counter to each other. So is the case with the interests of landlord vis-à-vis the tenants and the agricultural labourers. Since, the market economy strengthens the greed and acquisitiveness, the resourceful industrialists and the landowners perceive the claim of workers and tenants as a drag on their 'fortunes' and resist them. This results in mutual distrust, hatred, discontent and strife.

Further, the access to resources of all kinds, mainly material, determines the socio-economic status of an individual. The greater the degree of resourcefulness, the higher the status. This creates a feeling of the superiority in the minds of the resourceful who look down upon the resourceless. There is no social and cultural communication between them. While the economic relationships are involuntary, the tragedy gets worsened when the resourceless consider themselves inferior to the resourceful. What scope is there for the creation of the feeling of fraternity, let alone its sustainability, in a society fragmented into antagonistic socio-economic classes?

In the Indian context, it is the caste system that has destroyed the spirit of liberty, equality and fraternity to which we now turn.

III
The Caste System

The eradication of untouchability and the caste system was the mission of Ambedkar's life. He therefore analyzed every problem of the Indian society – economic, social, political, cultural and educational, keeping this mission in view. This is because each one of these problems has a caste dimension, the implications of which are disastrous for the low-caste people, variously known as the untouchables, the depressed classes, the scheduled castes, the scheduled tribes, and so on. What the caste system inflicted upon these disadvantaged social groups for centuries is too well known to be repeated here. Suffice is to say that the caste system made the low-caste people, and mainly the untouchables, social outcasts, economically slaves and politically handicapped. They were oppressed, exploited and marginalized in every walk of life.

While suggesting solutions to various problems of this country, Ambedkar remained preoccupied with the implications they have for the depressed classes, though he did not spell out how the depressed classes would benefit from state socialism. For him safeguarding the interests of the depressed classes was of paramount importance, not just because they were destitute in every conceivable sense, but also because according to him, nobody, neither an individual nor an organization, had championed effectively the cause of this deprived lot. Ambedkar therefore went to the extent of saying that he would not hesitate to give priority to the interests of the Depressed Classes should there be a conflict between them and the interests of the nation. His early position towards India's freedom struggle under the leadership of the Indian National Congress and its supreme leader Gandhi, and his urge and constant struggle to seek constitutional safeguards for the depressed classes in every sphere of social life have to be seen in this perspective. Obviously, Ambedkar's advocacy of state socialism too is no exception to this general framework of his thought and action.

The caste system would not have been perpetuated for centuries only through subjective prejudices and the idea of pollution. A formidable factor that provided enduring sustenance to the caste system was its material foundation, which was sanctified by the Hindu religious scriptures, and like other discriminations, it was deeply internalized.

To begin with, the caste system played an ascriptive role inasmuch as it allocated economic functions in society. Such distribution of economic activities among different individuals has been a characteristic feature of a human society, either in its very crude or very complex form. The unique feature of the caste system, however, was that it assigned an occupation not to an individual but to a group of individuals. A particular individual was to undertake a particular occupation just because he belonged to a particular group, by birth.

This led Ambedkar to argue that the caste system did not result only in the division of labour, but culminated in division of labourers. The former is the result of preference, choice and aptitude of an individual; the latter is independent of individual will. The former is voluntary, the latter is not only obligatory, but also coercive. Thus, as in the social sphere, in the economic sphere too, the caste system amounted to a travesty of individual freedom.

But that is not all. The effects of birth-based occupational arrangement on different castes was entirely opposite in nature. It proved to be a divine privilege of the upper castes to enjoy the exclusive rights to education, industry, trade, commerce and so on. On the other hand, it spelt disaster for the lower castes. This is because the latter were assigned the tasks involving only menial labour. They were thus prevented from earning, let alone accumulating wealth, which restricted their needs to bare existence. Even more deplorably, menial labour was stigmatized. Thus, absence of freedom of occupation, low earnings, implicit restriction on needs and stigma on menial labour destroyed the economy of the lower castes. They came to be wholly dependent on the upper castes for bare subsistence.

Under such circumstances, Ambedkar must have visualized that the free enterprise economy based on the private ownership of means of production would have very little to offer to the depressed classes. For in such a society the depressed classes, along with the other, may have a fundamental right to property, but it would be devoid of any practical significance. The depressed classes neither owned land nor capital. As a result, the right to property is *real* only in the case of owners of property, but notional for the property-less. Ambedkar therefore must have thought that the depressed classes stood to benefit only under collective ownership of major resources of production, particularly land. When he recommended collective farming where the state was to acquire land and distribute it among the village residents without distinction of caste to ensure that 'there is no landlord, no tenant and no agricultural labourer', Ambedkar was doubly sure that in the absence of collective farming only the upper castes would be the landowning classes, while the Depressed Classes would get the dubious distinction of being agricultural labourers. Regretfully, Ambedkar's prophecy with regard to the socio-economic conditions of the depressed classes proved true.

After independence, under the guise of mixed economy, India adopted the capitalist path of development. The benefits of the progress achieved during the last fifty years are enjoyed largely by the resourceful in proportion to the amount of resources held. This cannot be otherwise. The access to and the amount of resources, yield power to shape and influence both the decision-making process as also the policy implementing apparatus. The resourceful classes use these mechanisms to serve their own interests. Many a time, the resourceful classes divert to their own interest even the benefits of schemes and programmes meant for the poor.

IV
Faith in the Constitutional Means of Social Transformation

Ambedkar's belief in the adequacy of constitutional means for securing socio-economic transformation arose from three factors: (a) his disapproval of violence as a matter of principle; (b) his rejection of dictatorship of any kind; and (c) his conviction that social change secured through peaceful means and consent of people is more durable and sustainable. Reacting to the communists' dictatorial ways, he wrote:

> The end of dictatorship is to make the revolution a permanent revolution. This is a valuable end. But can the communists say that in achieving this end they have not destroyed other valuable ends? Dictatorship is often defined as absence of liberty or absence of parliamentary government. Both interpretations are not quite clear. There is no liberty even when there is parliamentary government. For law means want of liberty. The difference between dictatorship and parliamentary government lies in this.
>
> In parliamentary government every citizen has a right to criticize the restraint on liberty imposed by the government. In parliamentary government you have a duty and a right. A duty to obey the law and a right to criticize it. In dictatorship you have a duty to obey and no right to criticize it (GoM, 1987: 452-53).

He again maintained:

> They [the communists] have destroyed private property. Assuming this is a valuable end, can the communists say that they have not destroyed other valuable ends in the process of achieving it? How many people have they killed for achieving their end? Has human life no value? Could they have not taken away the property without taking the lives of the people? (p. 452).

This does not however, mean that Ambedkar was totally averse to the use of force. But he wanted that "the use of force must be so regulated that it should serve as many ends as possible while destroying the evil ones" (p. 451).

Ambedkar was sometimes inclined to justify temporary dictatorship to strengthen democracy, but not as a permanent feature of social life. He asked: "Why should not dictatorship liquidate itself after it has done its course, after it has removed all the obstacles and boulders in the way of democracy and has made the path of democracy safe?" (p. 459). The following passage gives an indication of his thinking on the subject:

> It has been claimed that the communist dictatorship in Russia has wonderful achievements to its credit. There can be no denial of it. That is a why I say that a Russian kind of dictatorship would be good for all backward countries. But this is no argument for permanent dictatorship. Humanity does not want only economic values; it also wants spiritual values to be retained. Permanent dictatorship has paid no attention to spiritual values and does not seem to intend to. Carlyle called political economy a pig economy. Carlyle was of course wrong, for man needs economic comforts. But the communist philosophy seems to be equally wrong. For the aim of their philosophy seems to be fatten pigs as though men are no better than pigs. Man must grow materially as well as spiritually. Society has been aiming to lay a new foundation as summarized by the French Revolution in three words: Fraternity, Liberty and Equality. The French Revolution was welcome because of this slogan. It failed to produce equality. We welcome the Russian Revolution because it aims to produce equality. But it cannot be too much emphasized that in producing equality the society cannot afford to sacrifice fraternity or liberty. Equality will be of no value without fraternity or liberty. It seems that the three can co-exist only if one follows the way of Buddha. Communism can give one but not all (pp. 461-62).

Ambedkar ultimately embraced Buddhism as a means of securing spiritual development of the individual as well as that of society.

V
Relevance of Democratic Socialism to the Contemporary World

Having argued that Ambedkar advocated democratic socialism, it is now imperative to briefly examine its relevance. In the contemporary world the concepts of state and the market have undergone dramatic change. To the fore have come issues relating to the nature and ethos of the development paradigm, the role of democratic institutions in the governance of society, as also the basic freedom of the individual and human rights. Again, the so-called process of globalization does not seem to ease the conflict between developed and developing nations and within developing countries. There are serious economic problems of poverty, unemployment, inflation, external debt, socio-economic inequalities and imbalance in development. The problems are complex in nature and defy easy solution. Yet, we are inclined to argue that as a broad socio-political doctrine, democratic socialism provides guiding principles for organizing the political and economic life of society, on three grounds:

First, the collapse of socialism in eastern European has brought into question the sustainability of centrally planned command economies. Some argue that this is not the collapse of socialism, because the socialism as practised was not the one Marx visualized. This argument leads us nowhere, for there can be a ceaseless experimentation with socialism. The Soviet and East European economies did manage to free their people from the fear of hunger, malnutrition, illiteracy and basic health problems. But these economies failed to secure sustained economic growth, due, among other factors, to slow pace of technological adaptation on one hand and absence of work ethic on the other. The latter may be largely attributed to the lack of incentive in these economies.

This was true of state enterprises as well as collective farming. Again, in the absence of market, these economies came to face serious problem of allocation of scarce productive resources as also fixing product and factor prices. Further, the whole economy came to be controlled by bureaucrats and technocrats, who wielded enormous political and economic power and reaped the benefits of economic development much more than the common people.

The growing inability of the socialist economies to secure sustained economic growth made economic reforms imperative. All these economies initiated reforms at some stage or the other, but these reforms could not make much headway. One reason for this failure was the absence of democratization in these societies. One-party rule, popularly known as dictatorship of the proletariat, deprived the common people of basic individual freedoms of expression, criticism and dissent. Ultimately, these regimes disintegrated and collapsed due to their own contradictions and eventually made the transition to market-driven economies, to be known as 'market socialism'.

China has since 1978 initiated wide-ranging economic reforms under the leadership of Deng Xiaoping. These reforms include thorough restructuring of agriculture, including de-collectivization of farming and replacing it with the so-called household responsibility system, rationalization of state enterprises and autonomy to the management, boost to foreign investment, technological collaboration and thrust upon exports. Deng described this departure as socialism with Chinese characteristics.

These reforms have paid rich dividends: the growth rate is impressive and sustained, there is increase in foodgrain and industrial production, foreign direct investment is increasingly flowing into China, foreign exchange position is very comfortable, and standard of living is rising.

But disturbingly, along with the fear of rise in unemployment, and income and regional inequalities, there is emerging in China a major contradiction with regard to political management. The single-party rule, 'People's Democratic Dictatorship' as Deng called it, endures, and there are no signs that the party is inclined to go for a liberal democratic order based on a multi-party system. There is no individual liberty, no free debate or discussion or criticism of the official policies.

In brief, China will find it extremely difficult to manage and live with the contradiction of market-oriented liberal reforms in economics and one-party dictatorship in politics. This may jeopardize its economic reforms in the long term. As Saito (1991) eloquently puts it:

> (Thus) there is a serious danger also in China that economic reforms which maintain the previous political system of a rigid one-party rule cannot attain the expected success. Without any serious efforts of democratization, but with recurrent suppression of democratization movement, there would be accumulated political dissatisfaction of common people because of the failure of the economic reforms. Thus, the needs for political reforms, the needs for democratization, first of all the needs for radical change of the existing political system (the one-party rule of Communist party of China) are clear also in China.

Meanwhile, the collapse of the Soviet type of socialism may not be construed as the triumph of capitalism or the market economy. True, capitalist economies did not collapse, but they too are not free from grave economic problems. The superiority of their technological advances was their major strength vis-à-vis the erstwhile socialist countries, but that also acts as the main contributor to the worsening unemployment problem. All these countries have faced prolonged recessions, worst ever since World War II. Their monetary and fiscal arrangements are far from satisfactory, and they are forced to find suitable means to overcome their chronic economic problems. First, they continue to rely on war industries as a source of sustenance of their economic growth, notwithstanding their empty rhetoric of world peace. Second, they are forcing the developing countries to restructure their economies in such a way that the former could get easy access to their surplus capital and technology, notwithstanding the long-term implications of these policies for the latter. Their hegemonic position in the international financial institutions, such as the IMF and the World Bank, is making their task easy. But, the question remains: why did western capitalist economies not collapse?

There could be many reasons, but primarily it is because the western capitalist countries have democratized their societies. Full liberty to individuals and the press to criticize and dissent with the policies of the government or the establishment, as also the network of democratic institutions in every sphere of national life, acted as a great correcting factor. Again, free debate and discussion provided a mechanism to the ruling establishment of knowing a variety of views and aspirations of the society and ultimately securing a broad consensus over a given policy or programme. This gave sanction or legitimacy to the rule of the party in power. Thus, the so-called bourgeois democracy turned to be the major strength of the capitalist societies and helped them survive.

In the last two decades or so, almost all developing countries, including India, have launched comprehensive economic reforms based on globalization, liberalization and privatization. As a result, the role of the state in the economy has been considerably restricted. Now, as far as relaxation or total withdrawal of certain policy instruments, such as licence-permit-quota system, regulation of foreign exchange, etc., is concerned, one need not lament. But, due to the excessive preoccupation with controlling fiscal deficit as dictated by the IMF-World Bank, governments have been reducing even the productive investment in the economy. For instance, the ratio of capital expenditure (both plan and non-plan) to the GDP declined from 5.88 per cent in 1990-91 to 3.09 per cent in 1997-98. Again, the ratio of gross domestic capital formation on public account to the GDP was 10.5 per cent in 1990-91, which declined to 7.5 per cent in 1995-96. Since the public and private industrial investments in India have been complementary, a fall in the former is bound to adversely affect the latter. Thus, the reduced role of the state in the economy, demonstrated by the relative fall in capital expenditure/public investment, among other things, is constraining the growth prospects of the Indian economy.

But even if, we assume, that economic reforms help secure higher rates of economic growth, the needy sections of society may, yet, remain largely deprived of the benefits of growth. This is mainly because the pattern and structure of growth is likely to be capital-intensive, which may aggravate the problem of unemployment further. Again, in a country like India, the growing tendency towards privatization of social services, such as education, health, etc., may reduce the access of the poor to these services and hence, their well-being may be further impaired. Lastly, the depressed classes, such as the SCs and the STs, are likely to suffer the most.

Thus, while doing away with growth-hampering intervention of the state in the economy, even the welfare role of the state is getting eroded. This will not only reduce the poor people's access to the benefits of growth but will further narrow down their participation in the process of growth. As a result, in the developing economies, highly inegalitarian as they are, the socio-economic tensions are likely to assume serious proportions.

VI
Final Remarks

The foregoing discussion would lead us to conclude that although Ambedkar described his scheme of economic organization of the Indian society as state socialism, in view of its other features, we considered it appropriate to call it democratic socialism. However, collective farming, one of the major features of his model of democratic socialism, needs to be thoroughly reconsidered as it lacked viability.

The collapse of Soviet-type socialism has proved beyond doubt the importance of democratization of society, as also that of the parliamentary/constitutional means of securing/sustaining social change. Further, the disintegration of the Soviet Union and Yugoslavia seems to confirm that a society (particularly the one consisting of heterogeneous socio-cultural-ethnic entities) cannot be kept integrated through coercive and dictatorial means. This reinforces the relevance of the multi-party democratic system as a method of governance of society.

The collapse of the Soviet type of socialism on the one hand, and the prolonged economic crisis facing the capitalist economies on the other, vindicates that as excessive state intervention in the economy and its bureaucratization is harmful for securing sustained economic growth, so also is the case with reliance on the market which may perhaps help obtain relatively higher growth rates that may not be socially relevant. Thus, the roles of the state and market have to be judiciously defined so as to ensure optimum allocation of resources, efficiency and higher rates of economic growth on the one hand, and a sustained increase in the levels of employment, stability of prices and progressive reduction in income and regional inequalities on the other.

References

Friedman, Milton, 1962. *Capitalism and Freedom*, Chicago University Press, Chicago.

Government of Maharashtra (GoM), 1979. *Babasaheb Ambedkar: Writings and Speeches*, Vol. I, Education Department, Mumbai.

Government of Maharashtra, 1987. *Babasaheb Ambedkar: Writings and Speeches*, Vol. III, Education Department, Mumbai.

Government of Maharashtra (GoM), 1991. *Babasaheb Ambedkar: Writings and Speeches,* Vol. X, Education Department, Mumbai.

Hayek, F.A., 1944. *The Road to Serfdom*, Routledge and Kegan Paul, London.

Okun, Arthur M., 1975. *Equality and Efficiency: The Big Trade Off*, Oxford & IBH, New Delhi.

Palme, Olof, 1980. *What is Democratic Socialism*? Progress Publishers, Moscow.

Saito, Minoru, 1991. "The Collapse of Soviet Type Socialism in Europe and the Lessons for China", *Journal of International Economic Studies* (Tokyo), No. 5, (March).

7 Good Society: Rights, Democracy and Socialism

VALERIAN RODRIGUES

Ideological persuasions prefixing or suffixing 'democracy' or 'socialism' are common in the intellectual market place, such as democratic socialism, socialist democracy, liberal democracy, Marxian socialism and even Gandhian socialism. Although such coupling makes them conceptually much more elastic than taken singly, incorporation in ideological discourse has imparted to them determinate connotations and range of meanings.

There have been several attempts to hang an ideological name-plate on Ambedkar, particularly in the heyday of ideological polarization, which, one tends to think, is no longer trendy. Such a name-plate was felt necessary not merely to locate Ambedkar's richly and sometimes widely scattered ideas and polemical stances but also for discerning, discriminating and interpreting kindred and hostile influences. More prominently, the political necessity of mobilization, coalition building and alliances demanded it. Unlike Gandhism, attempts to prop up Ambedkarism as a self-contained ideology have been rare, although attempts at identity construction around Ambedkarism are widespread.

However, ideological naming of Ambedkar does not seem easy. It is not because his intellectual and political stances are devoid of consistency, although he derided it sometimes. In fact, a remarkable consistency can be seen both in his explanatory concepts such as 'graded inequality' as well as in his deployment of normative concepts such as liberty, equality and fraternity. In fact, Ambedkar often explicates the nuances of the concepts that he deploys and sometimes even goes to illustrate them by citing specific thinkers. However, all such engagement is in practical state. Concepts do not engage with concepts but with issues and concerns at hand although the latter may be a research investigation, a legal battle, a political rhetoric or a pedagogical engagement. Practical considerations often impute a set of meanings to the concepts deployed. Besides, depending upon the need forays are made into a range of ideological kitties. Such an employment of concepts and ideological persuasions in Ambedkar goes along with an avowal of pragmatism, which is reflectively adhered to, from his early association with Dewey and the Fabianism of the Webbs.

This paper suggests that Ambedkar subscribed to a political order informed with rights, democracy and socialism. He employed socialism to critique an order based merely on rights, while socialism without a commitment to rights would tend to authoritarianism. A good society cannot but be democracy – a democracy informed with rights and socialism. In constructing the relation across them Ambedkar laid great stress on human agency and a strong state.

Rights

Avowal of rights is central to Ambedkar's entire projects. A political order based on rights has come to be universally accepted following the French Revolution. It begets a free social order in which the individual comes to be considered an end in himself and the aim and object of society becomes the growth of the individual and the development of his personality. It places the human person at the centre of things. He quotes the philosopher Jacques Maritain:

> Human person is both a physical and spiritual microcosm; subsistent in an independent manner; more a whole than a part; while being a minute fragment of matter, he is at the same time a

universe; image of God; belongs to the order of things naturally sacred.[1]

The terms of association among such human beings have to be based on liberty, equality and fraternity, claims ordered in sequence that we find replete in his writings. Human beings are equal, as they 'possess, in degree and kind, fundamental characteristics that are common to humanity'. Besides, equality denotes 'moral equality'. It asserts an ethical value, "a belief to be sustained and recognition of rights to be respected".[2]

The right to equality occupies the central place in Ambedkar's priorities. In fact, equality-related rights precede those of liberty in the enumeration employed in Chapter 3 of the Constitution of India dealing with fundamental rights. Ambedkar acknowledged that men are "born unequal". Some are robust, others weaklings; some have more intelligence, others less; however, he felt, 'in the struggle for existence if inequality is recognized as the rule of the game the weakest will always go to the wall.' It may enable the fittest to survive. But, he asks rhetorically, 'who is the fittest and are the fittest the best from the view of society?' He then argues that equality may help the best to survive even though the best may not be the fittest.[3]

Fraternity meant for Ambedkar "a sense of common brotherhood, the principle which gives unity and solidarity to social life".[4] He says fraternity is "the name for the disposition of an individual to treat men as objects of reverence and love and desire to be in unity with his fellow beings".[5] It strengthens sociability and the inclination to dispose oneself towards the welfare of others. Sympathy and fellow feeling are integral to it.[6]

For Ambedkar liberty was the effective power to do specific things. He saw it as the basis of intellectual, moral, political and social progress. It was like Mill's salutation to liberty. However, real liberty exists only where "exploitation has been annihilated, where no suppression of one class by another exists, where there is no unemployment, no poverty and where a person is free from the fear of losing his job, his home and his food as a consequence of his action".[7] Liberty politically expresses itself by the "right of individual to share in the framing of laws and in the making and unmaking of governments".[8]

Rights that embody liberty, equality and belonging cannot be endowed merely in a discrete way. While being separate they also constitute a unity. Ambedkar employs the metaphor of 'Trinity' – the three gods in one – to denote their net aggregate value.

These principles of liberty, equality and fraternity are not to be treated as separate items. They form a union of trinity in the sense that to divorce one from another is to defeat the very purpose. Liberty cannot be divorced from equality; equality cannot be divorced from liberty. Nor can liberty and equality be divorced from fraternity. "Without equality, liberty would produce the supremacy of the few over the many. Equality without liberty would kill individual initiative. Without fraternity, liberty and equality could not become a natural course of things. It would require a constable to enforce them."[9]

Ambedkar inveighs against the Indian social order for being hostile to the fostering of these rights. The Indian social order, he thinks, is based on graded inequality embodying deference upwards and contempt downwards. Such a consciousness is not merely extremely regulative but is deeply internalized. Socio-economic relations are deeply stamped with it. Ambedkar is therefore often at a loss on how such a condition can be overcome. The constitutional and legal order and organized power of the state can provide a degree of support for the purpose. However, any long-term transformation can come only through social arrangements, which embody these values. Therefore, such interventions as personal codes, education and eventually Buddhism seem so significant to Ambedkar.

Ambedkar's conception of the range of rights as eventually enshrined in the Constitution is not merely comprehensive but conceptually highly discriminating. It has been suggested that Ambedkar was merely a hack doing the bidding of others as chairman of the drafting committee of the Constitution.[10] Some of Ambedkar's subsequent posers along with the debates in the Constituent Assembly have contributed to this view.[11] Nothing can be further from truth.

In fact, the organization and presentation of the scheme and enumeration of rights was well developed by Ambedkar much earlier in several of his memoranda and representations submitted in earlier years. Of course, it had become part of the public reason by the time the Constitution-making process was inaugurated, feeding on the contribution made by several sources. One could illustrate this by looking at one such document, the memorandum submitted by him to the Minorities Committee of the Round Table Conference in November 1930. In it Ambedkar argued that the untouchables were prepared to submit to majority rule under certain conditions. The first condition required that majority rule should not perpetuate the existing state of affairs, wherein untouchables were being treated as hereditary bondsmen. There had to be a concerted move to abolish untouchability. The government of the majority needed to create equality of citizenship, guaranteeing fundamental rights through the Constitution of India. The second condition required provision of remedies along with the declaration of rights. Infringement of the right of the people for the full enjoyment of accommodations, advantages, facilities, privileges of inns, educational institutions, roads, paths, streets, tanks, wells, etc., needed to be awarded exemplary punishment. Social boycott of untouchables had to be considered a cognizable offence. The third stipulation was that discriminatory conditions in the matter of possessing property or in the enforcement of contracts had to be done away with. Every citizen had to be eligible to serve in civil, military or educational institutions and access to and full enjoyment of accommodation, educational institutions and places of resort had to be made available to all. The fourth condition demanded adequate representation to the depressed classes in the legislatures to elect their own representatives through adult suffrage and by separate electorates. The subsequent conditions demanded adequate representation of the depressed classes in the services, the establishment of a machinery for the redressal of grievances, special departments to ensure equality of status and equality of treatment to depressed classes. Ambedkar's stipulation of the operationalization of the principle of preferential treatment in India was as follows:

> The weightage taken from the majority should be distributed among the minorities in inverse proportion to their social standing, economic position and educational condition so that a minority

> which is large and which has a better social, educational and economic standing gets a lesser amount of weightage than the minorities whose numbers are less and whose educational, economic and social position is inferior to that of others.[12]

Ambedkar's categorization and organization of rights trace an interesting trajectory. Their significance can be appreciated only by hindsight, particularly in terms of the contemporary debate in the UN fora about the different types of rights – civil and political, social and economic and right to community and environment, etc. Ambedkar acknowledges both individual rights and group rights although group rights remain primarily ameliorative and protective and primacy is accorded to individual rights. Rights of equality have definite preference over other claims. Rights of liberty are much more qualified and a strong state is ensured.[13] Ambedkar initially suggested incorporation of certain socialist principles as integral to fundamental rights and was against Article 31 upholding the right to private property. However, when it could not be done, the directive principles of state policy were brought to the fore, which except for a few provisions directly bears Ambedkar's stamp.[14] In fact, except for the legality, i.e., whether justiciable or not, Ambedkar himself sees the directive principles as continuation of the fundamental rights. So they are arranged too. In fact, Ambedkar initially toyed with the idea of defending their justiciability.

The complex construction of rights embodied in the Constitution and their affiliation to an egalitarian democratic order could not be realized, as the vision that infused this document was not widely shared. Given an option the other stalwarts in the Constituent Assembly would have articulated the constitutional regime of rights very differently from the way Ambedkar went around the task. The constitutional possibilities in this respect are still to be explored.

Socialism

Ambedkar's relation with socialism as an ideology remained ambivalent, particularly in its Marxist formulations. He accepted the concept of class struggle, although he felt that in the Indian context it had to be substantially redefined; took overboard the concept of social justice and ascribed a similar agenda to the Buddha and agreed that one of the major contradictions of capitalism was the social basis of its production in contrast to private appropriation. He criticized Marxism for subscribing to economic determinism, for its inadequate grasp of liberal democracy, for its inability to adequately understand the realm of ideologies and for considering moral values as historically conditioned.[15] He found existing socialism as far practised too authoritarian and its theoretical postulates did not allow it to subscribe to basic values constituting societies. He held the view that shorn of a moral basis, the Soviet Union would not endure for long, unless it accepted Buddhism as its moral foundation. He felt that Buddhism could constitute the moral foundation of a socialist society as it did not subscribe to the idea of God or soul and believed in socialism, secularism and a communitarian way of life.

Although Ambedkar suggested socialist measures in response to several situations, his response to the socialist agenda remained essentially piecemeal. However, Ambedkar was deeply dissatisfied with Nehru's stance on economy in the objective Resolution[16] as with certain other themes.[17] Ambedkar thought that a clear stance on socialism was required and it needed to be an integral part of the Constitution of India and should not be subjected to the vagaries of party fortunes. He suggested, among other measures, that the United States of India should declare as follows:

1. Key industries would be owned and run by the state.
2. Basic industries would be run by the state or corporations established by the state.
3. Insurance would be a State monopoly. Every adult citizen would have a life insurance policy.
4. Agriculture would be organized under the state cooperative sector with compensation to the owners. The cooperatives would be organized with no regard to the caste of members.

Ambedkar's agenda of state socialism seems akin to the concept of state socialism advanced by Lenin following the Soviet Revolution. At that juncture Lenin advanced the argument that the immediate enemy of the nascent socialism in Soviet Russia was the petty-bourgeois production and the petty-bourgeois mentality that went with it. He argued that the development of the productive forces in Soviet Russia should be modelled on the state capitalism prevalent in Germany. Large industry under the state with dictatorship of the proletariat would place Soviet Russia at the corridor of advanced socialism. Lenin's enthusiasm for state socialism did not last long as internal war broke out.

Ambedkar did not advance such a comprehensive agenda of socialist construction subsequently.[19] If his agenda were to be carried out as a constitutional act, it would have meant a war of the Indian State against the broad layers of Indian society. It would have provoked greater animosity than what the Hindu Code Bill generated. In Soviet Russia, when the CPSU led by Stalin attempted to bring agriculture under the cooperatives, first hesitantly in 1927 and then briskly from 1929, it became truly a war between the Soviet State and the peasantry with awesome consequences to the Soviet Revolution. In China, when the CPC attempted to build peasant cooperatives from 1949, there was widespread resistance from the peasantry, in spite of the better presence of the CPC in the rural areas compared to that of the CPSU in 1929. Ambedkar's agenda included both agriculture and industry to be brought under the nationalized sector, which would have been well nigh impossible given the kind of party that the Indian National Congress was on the eve of independence.

Ambedkar was not to press for his socialist agenda, although to be fair to him, the form of political authority that he envisaged to carry out such a socialist agenda was parliamentary democracy.

Later, when K.T. Shah moved a resolution to characterize India as a socialist state, Ambedkar opposed it, holding that given the vagueness of the concept of socialism it was improper to introduce it into the Constitution.

Ambedkar's sympathy for a socialist agenda was to continue in spite of such debacles. As mentioned earlier, he was not keen on Article 31 dealing with private property and he was keen on the directive principles of state policy. His position need not be seen as his strong commitment to socialism but to a form of egalitarian liberalism wherein a socio-political order of equal liberties is upheld with a positive consideration towards the disadvantaged.

This does not mean that Ambedkar's commitment to socialism was superficial and opportunistic. He saw socialism as one of the directions of the march of Indian democracy, the other being retention of a regime of rights all through. He argued: "We must not be content with mere political democracy. We must make our political democracy a social democracy as well. Political democracy cannot last unless there lies at that base of it social democracy."[21]

Democracy

In Ambedkar's ideological map, democracy occupied the central place. We find him often making a distinction between democracy as the institutionalized structure of power and democracy as a way of life. Between the two he definitely favoured the latter and suggested that institutional democracy could not endure unless democracy became a way of life. He defined it as "a mode of associated living which enables every human being to unfold his or her limitless potentialities to the maximum possible extent without in any way jeopardizing the equally legitimate interest and aspirations of the other.[22]

This definition of democracy resonates with the Athenian conception of democracy. We often find Ambedkar repeating Lincoln's formula of democracy, i.e., rule of the people, by the people for the people. Among the democratic forms, he specially favoured representative democracy and parliamentary democracy.

He draws upon the Madison's arguments in favour of representative democracy – in the process of the electoral battle the potential representatives get tested and their programmes and policies are approved or rejected. Therefore, unlike direct democracy of the Athenian kind, representative democracy brings to the fore the best elements in society and policies and the programmes that have been tested against popular criticisms. Besides, Ambedkar finds that given the largeness and complexities of modern societies, direct democracy is not feasible.

In defence of parliamentary democracy, Ambedkar develops a set of interesting arguments. First, Indians have been exposed to parliamentary democracy, however limited. Such might be valuable assets when Indians have to operate these institutions. Secondly, Ambedkar finds that progressive constitutional reforms have been introduced in India and Indians have shaped these constitutional reforms to a great extent. Opting for other institutional forms will result in a great loss of such legacies. Thirdly, given the diversity and plurality obtaining in India, he felt that even small groups could find representation, limited though it might be, in the legislative bodies. A presidential form of democracy, he felt, was likely to benefit the privileged section with their capacity to network over large parts of the country. Besides, given the authoritarian and hierarchic values infusing Indian society, the presidential form, instead of undercutting such values, is likely to reinforce them.

Ambedkar's avowal of representative and parliamentary democracy, however, did not make him very sympathetic to decentralization of power. In fact, he continued to believe all through in a strong state. He felt that decentralization of power was more likely to benefit the established vested interests of caste, community and class. Given his emphasis on evolving relations conducive to the emancipation of the oppressed, he felt that such mediating political structures are likely to obstruct the emancipatory striving of the depressed classes.

For Ambedkar, society in India is suffused with values unfavourable to democracy, with its values of liberty, equality and fraternity. One found conformism, graded inequality and ghettoization through the breadth and length of India and any affront to the latter called forth immediate sanctions from vested interests. To incorporate values conducive to democracy, Ambedkar put forth several strategies. Negatively, he identified Brahmanism as upholding values hostile to democracy, he fostered agitation against it and suggested alternative ways of looking at traditions; he identified Buddhism as conducive to a democratic way of life; he challenged modern forms of authoritarianism, including Gandhi, and felt that they basically reinforced values and attitudes not conducive to a democratic temper. Positively, Ambedkar suggested the constitution of political power based on popular sanction with one man as one value, accountability of power under the rule of law, majoritarianism with appropriate protection to minorities, education and organization of people for forceful but non-violent struggle and developing values and attitudes in families and institutions conducive to democracy. In his later days Ambedkar felt that to strengthen the foundations of democracy in India a new cultural basis was required and that Buddhism met such a need. Given the hierarchic and authoritarian values prevailing in India, socialism without democracy might not provide an emancipatory alternative. In fact, socialism might strengthen the existing authoritarian foundations in society. Therefore, while he wanted democracy to work towards socialism he always wanted to have its basis in a regime of rights.

Notes

1. B.R. Ambedkar, *Writings and Speeches*, Vol. 3, part II, *India and Prerequisites of Communism*, pp. 95-96, Bombay, Government of Maharashtra.
2. Ibid., p. 97.
3. *Constituent Assembly Debates*, Official Report, Vol. X, 25 November 1949, pp. 972-81, reproduced in *Dr. Babasaheb Ambedkar: Writings and Speeches*, Vol. 13, Bombay, Government of Maharashtra, p. 1216.
4. B.R. Ambedkar, *The Buddha and His Dhamma*, Mumbai, Siddharth (2nd ed.), 1974.
5. B.R. Ambedkar "India and the Prerequisites of Communism", nd. p. 97.
6. Ibid.
7. Ibid., p. 98.
8. Ibid.
9. *Writings and Speeches*, Vol. 13, p. 1216.
10. See G. Austin, *The Indian Constitution, Cornerstone of the Nation*, New Delhi, Oxford University Press, 1966.
11. He said on 2 September 1953, "I drafted the constitution on the request of the majority party. I was compelled to incorporate provisions which I disliked most". See *Ambedkar and Social Justice*, Vol. I, New Delhi, Government of India, p. 241.
12. B.R. Ambedkar, *Communal Deadlock and a Way to Solve it*, Jullundar, Bheem Publication, 1958, p. 30.
13. For Ambedkar's justification, see *CAD*, Vol. VII, p. 41.

14. See Sharda Prasad Singh and Anil Kumar Singh, *Ambedkar's Vision of the Indian Constitution*, Patna, Swarna Prakashan.
15. See B.R. Ambedkar, *Buddha or Karl Marx*, *Writings and Speeches*, Vol. 3, p. 451.
16. Nehru moved the objective resolution in the Constituent Assembly on 13 December 1946, four days after its meeting.
17. See *CAD*, vol. 1, 17 December 1946, pp. 99-103.
18. See Lenin, *Collected Works*, Vol. 27, pp. 256-75.
19. When Ambedkar attempted to align with the socialists, a weak socialist platform of an indigenous kind was devised.
20. *CAD*, Vol. VII, p. 402.
21. See Ambedkar, *Writings and Speeches*, Vol. 13, p. 1216
22. Singh and Singh, n. 14.

8 Concept of Political Power

GOPAL GURU

Taking his or her clue from Ambedkar, every dalit leader, whether or not representing a formal political group, makes repeated pronouncements in public fora that dalit should become the ruling class of this country. After more than five decades of experience with parliamentary democracy, the dalits in this country cannot, however, claim that they have fulfilled the aspiration of becoming the ruling class of this country. They cannot claim to have achieved even an effective bargaining political power in the pluralist setting of political power. On the contrary, dalit consciousness, complex and complicated, still represents deprivations stemming from inhuman conditions of material existence, powerlessness and the ideological hegemony of the dominant forces in the country. This dalit scenario compels us to raise a few relevant questions regarding Ambedkar's problematic of political power *vis-à-vis* the dalit perception, in the liberal democratic framework that India has adopted.

Ambedkar rightly visualized that political power was the key to social progress of dalits. This idea appears regularly in his writings and speeches. His concept of power, though complicated, can be understood, when it is related to two major aspects of power – descriptive and normative. The descriptive dimension involves the aspect of description regarding different modes of exercising power in a given society. The normative aspect entails an element of ethics, which raises the question of value in the exercise of power.

Ambedkar held the normative aspect of power to be very important in the process of human emancipation. In *Muknayak* he says that it is not enough to have an independent state but it should be a good state.[1]

Further, a class holding power should have the will to perform and deliver the goods for the people. If this class is unselfish it can represent the society properly. The efficiency of the governing class is not enough to run the government because such class, if plagued by selfish motive, however efficient it may be, may exploit the poor sections of the society. But, the protagonists of democracy seldom understand the need to have an impartial governing class.[2]

In India, he says: "The governing class (Brahmin and Bania) has misused the political power with no sense of responsibility. This power-hungry insatiable class posed a serious threat to democracy and created an imbalance in the political field."[3] He suggests elsewhere that the dalit should become the repository not of the malignant power but of a benign face. He was making the observation in the context of the treatment the mainstream parties were giving to the Dalits who were elected on the ticket of these parties.[4]

Ambedkar's concept of political power distinguishes between the enabling aspect of power and its constraining aspect. In this paper, we shall examine, which aspect of power Ambedkar advocated his lifetime? And, what mechanism and strategies he suggested for capturing the political power. Secondly, whether his followers had become the repositories of the malignant power, and if the answer is in affirmative, how?

Ambedkar followed the normative aspects of political power throughout his life. To capture this redeeming aspect of political power, he imagined or positively identified comprehensive ideals like freedom, justice and equality with institutional arrangements like representative democracy with majority vote. He invested considerable faith in these institutional arrangements as a mechanism to empower the dalits or to make them the ruling class in the country. In the context of the disabling caste-ridden feudal structure, he appreciated how human empowerment depends upon the development of political practices, institutions and belief.

We need to ask: what sort of relationship did Ambedkar visualized between the liberal institutions and dalit political power? What corresponding political practice and strategies did he suggest in redeeming this power? Did he succeed in his mission to use this institutional framework for empowering the dalit? If yes, did he make a fetish of this institutional framework of power? If the answer is in the negative, it will be interesting to examine the political practice, power perception and belief of his followers who do not lose an opportunity in quoting Ambedkar who said, 'dalit should become the ruling class in this country'.

Ambedkar's concept of political power, though not implying intra-individual relations, introduces the requirement that the impartial exercise of power can occur in circumstances, which seek to maintain balance of power among the different forces striving for power. Ambedkar's concept of power, as we shall see in the following paragraphs, calls into question the effectiveness of power inasmuch as it leads to the seizure of power through compromise rather than conflict.

The political strategy that Ambedkar suggests also fits into the liberal framework of instrumentalist and electoral arithmetic. He suggests seizure of power through sharing it with the Muslims.[5] For sharing such power, Ambedkar expressed the need for special safeguards. He considered adult franchise an inadequate device to check such a deeply entrenched governing class as Brahmin and Banias in India.[6] Ambedkar was fundamentally opposed to the political domination of one community over another and therefore wanted to maintain a balance of political forces in Indian politics. He advised the dalits to organize themselves into a third force which he thought was necessary to hold the balance of power between rival political parties.

While emphasizing the need to form a dalit party as a third force, Ambedkar argued that it was only through this force that dalits would be able to acquire effective bargaining power, especially when there was no single party with an absolute majority. In such a situation, he believed, the other parties (Socialist and the Congress) would come to the dalits for their support, which would enable the dalits to hold the balance of power.[7]

To put dalits into the commanding position, Ambedkar has suggested political alignment of those forces which were natural allies of dalits due to their being equally deprived like the dalits.[8] Thus, Ambedkar suggested broad political unity of the SCs, STs and the OBCs in the country. He categorically said that these classes formed the majority of the population and there was no reason why they should not rule the country. All that was necessary was to organize for the purpose of capturing political power which, was their own, because of adult franchise.[9]

Ambedkar seems to argue in favour of SC, ST and OBC alliance by invoking examples from UP politics. He observed that if the combined strength of one crore scheduled caste and one crore backward caste people in UP joined hands against a common target, they could return 50 per cent of their members to the legislature and capture political power.[10] In trying to create a common force of the Bahujan, Ambedkar was willing to change the name from Scheduled Caste Federation to Backward Class Federation.[11] He did not, however, have a mechanical understanding of the alignment or the constitution of a historical bloc, being aware of the cultural contradiction among these classes.[12] Nevertheless, he was hopeful that these contradictions were temporary and could be overcome through mediation and constant negotiation. To recapitulate his argument, Ambedkar suggests at least in the beginning, not a conflict model but a compromise model within the limits of bourgeois democracy.

Such a theoretical model implies that the distribution of power undergoes changes in which the weaker sections have a chance to gain power. It is a concept with a bent of reformism. Second, Ambedkar's argument assumes the plural context of power exercise and operation. In such pluralism, any class or social group has as much power as another does not have, and any reduction of its power (in Ambedkar's sense the dominant caste) is directly translated into an increase in the power of the latter (in Ambedkar sense, dalit). Third, Ambedkar's concept of power, on an ideological plane, has a functionalist connotation signifying the conception of a social whole composed of equivalent elements, which are in an integrated equilibrium. The zero-sum power concept also assumes equilibrium, through sharing power or, countervailing power, as far as it intends to check the power of the dominant groups through competition and bargaining capacity. Finally, Ambedkar's concept deals in the beginning with only the formal aspect of power and does not discuss the deeper level of structures of power, which normally operates outside the sites of formal political power.

Ambedkar seems to substantiate this kind of framework in the context of the monopolization of power by the Brahmins and their allied castes. He cites the memorandum submitted by the backward class people to the UP government: "In the UP as a whole the four leading Hindu castes, Brahmin, Thakur, Vaishya and Kayastha form 21.5 per cent of the total Hindu population. But these castes have supplied no less than 93 per cent Hindu members to the council."[13] Ambedkar's concept at least in the beginning looks reformist in nature but certainly has a democratic agenda in as much as it challenges the hierarchical structures of power that existed in India. He did suggest balancing with the partners in the zero-sum game who he thought should be politically radical and not reactionary like the Hindutva forces. (The BSP, on the other hand, has no such inhibition in making an alliance in electoral politics.)

Did Ambedkar remain fettered within the narrow contours of this liberal notion of political power or did he transcend this self-limiting notion of power? How did he transcend this modernist valorization or triumphant mood to knuckle down the Congress and Socialist under its bargaining political power model?

Ambedkar slowly and gradually realized the limitation of this liberal concept of political power. He realized that the model, instead of making the dalits the repository of benign or liberating power, made them the repository of humiliation. The dalits became the repository of humiliation because they lost their independent voice and became puppets in the hands of the dominant party, which sponsored the political mobility of these dalits. He commented: "In Parliament there are 30 Untouchable MPs belonging to the Congress party. I ask them, have they done anything for our people? They never asked any question, they never moved any resolution and they never submitted a bill in Parliament because their voice is suppressed by the Congress leaders."[14] Thus, though, Ambedkar earlier seemed to have suggested that the dalits should send more sincere and committed dalit members to Parliament,[15] he became aware of the ineffectiveness of these dalit members in Parliament. Realizing limits of such institutional mode of political power, the committee presided over by Ambedkar at Bombay in 1955, passed a resolution calling for abolition of political reservations at the centre, in the state legislatures and at the local self-government district level.[16] Clearly, Ambedkar did not make the fetish of the institutional arrangement.

Another occasion when Ambedkar realized the limitation of these institutional structures in providing the proper context for creating a transformative framework for dalit emancipation was when he could not get the Hindu Code Bill passed in its entirety, though it contained clauses concerning the liberation of women in general: he was forced by the Hindu majority in Parliament to modify it, thus making it innocuous.[17] Ambedkar considered the allocation of portfolios based on the ability of the minister as much more respectful and dignified and really empowering as far as the dalits are concerned. With this in view, Ambedkar considered Finance, Home, Revenue and Industries as the most important departments.[18] But, the Congress gave him the Law portfolio when he had ability to handle any of the other four departments. He considered this a humiliation. He demonstrated this by pushing forward the Hindu Code Bill and finally resigned on matters of principle. But his followers have become the repository of malignant power as many of them, howsoever competent, are given the portfolio of Social Welfare, which is treated by all the ruling parties as a stigmatized department.

Ambedkar suggested that real power resides not within the formal structures of power but underneath them. He argued that state institutions are controlled by the propertied class and the elected representatives are merely in charge of this state.[19] The Brahmins and the Banias were the governing class, with the ability to get possession of executive authority.[20] But Brahmins could not maintain their supremacy as a governing class without an ally, on account of their numeric inferiority. They also needed an ally to aid them with finances to contest elections.[21] The Banias as collaborators fulfilled both these conditions.[22] The Banias would join the Brahmins and invest money because they knew that money invested in politics gives large dividends. In UP and Maharashtra, though the Brahmins are less in number, they have become the governing class by acquiring material assistance from the Banias and through enlisting the numerical support from the OBCs. Ambedkar's stance in this matter suggests that he never placed unconditional belief in the ability of the state to provide justice to the dalits.

In the post-Ambedkar period, however, dalit perception of political power supplanted the need to capture state power. Instead of attacking the state, both from within and outside the parliamentary structures, they have made the state and other institutions a sole repository of politics, reflected in the routine, everyday petty politics and the manipulation of the state structure for personal aggrandizement. The strategy of bargaining, adopted by the dalits in the post-Ambedkar period, howsoever, ineffective it may have been, has definitely contributed to stable, coherent and manageable politics of the dominant forces who are always on the edge of the unstable equilibrium in this country. In the process, the fundamental relations of property have not been altered. In fact, this process of bargaining has become the vehicle for reinforcing the dominant social and political values of society rather than providing the medium of a positional ideology. This in effect has led the dalits to treat the state as a neutral arbitrator, not discriminatory and exploitative. The dalits have placed the state above the contradictions in the civil society. They treat the state as the constitutionally mediating force among the different competing social groups, thus, ending up as ardent supporter of constitutional liberalism. This contradiction was seen as early as 1964, when in Maharashtra, Bhaurao Gaikwad, a staunch supporter of Ambedkar, led the massive struggle of the dalit masses for the redistribution of government land and B.C. Kamble, a dalit, was busy condemning Gaikwads struggle as unconstitutional.[24] Apparently, the latter was oblivious of the radical views Ambedkar held on the Indian Constitution.

Dalits after Ambedkar have not fully realized the nexus between the state and the dominant castes. They also have shut their eyes to the fact that the political power of the dominant class is based on an unstable equilibrium of compromise of which the dalits themselves are a part, such as the BSP-BJP compromise in UP.

To recapitulate, one finds in Ambedkar the dialectical progression of the concept of political power. This process involves the appreciation and negation of liberal political power. The alternative he seeks to this kind of political power is in Buddhism, more particularly in Dhamma. Of course, one will have to problematize this Dhamma concept of Ambedkar in terms of its transformative potential, and this definably is not an easy task. In fact, it is attendant with risk, considering that many Buddhists deny any kind of political status to Buddhism. But Ambedkar provides some kind of answer to this, which has to be sought in the streets, and not only in the corridors of Parliament or any other such structures. Talking a cue from, Ambedkar again, the political task in a society such as ours would be to criticize the working and even withdrawal (particularly in the age of globalization) of the institutions. Because political power in the liberal set-up goes much deeper than one suspects, there are centres and little-known points of support within the liberal structures like the very democratic space that the liberal system provides. These points certainly are not confined to adult franchise or political reservation. Perhaps Buddhism and its Dhamma provide a new space for inter-subjectivity that will lead to social transformation.

Notes

1. *Muknayak* (Marathi), 14 February 1920, Mumbai.
2. B.R. Ambedkar, *What Congress and Gandhi Have Done to the Untouchables*, Thacker & Co., Bombay, 1945, p. 740.
3. Ibid.
4. Ibid.
5. Ibid.
6. Bhagvandas (ed.), *Thus Spoke Ambedkar*, Bangalore, Ambedkar Sahitya Prakashan, Vol. III, p. 134.
7. Ibid., Vol. I, Buddhist Publishing House, Jalandhar, p. 81.
8. C.B. Khairmode, *Bhimrao Ramji Ambedkar* (Marathi) Maharashtra Sanskruti Mandal, Vol. 10, p. 164.

9. Bhagvandas, Vol. I, p. 87.
10. Ibid., p. 83.
11. Ibid., p. 164.
12. B.R. Ambedkar, *Writing and Speeches,* Education Department, Government of Maharashtra, Vol. I, p. 87.
13. Ibid.
14. Khairmode, Vol. II, p. 176.
15. Ibid.
16. Khairmode, Vol. II, p. 179.
17. Ibid., p. 70.
18. Ibid., Vol. 9, p. 437.
19. Ambedkar, *What Congress and Gandhi have Done,* nd., p. 243.
20. Ibid.
21. Ibid.
22. Ibid.
23. Ibid., p. 212.
24. Raosaheb Kasbe, *Mahrashtratil Dalit Chalval* (Marathi) Sugawa Publication, Pune, 1989, p. 18.

Part Three

Nationalism, Representation and State Formation

9 Caste and Nationalism

G. ALOYSIUS

I

While a conspiratorial silence prevails within social sciences as to Ambedkar's contribution to the understanding of modern India, in the quasi-sacred realm of 'nationalism', his touch is considered positively polluting.[1] The trend was set early in the century by the nationalist leaders: Ambedkar stood away from the Indian National Congress (INC) in its struggle against the British; this posture often landed him, wittingly or not, in the camp of the latter; this clearly meant that he was a stooge of the British, worked against the freedom of the country and hence an anti-national. This simplistic and mindless argument repeated *ad nauseam* by many, from C. Rajagopalachari to Arun Shourie, is faithfully reflected by the academics, particularly by the historiographers, whether imperialist or nationalist, elitist or subalternist. Ambedkar became also an academic untouchable.[2] For the universal tactic is to pretend ignorance of the existence of the man, his life activities and thought. Despite this collective amnesia of the dominant-stream academia, the flame of Ambedkar thought has been kept alive, down the century by a small band of largely marginalized intellectuals. Within this small group itself, consideration and evaluation of Ambedkar's contribution varies – a Mahar leader, spokesperson of the depressed classes, symbol of revolt and of course occasionally a social revolutionary. Specifically with regard to nationalism, they all tend to be defensive, protesting that the learned doctor too was 'national' in the same sense or within the same nationalist paradigm as that of the mainstream leaders: that Ambedkar too was anti-British, that he too desired independence as an absolute value and that he considered when compared to *swarajya* beneficial to the masses, particularly the lower castes. However, *vis-à-vis* the onslaught of the dominant ideology of the nationalist leaders, Ambedkar's nationalism and patriotism in the traditional sense could not be made to appear vibrant and compelling.

What is being claimed here, however, is different: that in view of the sea-changes that have taken place in theory, advances in the understanding of the nationalist phenomena and the new initiatives in modern Indian historiography on the one hand and the spread of sociopolitical consciousness among the subaltern classes, the world over, on the other hand, a review of Ambedkar's ideology of nationalism is in order and within such a review, the marginalized personality and his ideology is likely to emerge as strikingly modern, meaningful and challenging. Two preliminary points require to be made at the outset. Of all the modern Indian ideologues, Ambedkar alone attempted to elaborate a full-fledged theory of nationalism and sought to apply it critically to the Indian situation. Within the nationalist movement itself theoretical reflections and justifications were virtually non-existent. While one section asserted that India as Hindu has been eternal and that the nation is merely waking up from its long stupor, imposed on it by its external enemies, the other section kept repeating the phrase "a nation-in-the making" whenever difficulties arose. One could almost sense in general a theoretical unease with the concept of nationalism, which was duly branded as western, whenever the situation demanded. Against this, Ambedkar alone grappled with this idea and ideology of nineteenth-century Europe, deconstructed it as to what is perennial and peripheral in it and showed how it could critically be applied to the peculiarities of the colonial Indian situation. Secondly, Ambedkar's thoughts in general and on nationalism in particular are not merely ideas or opinions of a great thinker. They are aspects of a collective ideology operating as a motor-force, and in struggle with other ideologies in a fast-changing society. This means that to discuss the nationalist thought of Ambedkar is to engage in the exercise of deconstruction of the INC with which it was locked in irreconcilable conflict. Those who prefer to move away from this rather, unpleasant task and to camouflage the antagonism between the two ideologies not only misrepresent Ambedkar but also do not advance the cause of social sciences. This note is limited to the highlighting and clarifying of the central point of contestation between the two forces and thought processes.

II

From the beginning of his public life till his death in 1956, the basic socio-political posture of Ambedkar, despite short periods of programme-based collaboration, had been one of insistent and consistent opposition to the INC-led freedom movement. It is this opposition and antagonism that requires to be problematized in order to understand the crux of Ambedkar's nationalist ideology. The collective-existential context of this antagonism as well as the resultant issue of contestation between the two ideologies can be summarized thus: the nearly two hundred years-long and mostly pragmatic British colonialism, though it unified the subcontinent into one central state, had simultaneously deepened and widened the existing cleavages within society. These, though numerous, based on language, religion, race, territory, etc., as a consequence of political unification at the level of the state tended to become monolithic and revolve around the single basic cleavage which was caste as varna.[3]

This meant that caste as varna tended to divide society along the traditional lines of the pure and the polluted or the upper and the lower castes now released from its local circumscription, not only spread to the entire extent of the colonial state engulfing also the newly emerging urban opportunity structure but also became a model of super and subordination for all other – language, religion, etc. – cleavages of society as well. In other words, caste as varna under colonialism became the take-off point to the emerging process of class-like horizontal polarization everywhere within the newly unified subcontinent. Expressed within the problematic on hand, caste as varna became 'national', setting off a process of the formation of two polarized blocks, having vested interests either in its perpetuation and promotion or in its neutralization and eventual abolition. Such a dichotomous vested interest was indeed the platform for the rise of political consciousness which in turn was also bifurcated; the upper-caste cluster, which stood to benefit by the perpetuation of caste privileges and priorities, while actively engaged in appropriating the emerging opportunities and resources, was also simultaneously busy in preventing the indiscriminate expansion of civil society in the name of "safeguarding tradition and culture". It is from within groups engaged in this double-edged process of resource appropriation on the one hand and prevention of the others on the other, that perceptions of a threat to 'national ethos' by the British came to be articulated.

The lower-caste cluster, on the other hand, broke all over the subcontinent into a multiplicity of socio-economic and socio-religious movements, diverse though in form, extent and emphasis, having this single trajectory of moving away from the caste-imposed occupational, religio-cultural and educational restrictions and liabilities, and seeking to create either implicitly or explicitly a more homogenized and democratized form of an anonymous civil society.[4] To these latter the political plank and banner of the former – protection of tradition and culture – within the current existential conflicts seemed to be plainly a call to reinforce by reinstating caste as varna; and the situation became alarming as the battle cry was raised in the name of nationalism. When open debate on caste could not be avoided, a section within the movement claiming to be more nationalistic than the rest, openly defended caste as being the superior principle of social organization; another finding it profitable silently condoned it in practice; while a third pretended ignorance of it. To top it all, the organization called 'national' seemed to be bordering on the verge of upper-caste exclusivism.

Within such an existential context, whenever the cry of nationalism was raised, it sounded very different to those on the other side. Anti-British seemed to have had something serious to do with social and political relations within society. It was thus that caste as varna – its perpetuation or abolition came to be implicated in the debate between the classes and masses on nation-formation and nationalism. And Ambedkar's ideological elaboration as the aspiration of the lower-caste masses and movements are to be situated, analyzed and understood within such a confluence of forces and movements.[5]

III

This then is the first and fundamental premise of all Ambedkar thought and hence also of his nationalism: that the concrete Indian society of the early twentieth century was not only a caste-based and fragmented society, a continuation of at least a millennium of tradition but also one in which empowerment and impoverishment as well as positive and negative consciousness have far advanced along the caste cleavage. Against this, the two concepts, caste and nation, in Ambedkar's opinion, represent a contradiction and a tension between the actual and the ideal or between the present and the future. For Ambedkar, caste and nation stand in sharp contrast to each other. They are incompatible as the two are constructed on two different and mutually opposed principles of social organization. This contrast is essential to Ambedkar's thought, and in this disjunction his subsequent elaboration of nationalism rests. Caste calls for closure and nation, for openness; the one is based on rigidity and stability and the other presumes flexibility and mobility; and again, the one insists on graded inequality and the other aspires to a standardized equality.

To say that the people of India everywhere, at least the majority of them who have come to be known as Hindus, are found to be members of one or another identifiable caste, more or less distinct in habits, customs, traditions and even belief and worship, is to state the obvious. Despite functional interactions and mechanical cooperation, these castes are generally *exclusive* and inward looking and their insulation is underwritten by mandatory endogamy.[6] In this way, communication, common participation and mutual sharing are severely restricted between individuals and groups belonging to different castes. Secondly, these castes, numerous though they are, form among themselves some sort of *hierarchy* embodying differential rights and liabilities. The rights increase as one ascends the ladder, and so the liability as one descends it. As Ambedkar repeatedly states, the castes form "an ascending scale of reverence and descending scale of contempt".[7] Varna ideology is the single most articulated and religiously sanctioned hierarchy. Such a graded inequality tends to promote specific and exclusive caste interests: "What a caste or a combination of castes regard 'as their own interest' as against other castes remains as sacred and inviolate as ever."[8] The general intercaste feeling is one of animosity: "the castes are not merely non-social. Often they are anti-social."[9] And shows that it is true particularly of the Hindus towards the untouchables. Thirdly, the caste system and spirit promotes rigidity of station in life and fixity of occupation. While this is generally true for all castes, its application is more rigorous in the case of the lower ones – Shudras and Ati-Shudras – who anyway do not have much choice in the matter. One is encouraged to continue doing whatever one's ancestors always did. These practices and characteristics of caste to point out "are not accidental or incidental. It is the religion of the Hindus. It is the official doctrine of Hinduism. It is sacred and no Hindu can think of doing away with it. Therefore, they are a permanent fact and a menace forever".[10]

In contrast to these characteristics of caste as an existential and dominating reality in the Indian social life, nation as a social category of collective aspiration has diametrically opposing ideals and principles of social organization. "What is a nation?" asks Ambedkar rhetorically, explaining that 'nationality' (or nationness) is a social feeling. It is a feeling of corporate sentiment of oneness which makes those who are charged with it feel that they are kith and kin. Again it is a feeling of "consciousness of kind", "like-mindedness", "possessing things in common" in a life of communication, participation and of sharing with all those who constitute one nation.[11] There is no ambiguity here. What Ambedkar tried to point out several decades ago as the core of the nation is affirmed within the recent scholarship on nationalism. Benedict Anderson states: "Nation is always conceived as a deep horizontal comradeship."[12] Ernest Gellner elaborates it: "a mere category of persons becomes a nation if and when the members of the category firmly recognize certain mutual rights and duties to each other in virtue of the shared membership of it. It is their recognition as fellows of this kind which turns them into a nation."[13] In Ambedkar's writings the terms nation, society (ideal) and democracy (social) all are used interchangeably to express a social reality for which we may be more comfortable with the term 'civil society'.[14] In this sense nation is a society where there is an unlimited scope of 'social endosmosis'. Nation is a democracy, a mode of associated living, of conjoined communicated experience. Ambedkar could not be more precise and his import could not be clearer.

Caste insulation and exclusivism is incompatible with the ideal and ideology of the nation. This basic social posture of indiscriminate openness towards one and all members of the presumed nation is called *fraternity*. To quote Anderson again, "ultimately it is this fraternity that makes it (the Nation) possible.."[15] Fraternity in its turn engenders a mental attitude of fair play and equality towards the co-nationalists. The nucleus of caste as varna – graded inequality or hierarchy or differential privileges and liabilities, in short the consideration of superiority/inferiority on the basis of birth – will have no place in the nation. Bryan Turner says: "the existence of the citizens presupposes a certain decline in the dominance of hierarchical social structure and emergence of egalitarian horizontal relationships."[16] Social endosmosis along with homogenization of power within society as equality leads to a situation in which every man has a right and *liberty* "to property, tools and materials as being necessary for earning a living of his own choice". This again is contrary to a caste-based society where persons "are compelled to carry on certain prescribed callings which are not of their choice".[17] Gellner again affirms the virtual cession of all hereditary occupations in a nation.[18]

Nation, then, according to both Ambedkar as well as the recent social science theorists, refers to a segment of people larger than those constituted by primary relationships but suffused with the socio-psychological feeling of mutuality and comradeship, and engaged in actual and active sharing and communion. Quoting profusely Renan's celebrated essay, Ambedkar explains that nation is a plebiscite demonstrated and thereby renewed and strengthened daily through innumerable ways of collective and corporate thought processes and activities.[19] It is not a physical thing in which certain objective characteristics, such as commonality of language, race, territory, etc., could be mechanically identified, as claimed by a section of the orthodox and upper-caste Hindus. Nation, on the contrary, is a spiritual reality binding a people into a deep comradeship.

The three characteristics, which Ambedkar found operative within caste – exclusivism, gradedness and rigidity – meet their opposite in the three virtues of fraternity, equality and liberty as functional and foundational for any nation. If pre-modern India was composed of several castes as quasi-culture or power groups, the modern Indian nation is to be comprised of the principles and ideology, precisely of castelessness. If castelessness is translated into modem political theory as equality, this does not mean that these are peculiar to the western societies. They are to be found in varying degrees within all cultures as the aspirations of the lower orders and, as Ambedkar points out, certainly within the Indian heterodox traditions.

Why and how caste and nation cannot co-exist is explained by Ambedkar: within a formally unified society the danger is that the groups will develop what are called 'their own interests' and these would cause mischief to others outside them. This practical insight of Ambedkar can easily be grasped within the theoretical elaboration of nationalism as congruence between culture and power. In the context of the nation's emergence the ideal is that the totality of power goes along with the totality of culture: in other words, there is equal spread of power over culture. The presence of castes as quasi-culture groups would result in multiple, therefore differential and conflictive congruences of power, and society would become faction-riven. Again, without this equal spread of power over culture, imagining of the nation will certainly not be in the singular but plural, competitive and conflicting.

Within Ambedkar's thought the concept as well as the reality of nation looms very large. Nation is an ideal-typical construct, a social category built around certain principles. A serious and ideological commitment engendering an equally serious change in social and societal relations at least is a necessary prerequisite to actualize the nation as a political entity. In the concrete context of the subcontinent, this demands that caste in all its dimensions, both the system and spirit whether understood in its pristine *vedic-shastraic* purity or in its degraded and distorted nineteenth-century form, be renounced once and for all as an ideology and principle of social order and organization; and socio-politically move towards and aspire to another form of society and social relations. This ideological renunciation and a 're-socialization' is the *conditio sine qua non* for the desire to constitute an independent polity. This brings us to the question of nationalism.

What, then, of nationalism? Nationalism for Ambedkar is the "desire for a separate national existence for those bound by this tie of kinship". It is a will to live as a nation in the full sense of the term not only socially but also politically. Nationalism as an ideology and a movement succeeds the nation as the corporate feeling. It is a praiseworthy desire for those bound by this tie of kinship. Ambedkar is categorical on this point: "there cannot be nationalism without the feeling of nationality in existence".[20] It is precisely this feeling of corporate and communicative oneness that legitimizes the demand for self-determination and then the claim for nation-statehood becomes irresistible. What happens if the cry of nationalism is raised without a simultaneous effort towards or at least an ideological commitment to bring forth the nation or the nationality feeling of social-corporate sentiments? What indeed happens, if the cry of nationalism is raised on the very basis or glorification of a social organization built around an anti-nationality/national (caste) system and ideology? Or worse still, what happens if a nationalist movement itself takes upon to discourage or even stifle through traditional dominance as well as modern political tactics, all those small and big collective attempts to bring forth the nation/nationality or "consciousness of kind" by breaking through the stranglehold of caste barriers?

IV

Such, unfortunately, was found to be the case according to Ambedkar with the governing class in India, the Indian National Congress, and their call for the freedom of the county. Ambedkar observed that the Congress, which had raised the banner of nationalism in the last quarter of the previous century, was basically a Hindu body not very different from the Hindu Mahasabha. Congress for Ambedkar is "a body which is Hindu in its composition and is bound to reflect the Hindu mind and support Hindu aspiration".[21] However, "the Hindu society itself is a myth. Hindu society as such does not exist. It is only a collection of castes, each conscious of its existence and the survival of which is the be-all and end-all of its existence".[22] As the governing class of this mythical society is by and large composed of the Brahmin and Bania castes, Hindu – its consciousness, aspiration, ideals, etc. – merely means and refers primarily to those of the governing class.[23] For, in every "Hindu the consciousness that exists is the consciousness of his caste".[24] Evidences for this was certainly not lacking even at the highest level of the leadership within the nationalist movement.[25]

One needs, therefore, to assess accurately the very character of this coming together of the governing class under the banner of "freedom for the country". Far from being a political act in the modern sense of the term, the basic impulse behind this Congress motive is its own survival, perpetuation and further strengthening. In other words, the majority that the Congress sought to demonstrate is primordial – communal; not issue based – political.[26] These observations of Ambedkar on the nature of the Congress are not mere allegations or wild accusations but a result of empirical investigations into the existential situation, particularly of the collective behaviour of the Congress politicians within the movement and their kith and kin outside it.

There were those who openly praised the caste system as a wonderful and sacred device for a harmonious collective life, particularly expressive of native Indian genius and worthy of emulation by other cultures. They saw or at least pretended to see no contradiction between caste and nationalism. Then, there was this majority who discovered a double benefit in retaining traditional caste privileges while at the same time aspiring for nationalist power and they behaved like the ostrich. There indeed was an uneasy consciousness of the incompatibility between caste and nation expressed by a handful, but the determining majority easily silenced their all too feeble resistance.[27]

At the level of social and political behaviour, however, the entire Congress and its base – the governing class – did not waver from the time worn tradition of caste – exclusivism, sense of gradedness and rigidity. Their antagonism was particularly strident when the lowest levels of the caste society sought to shake off their chains and emerge into civil and political society through a number of ways – education, employment, entry into temples, etc. Within the movement, this also took the form of claim for monopoly representation of the entire mass of people and of refusal to share power with any other socio-political organizations, particularly those of the 'untouchables'.[28]

Ambedkar's deconstruction of the Congress was ruthless and his critical pursuit relentless. Transition to nation and nationalism everywhere in the world has involved social change in general and in particular giving up of traditional and ascriptive privileges by the dominant classes in society. This also meant equalization in a certain real sense between the dominated and the servile masses. From the point of view of the latter this definitely was a gain. Ambedkar cites the examples of France and Japan:

> When the Revolution broke out and demanded equality, the governing class in France voluntarily came forward to give up its powers and its privileges and to merge itself in the mass of the nation... The attitude of the governing class in Japan during the period between 1855 to 1870 – a period in which the Japanese people were transformed from a feudal society into a modern nation – was even more patriotic. The Damiyos and the Samurai realized that it was – impossible to transform this feudal society with its class composition and class rights into a modern nation with equality of citizenship. Accordingly, the Damiyos charged with the spirit of nationalism came forward to surrender their privileges and to merge themselves in the common mass of people.

How do these examples of nationalism of the governing classes elsewhere compare with that of India where caste/varna sanctified by religious beliefs defined the differential privileges and liabilities for different classes and communities? Just the opposite. The governing class in India has no such intention of making any sacrifice on the altar of Indian freedom. Instead of "surrendering its privileges in the name of nationalism, the governing class in India is using or misusing the slogan of nationalism to maintain its privileges".[29]

In the context, then, of the absence of a commitment to renounce its own traditional and ascriptive privileges, the cry of nationalism sounded hollow. As though this was not bad enough, what the so-called nationalists did was to glorify the very anti-national principle of caste as the unique national synthesis and in addition explained that the imperialists were to be driven out precisely because they were a threat to this tradition, culture and religion. This certainly was alarming, particularly for those who were beginning to emerge out of their socio-political limbo. Against such a scenario, the nationalism of the governing classes could not be taken at face value. It needed to be interpreted as something other than nationalism. To quote Ambedkar: "The patriot's one cry is power and more power for him and class."[30] Again, "the Congress' fight for freedom is nothing more than mere tactics".[31] And again, the fight for freedom "led by the governing class from the point of view of the servile classes is a selfish, if not a sham struggle. The freedom, which the governing class in India is struggling for, is to rule the servile classes. What it wants is the freedom of the master race to rule the subject race which is nothing but the Nazi or Nietzschean freedom for superman to rule the common man".[32] And, indeed, "the Congress is deceiving the world by using nationalism as a cloak for a free field for rank communalism".[33]

This view of the origin and growth of the nationalist movement is in total variance with that we are accustomed to, either as Marxist or imperialist or nationalist or subalternist historiography. From the point of view of Ambedkar – and also that of several other leaders of the anti-caste movements – the origin of the Congress upper-caste, anti-Britishism itself is to be traced to the time when the British were being forced to take note of the struggle of the lower castes' emergence into civil society. The threat and danger to 'custom and tradition' so accurately perceived by the nationalists are to be contexualized here and recognized for what it actually was – the prevention and preemption of the new arrivals on the socio-political scenario.[34]

Under the circumstances, the question 'why more than half the population does not cooperate with the Congress in this fight for freedom' assumes a different connotation. The Congress had a readymade answer that the untouchables are tools of British imperialism. Reputing this charge Ambedkar says:

> ... The untouchables have not joined the freedom struggle not because they are the tools of British imperialism but because they fear that the freedom of India (without the minimum requisite, social, ideological change) will establish Hindu domination which was sure to close to them and forever all prospects of life, liberty and pursuit of happiness and that they will be made the hewers of wood and drawers of water."[35]

Commenting on *Swaraj*, Ambedkar suspected that "*Swaraj* would make Hindus more powerful and untouchables more helpless and it is quite possible that having regard to the economic advantage which it gives to the Hindus, *Swaraj*, instead of putting an end to untouchability may extend its life."[36]

V

About the transition from imperialism to nationalism also the relative positions of Ambedkar and the Congress were in contrast. Within the latter's scheme of things the transition was envisaged merely as from British to Indian rule. To quote Ambedkar, "the Congress on the other hand regards the freedom of India from the British imperialism to be the be-all and end-all of Indian nationalism".[37] But this in itself was not dismantling colonialism. Instead, "it would be creating another imperialism", that of caste. The Congress expected that the entire population of the country would non-problematically accept its leadership merely because of the fact that it was Indian and the opponent were the British. In the absence of a definite plan for a minimum social and ideological change demanded and struggled for by the masses that stood to lose by the perpetuation of the existing social order, the appeal was to sentiments of racism. This at its worst would be xenophobia and at best patriotism, but certainly not modem nationalism.

Within the scheme of the lower rungs of the caste ladder, the transition itself is viewed as from bureaucracy to democracy. Ambedkar takes pains to point out the distinct nature of his stand from that of the Congress:

> Ours is an independent decision. We have judged the existing administration solely in the light of our own circumstances and we have found it wanting... They are quite incompetent to tackle our problems.. The British government in India suffers from two very serious limitations. There is first of all an internal limitation which arises from the character, motives and interests of those who are in power. The second consideration ... is the mortal fear it has of external resistance ... that its intervention to amend the existing code

> of social and economic life will give rise to resistance... We must have a government in which men in power knowing where obedience will end and resistance will begin will not be afraid to amend the social and economic code of life which the dictates of justice and expediency so urgently call for. This role the British government will never be able to play. It is only a government which is of the people, for the people and by the people that will make this possible.[38]

Within this kind of transition the transfer of power from British to Indian was simultaneous with the more radical transition. In other words, while actualizing the nation-to-be, in laying the foundation of nationality-feeling and in the very act of the emergence of the nation, the lower orders were indeed advancing, promoting and strengthening the cause of nationalism itself.

Karl Deutsch has pointed out that the beginning of mass emergence in colonial countries is also the beginning of the end of colonialism.[39] They make, through their historic and democratic emergence, collusive colonialism impossible. Here, in this democratic process, we have a harmony and even identity of nation and nationalism, nation legitimizing nationalism and the latter advancing the cause of the nation.

Critics of Ambedkar and lower caste movements tirelessly repeat Ambedkar's statement at the Round Table Conference that the depressed classes were not anxious that there should be immediate transfer of power from the British. They certainly were not anxious, for they were seriously engaged in the much more arduous task of bringing to reality the nation – homogenization of power within culture without which nationalism becomes merely a cloak to hide communalism and communalist power mongering.

Where casteism leads directly to national power, nationalism is vitiated; it merely becomes a fig leaf to cover the nakedness of caste. While the nation does not emerge, the outcome is bound to be differential: for those who always gained by caste and its privileges, now it is double benefit; to the traditional caste dominance and privileges, is now added the national political power and prestige. But, to those who always stood to lose by caste, now it is double bondage – traditional liabilities as well as deprivation of the new opportunity structure. That the post-Ambedkar history and society have by and large demonstrated these, his insights and conclusions are there for all to verify.

If castes are by their very nature anti-national, what does one call those who seek to promote caste in the name of nationalism? Conversely, what does one call those scores of scattered attempts to break through caste restrictions and barriers, expand the emerging civil society, and strengthen the nascent democracy? These are questions to be decided not by following self-proclamations of groups and individuals but by observing and analyzing the consequences, both intended as well as unintended, of their collective behaviour.

VI

To conclude, the various aspects of Ambedkar's ideology of nation and nationalism anticipated by more than half a century, the theoretical advances on the subject: nation as a transition to a power-homogenized society leading to a civil and social democracy involves a certain abatement in the power of the traditional governing classes; and it is this homogenized or unified society that could lay claim for nationalism as self-determination.

Secondly, during the last quarter of receding colonialism, Ambedkar stood up not alone but as a national representative of the collective aspirations of scores of movements scattered all over the subcontinent. This certainly meant that political nationalism of social democracy was very much a reality, contending for power and legitimacy and contesting a retrograde type of cultural movement of the upper castes, although using the banner of nationalism.

Thirdly, the historic personality and ideology of Ambedkar rose on the political horizon, certainly and consciously as a historical continuity of the ancient past, looming large over the present and seeking to determine the destiny of the future. Ambedkar saw himself and in turn was seen by the lower-caste masses as the bearer of the rationalist, heterodox, pragmatic and humanist tradition, within the cultural streams of the subcontinent. The fact that this liberative tradition of yore could not become politically successful in a holistic sense is not a reason, why social scientists should not give it, its due in modem Indian intellectual history.

Notes

1. The conspiracy of silence with regard to Ambedkar's academic contribution was first highlighted by Upendra Baxi. See U. Baxi 1991, Collective Conspiracy to Hush up Babasaheb's Burning Thoughts, *Dalit Voice*, 1-15 April, pp. 15-21.
2. C. Rajagopalachari 1946, *Ambedkar Refuted*, Bombay, Hind Kitabis; Arun Shourie, 1997, *Worshipping False Gods-Ambedkar and the Facts which have been Erased*, New Delhi, ASA Publication; also see K. Santhanam, 1946, "Ambedkar's Attack", New Delhi, *The Hindustan Times*.
3. "It is my hunch that Varna model became more popular during the British period as a result of variety of forces". See M.N. Srinivas, 1966, *Social Change in Modem India*, Hyderabad, Orient Longman, p. 6.
4. "It was as though they suddenly woke up to the fact that they were no longer inhabiting a prison", ibid., p. 91.
5. This is a highly condensed version of the thesis elaborated in G. Aloysius 1997, *Nationalism without a Nation in India,* New Delhi, Oxford University Press.
6. See *Baba Saheb Ambedkar's Writings and Speeches* (*BAWAS*), Vol. I, pp. 50-51; Vol. IX, pp. 192-94.
7. See ibid., Vol. II, p. 504.
8. See ibid., Vol. IX, pp. 192-94.
9. Ibid.
10. See ibid., pp. 167-70.
11. See ibid., Vol. VIII, pp. 30-31.
12. Benedict Anderson, 1983, *Imagined Communities*, London, Verso, p. 16.
13. Ernest Gellner, 1983, *Nations and Nationalism*, Oxford, Basil Blackwell, p. 7.
14. Within recent scholarship there is a definite movement away from the earlier position that nationalism and democracy are incompatible, see Ghia Nodia, 1992, Nationalism and Democracy, *Journal of Democracy,* 3(4):

3-31 and Liah Greenfeld, 1996, Nationalism and Modernity, *Social Research,* 63(1): 3-40.

15. Benedict Anderson, 1983, p. 16.
16. Bryan Turner, 1986, *Citizenship and Capitalism,* London, Alien and Unwin, pp. 18-9.
17. See *BAWAS,* Vol. I, pp. 57-58
18. Ernest Gellner, 1983, p. 18.
19. See *BAWAS,* Vol. VIII, pp. 34-35.
20. For elaborations on this point, see E. Gellner, 1983 and G. Aloysius, 1997.
21. See *BAWAS,* Vol. VIII, pp. 38-39.
22. Ibid.
23. See ibid., Vol. VIII, pp. 47-98.
24. See ibid., Vol. I, pp. 50-1; in this context see the celebrated essay of Romila Thapar, 1989, Imagined Religious Communities, *Modern Asian Studies,* XXIII(2): 209-31.
25. See ibid., Vol. IX, pp. 214-17.
26. See ibid., Vol. I, pp. 50-521.
27. See ibid., Vol. IX, pp. 204-48.
28. For Ambedkar's discussion on the difference between communal and political majorities see ibid., Vol. I, pp. 168-70.
29. See ibid., Vol. III, pp. 308-09.
30. For an elaborate treatment of these themes, see G. Aloysius, 1997.
31. See *BAWAS*, Vol. IX, pp. 225-27.
32. See ibid., Vol. II, p. 599.
33. See ibid., Vol. IX, p. 180.
34. See ibid. p. 232-34.
35. See Ibid., pp. 170-73.
36. See G. Aloysius, 1997, for elaboration on this crucial issue.
37. See *BAWAS*, Vol. IX, pp. 167-73.
38. See ibid., p. 198.
39. See ibid., pp. 167-73.

10 Representation

A. GAJENDRAN

Ambedkar arguing for representation of the depressed classes (DCs) in the organs of the state of emerging India has its genesis in the diverse crises faced by them in the subcontinent. The hubs of all their crises in the DCs perspective were caste Hindus and the 'distrust' they assume day by day. The denial of even basic civic rights, such as taking water from any source like anybody else, walking on any street like anybody else, keeping names like anybody else, wearing any clothes and in any way like anybody else, etc., by caste Hindus, did not allow the DCs to believe that in the unfolding historical circumstances caste Hindus would represent their socio-economic and political rights in the evolving state of India.

The severe infliction of caste Hindus on the DCs was felt when they denied their very existence in the census as groups let alone their being accorded consideration in the bargain for citizenship.[1] Despite the dehumanization that the DCs suffered as untouchables, the gradual enumeration of castes and creeds by the second census of 1891 provided a space for them to be counted as humans, of course still as a separate group as untouchables, concretely since the fourth census of 1911. Still realizing the socio-political implication of the DCs knowing their numbers and brethren across the subcontinent, caste Hindus, while wanting to assert their majoritarianism out of the census, denied the very existence of the DCs in the diverse provinces. This was a grave dispossession that the DCs suffered. However, the 1911 census report proved through certain criteria that there were people who denied the supremacy of the Brahmins, denied the authority of the Vedas, denied worshipping the Hindu gods, ate beef and did not revere the cow, etc., and were therefore discriminated against as untouchables.[2]

The agitation of the Muslims since 1907 for adequate representation in the legislatures and it being legitimized through separate electorates along with other constitutional reforms for India in the Minto-Morley Act of 1909 created some hope for DCs. The temporary respectability the DCs had gained through participation in the British army, railways, mining, etc., which enabled them to challenge caste Hindus, was also prone to a threat, with the constitutional reforms favouring the upper castes. The British government was shirking the trust the DCs had placed on them by playing second fiddle to caste Hindus. Against this trend, representative organizations of the DCs such as the Panchama Kalvi Abhivarthi Abhimana Sangha, the Madras Adi-Dravida Jana Sangha and their leaders like N.G. Chandavarkar from Bengal objected to the political change and appealed to the British government to save them from the yoke of Brahmanism who in the new set-up would be like the snake that seeks guardianship of the frogs.[3]

The diminishing performance of the British government regarding the welfare of the DCs in terms of recruitment to jobs, allocation of resources to education of DCs, etc., was also alienating them from the government. The judicial structures too were bending the laws in favour of caste Hindus, especially to prevent the rights of the DCs in the commons such as water, land, etc.[4] The various social movements, such as those of the Muslims, Sikhs and DCs to elevate their position with better enfranchisement, received a partial treatment from the British government. The worst blow was struck with the DCs being accorded nomination to legislative councils, making them dependent upon the whims and fancies of the nominating authorities, who were either caste Hindus or informed by caste Hindus, and conferring on the DCs a limited franchise, thereby denying full citizenship as accorded to caste Hindus.[5]

The increasing assertions of the DCs *vis-à-vis* the British and caste Hindus brought forth a backlash from the latter. "The Hindu does not look at the revolt of the untouchables as an attempt on the part of the latter for socio-economic improvement of their people. He looks at it as an attempt directed against him, an attempt to equalize."[6] This was manifested in their atrocities on the DCs, for instance, when they tried to take water from Chawdar tank at Mahad. The assault by the Brahmins on DCs trying for temple and public school entry was no less terrorizing. The law did not give them redress. Ambedkar said: "The police are drawn from the ranks of the caste Hindus. The magistracy is drawn from the ranks of caste Hindus. The police and magistracy are the kith and kin of the caste Hindus."[7]

Ignoring the cause of DCs by the Indian National Congress and the national movement was no less significant in causing the political upheaval of the DCs. From the late nineteenth century diverse social reform movements such as the Prarthana Samaj and Brahmo Samaj vanished without a trace, having done nothing for the DCs.[8] The nationalists propagated a *de jure* conception of the Indian people's unity with a *de facto* conception of conflict in it. Gokhale voiced the moral evils of the British occupation as follows:

> There is a moral evil, which, if anything, is even greater. A kind of dwarfing or stinting of the Indian race is going on under the present system. We must live all the days of our life in atmosphere of inferiority and the tallest of us must bend, in order that the exigencies of the existing system may be satisfied. The upward impulse, if I may use such an expression, which every school boy at Eton and Harrow may feel, that he one day be a Gladstone or Napoleon or a Wellington, and which may draw forth the best efforts of which he is capable of rising can never be reached by us under the present system. The moral elevation, which every self-governing people feel, cannot be felt by us. Our administrative and military talents must gradually disappear, owing to sheer disuse till at last our lot as hewers of wood and drawers of water in our own country is stereotyped.

Ambedkar retorted:

> Whether these sentiments which have been voiced by a Brahmin (a noble Brahmin to be sure) to the disgrace of British bureaucracy can't be more fittingly voiced by the untouchables to the disgrace of the Brahmin oligarchy? May it, be said to the credit of the bureaucracy that it has disproved the charge of being wooden and shown itself susceptible to feeling by proposing changes in the system of the government which has dwarfed the personality of those for whom it was devised. But can the oligarchy claim anything half noble?[9]

Nationalists-cum-social reformers, such as Tilak, who presided over a conference on the removal of untouchability in 1918, replacing the Shankaracharya of Karvir, who preferred to leave on an urgent business, but refused to sign the proclamations[10] and Vallabhbhai Patel forcing the DCs to withdraw the case they filed against the caste Hindus of Kavitha for having molested them just because they had sent their children to a village school[11] have gone a long way in demystifying, whatever was called as nationalism and the movement for the DCs.

Gandhi's efforts to represent and remedy the DCs' pathos remained suspect while dealing with the British on the one hand and attempting to reform caste Hindus on the other. Gandhi seemed to have had aggrandized assumption of DC leadership[13] despite the challenge of the DCs and their leaders. The agenda of the DCs became secondary. His claim to represent the DCs was suspect despite his personal efforts at his ashram that were resented by other caste Hindus. His endeavour to redeem caste Hindus to redress the grievances of the DCs was too personal, apologetic, hierarchizing and paternalistic.[12] By denying the agency of the DCs to represent themselves Gandhi seems to have committed a historical blunder in not realizing the significance of 'organic liberative representation' for them.

Ambedkar's Conceptualization and Application of Representation

Beginning as a learned person to represent the DCs evolving as a leader as well, Ambedkar's career spanning more than three decades

(1919-1956), in India and abroad, enabled him to exercise a broad vision on representation in legislative, executive and in the services. For him, representation meant two things: representing opinions and representation of persons. In societies that cherish commonalities in terms of culture, religion, economy, etc., the institutionalization of representing opinions was possible. But, in multi-cultural societies, representation of opinions would not adequately fulfill the needs and interests of diverse groups. On the contrary, distortions of opinions in antagonistic terms can be expressed as manifested between Hindus and Muslims in India. In a society with majority and minority group's personal representation alone could secure their interests. In a democracy, a government could not claim to be democratic when it was merely a government for the people. It had also to be a government by the people, the governed being eligible to partake in the state organs so that the lawmakers were not always the privileged few.[13]

The two possible modes for personal representation were: one, reserved constituencies especially for the minorities in a society with more or less congruity; and two, communal electorates for a society with diverse communities. Given the infructuous implications on personal representation resulting from restricted franchise Ambedkar argues for deferring qualification. That is not merely the underdeveloped regions *vis-à-vis* more developed regions should be given more weightage in franchise but the uneducated and poor as well. However, the logic of the physical majority usurping franchise is anti-democratic in his perception. It should rather be determined by the condition and necessity reflected by the material and educational inadequacies of the population. Nomination, on the other hand, restricts the freedom of the representatives and retards their political education.[14]

Beyond electoral representation, Ambedkar theorized that representation in the offices of the state, i.e., in the administrative services, also formed an inalienable right of the citizens.[15] For him representation in all its forms is not a gift; rather it is 'self-determination' of the groups, and cultures determined by the rights of the individuals.[16]

Ambedkar argued for communal representation through reserved seats according to the population of the DCs. Untouchability and its continued survival benefited caste Hindus. Only DCs, therefore, could represent their own interests and none else.

When it was pointed out that such a system would perpetuate the social divisions, he argued, "those who uphold the divisions are the loudest in their expression of this argument". Communal representation was a way of dissolving the social divisions. When the isolated castes interact with others on an equal footing, "resocialization of the fossilized attitude occurs through cooperation and contact".[17] Normally, Ambedkar's modes of representation have been viewed as one for the DCs alone, despite his arguments and justifications to the contrary.

This vision of the twenty-eight-year-old Ambedkar presented before the Southborough Committee was rejected because the Srinivasa Shastri and S.N. Banerjee opposed it. He carried better conviction during the Round Table Conference of the early thirties. The professional historians of modern India chose to call these contributions as anti-national and pro-imperialistic.[18] In the meanwhile, the Simon Commission's report of 1929, despite Ambedkar's appeals and arguments, continued to recommend governor-approved DC members for elections in joint electorates with reserved seats only. The Nehru report preliminary to drafting the so-called swaraj constitution regarded reservation of seats as 'harmful and unsound', let alone separate electorates. Ambedkar rightly condemned the swaraj constitution as being Brahmanical and upper class oriented.[19]

Ambedkar's experience of the British and caste Hindus bargaining and then scuttling the DCs' 'right to adequate representation' convinced him of the inevitability of separate electorate. He was aware of the danger of thrusting a joint electorate on the DCs. In order to dismantle the stranglehold of caste Hindus, he also urged the need to establish public service commissions to execute 'decasteization in services'.[20] A supplementary memorandum corrects the previous demand of separate electorates for DCs for the first ten years and thereafter, joint electorates and reserved seats, changing into separate electorate only through a referendum, with the rider that no such referendum should be held until after twenty years under universal adult franchise.[21]

On this stand of Ambedkar, Gandhi made disparaging remarks that Ambedkar was not a plenipotentiary and he could not dictate terms of the DCs on the Congress.[22] In other words, Gandhiji again uprooted the organic representative character of the DCs. Secondly, Gandhiji rejected the minority pact that was arrived at between the Muslims, Christians, Europeans, Anglo-Indians and the DCs to urge the honourable treatment of the DCs in civil rights and recruitment in services. The result was that other minorities deserted the DCs' cause.[23]

Ambedkar's argument for the representative rights of the DCs resulted in the Ramsay Macdonald Award, which assured separate electorates for the DCs. This meant that the DCs would have their own constituencies and electorates, and own representatives, apart from voting in a joint electorate to elect caste Hindus also.

But Gandhi's fast against the Award and the Poona Pact nullified these gains. He retorted that neither Gandhi nor the Congress was immortal, that mahatmas had come and gone but the untouchables had remained so. Yet he had to yield to, the harassment and threats of the Congress, of the caste Hindus, to save Gandhi's life. The end result was that the DCs would have only joint electorates with reserved seats. But Ambedkar succeeded in getting a primary election for the DCs themselves who would in turn contest in the joint electorates. The number of seats was also increased to 148 in the provincial assemblies and 10 per cent in the Central Assembly.

The entire episode of the Poona Pact revealed that Gandhi's priority was to save Hinduism. His assumption that the DCs are Hindus and granting their organic representative rights through separate electorates would move millions away from the Hindu fold inspired him to pledge his life to stop it happening. To the question on how to redeem the dehumanized existence of the DCs he answered that it would be through the paternalistic representation of caste Hindus until the social reformers succeeded in changing the food and other cultural values of the DCs.[24] The Poona Pact meant a betrayal of the DCs. For his victory in mathematical calculation, through blackmail, Ravindra Kumar has compared him to Christ, which for the DCs is not easy to digest.[25]

Upendra Baxi says:

> The costs of victory would have to be rewarded by an untouchable historian of future India. But this much is clear. Whatever be the merits of the actual electoral proposals, Gandhi's victory represented for him and others, the victory of the idea that the problem of untouchables was a social problem and not a political one and that it was a problem of Hindu religion and not of a Hindu economy....
>
> One sincerely hopes that Gandhi was right, despite increasing evidence to the contrary, as otherwise historians in the coming centuries might deprive him of the cherished title of a social reformer ... In the meantime, much though one may deplore this, just as Ambedkar denounced Gandhi, Ambedkar too may come to he denounced by the present and coming generations of untouchables for having yielded to Gandhi and Nehru.[26] The results of the February 1946 elections revealed that the Poona Pact was loaded against the DCs. The DC candidate won because of caste Hindus and not because of the DCs. Secondly, the least favoured in the primary election became the most successful in the final election. Thirdly, the disparity in the voting strength between the caste Hindus and the DCs did not enable the DCs to return their true representatives. Finally, candidates rejected in the primary election were returned in the final election, which amounted to disfranchisement of the DCs themselves.[27]

Armed with the statistics of the election results, population, communities, etc., and the implications they would have in the post-independence scenario, Ambedkar's memorandum to the Constituent Assembly reveals him exhausting his ideas on representation in the form of fundamental rights of citizens and their protection against invasion by analytically specifying the protection of minorities and Scheduled Castes.[28] Visualizing the inevitability of the Hindu majority assuming the centre stage in post-British India, he rejected a homogenized majority rule of a community. Therefore, he advocated 'relative majority of representation' to prevent absolute majority from coming into being. Even this relative majority of a community was not to be allowed to establish its rule with the aid of the smallest groups. On the contrary, the smallest groups in a combined way were to be able to form their rule. His commitment to the representative rights of the smallest and the depressed minorities comes to the fore when he vouches for the weightage taken from the majority to be distributed in an inverse manner according to the socio-economic-educational positions. He categorically argues that joint electorate or separate electorate should be considered according to the purpose of group interests and not as rigid principle. Here, while recognizing the significance of separate electorate, he is not oblivious of the relevance of joint electorate to protect the interests of the minorities equally.

For dalits electoral representation has been a great failure. The reserved constituencies do not have the dalits as the majority voters, hence dalit candidate depends and suffers the manipulation of caste Hindus.[29] Likewise, dalit representation through reservation in services has not brought them out of their forced isolation.[30] The caste Hindu-dominated bureaucracy conceives the reservation programmes in such a way as to be "less expensive, easier to formulate, administer and monitor, and politically less risky than those involving major structural transformations"[31] to the detriment of the dalits.

While at the practical level efforts are on to negate what has evolved over the few decades for the restoration of the representation rights of the dalits, at a theoretical level, a challenge is constantly emerging to question the very logic of reservation from the point of view of efficiency and institutional well-being.[32] This argument emanates from a skewed logic which treats merit/efficiency as an absolute category rather than a relative one, especially in a hierarchized multi-cultural society. Secondly, that the merit criterion benefits the clever is, in itself, no reason to adopt it.[33] Thirdly, institutions – hospitals, universities, banks etc. – are evolved by societies. The socio-cultural landscape of a particular society is not irrelevant to those institutions as it is assumed to be. Otherwise, the privileged few would determine the well-being of those institutions in such a way as to prevent the entry of various hierarchized groups/cultures to which they do not belong. The institutional well-being theory, along with the theory of elitism that challenges the beneficiaries of representative reservation, neither interrogates caste Hindu's stranglehold in the socio-economic realms nor questions the failure to implement the constitutional programmes for the deprived sections, but seeks to remove, whatever meagre change occurs among the dalits and adivasis and now more so among the OBCs.

Given the worsening scenario in terms of escalating atrocities, let alone economic prosperity and cultural preservation, the dalits, adivasis and minorities need to interrogate the existing representative mechanisms to know their futility on the one hand and need to bring into the debate the relevance of separate electorate as an alternative, may be in a modified form, on the other. Undoubtedly, Ambedkar's perception of representation seems to be the only hope for the dispossessed and marginalized India, at least till a fundamental geopolitical transformation succeeds.

Notes

1. B.R. Ambedkar, 1989. *Babasaheb Ambedkar: Writings and Speeches* (henceforth BAWAS), Vol. 5, Government of Maharashtra. p. 230.
2. Ibid., p. 232.
3. Dhananjay Keer, 1991. *Dr Ambedkar: Life and Mission*, Bombay, Popular Prakashan.
4. BAWAS, Vol. 5, p. 251.
5. Ibid., Vol. 1, pp. 247-78.
6. Ibid., Vol. 5, p. 261.
7. Ibid., p. 268.
8. Ibid., p. 270.
9. Ibid., Vol. 1, p. 269.
10. Ibid., p. 270.
11. Ibid., Vol. 5, p. 264.
12. W.N. Kuber, 1973. *Ambedkar: A Critical Study*, People's Publishing House, New Delhi, pp. 99-119.
13. Upendra Baxi, 1978. Ambedkar Memorial Lecture, University of Madras, p. 10.

14. M.K. Gandhi, *Statements on Untouchability*.
15. BAWAS, Vol. 5, pp. 287-95.
16. Ibid., Vol. 1, p. 251.
17. Ibid., pp. 251-65.
18. Ibid., p. 256.
19. Ibid., p. 269.
20. Ibid., p. 266.
21. Bipan, Chandra, 1986. *Modern India*, NCERT, New Delhi. See also *Nationalism and Colonialism in Modern India*, Delhi, Orient Longman.
22. Ibid., 1979.
23. BAWAS, Vol. 5; Kuber 1973, pp. 99-119.
24. Ibid., Vol. 2, p. 521.
25. Ibid., pp. 669-72.
26. Ibid., Vol. 5, p. 314.
27. Ibid., pp. 320-24.
28. Ravindra Kumar, 1984. Gandhi, Ambedkar and Poona Pact, 1932, Teen Murti, New Delhi.
29. Ibid., p. 22.
30. Baxi, 1978, op.cit., p. 10.
31. BAWAS, Vol. 1, pp. 431-32.
32. Ibid. 383-449.
33. Devanesan Nesiah, 1997. *Discrimination with Reason*, New Delhi, Oxford University Press, p. 188.

11 Reorganization of States

SUDHA PAI

Over the years, there have been many demands for the creation of new states out of the existing ones formed in the immediate post-independence period based upon ethnic, regional, economic and such other grounds. The Sikh demand for the Punjabi Suba in the 1960s resulted in the concomitant demand for separate states of Haryana and Himachal Pradesh. In the 1970s the persistent demand for statehood and autonomy in the north-eastern hill regions remained a major source of federal tension. Since the 1980s the agitation in Assam on the domicile issue, and the Akali agitation alternating between the demand for greater state autonomy and a separate state of Khalistan, have disrupted the functioning of the Union. There have also been demands for separate states of Gorkhaland, Uttarakhand, Jharkhand etc., which have acquired considerable public support as expressed in massive popular demonstrations that led to creation of Uttarakhand, Jharkhand and Chattisgarh. This has led scholars and political leaders to speak of the need for a second States Reorganization Commission that would restructure the entire federal system in the light of the present requirements and people's wishes.

This paper briefly analyzes the rationale upon which the Indian states were formed based upon the recommendations of the States Reorganization Commission against the backdrop of the political situation and pressures of the time. It then examines in detail an alternative viewpoint, which was available, but was not discussed widely during that period – that of Dr. Ambedkar. The concluding section examines the relevance of Ambedkar's ideas on the reorganization of states, in terms of size and the linguistic principle, in the light of the present-day situation.

The Congress Party and the Reorganization of States

The demand for the formation of linguistic provinces at independence was in large measure a direct outcome of the development of regional languages and corresponding identities[1] in the nineteenth century. This had led to the emotional integration of different language groups and the development amongst them of a consciousness of being distinct cultural units. Although the British were aware of the importance of the linguistic principle in India, they gave it only qualified support, and in the last resort imperial interests were paramount.

The Congress party lent support to the linguistic principle as early as 1905, when it demanded annulment of the partition of Bengal that divided people speaking the same language. Another concession was the creation of a separate Congress province of Bihar in 1908, and Sind and Andhra in 1917. However, Congress opinion had not crystallized in favour of linguistic provinces and in fact in its 1917 session it was opposed by the group led by Annie Besant. It was at the Nagpur session of 1920 that the party under the leadership of Gandhi adopted the linguistic redistribution of provinces as a clear political objective and in the following year the Congress was reorganized along these lines. In 1927 the Congress adopted a resolution that "the time has come for the redistribution of provinces on a linguistic basis" and constituting Andhra, Utkal, Sind and Karnataka into separate provinces could make a beginning. Members supporting the resolution referred to the right of self-determination of the people speaking the same language, and bound by the same tradition and culture. The question was also examined by the Nehru Committee of the All Parties Conference in 1928. While other factors were mentioned, the committee held that "the main considerations must necessarily be the wishes of the people and the linguistic unity of the area concerned". Between 1928 and 1947, on many occasions, despite the growing demand for a separate state of Pakistan, the party reaffirmed its adherence to the linguistic principle. In its election manifesto of 1945-46 the party clearly stated that the reorganization must necessarily be on linguistic lines.[2]

The mobilization patterns adopted by the Congress during the National Movement also encouraged regional identities and loyalties. Two kinds of mobilizations took place, namely, horizontal and vertical. Under horizontal mobilization, with Gandhi's leadership, large masses joined the movement in parts of the country. However, the latter process saw the integration of certain regions under the growing middle classes who later emerged as a regional elite.[3] However, the partition of the country and the riots immediately following it brought a change in the thinking of Congress leaders. In the Constituent Assembly, on 27 November 1947, soon after partition, Prime Minister Nehru argued, "First things must come first, and the first thing is the security and stability of India." This change is also reflected in the reports of the Dar Commission and the JVP Commission, which showed that the reconstitution of provinces solely on a linguistic basis was no longer taken for granted.

Both these commissions, the former appointed by the Constituent Assembly to fix the boundaries of Andhra, Karnataka and Maharashtra, and the latter by the Congress at its Jaipur session in December 1948 at the insistence of party members, were clearly concerned with the supreme need to concentrate upon security, unity and economic prosperity, and to discourage separatist and disruptive tendencies. Both also strongly expressed themselves against any reorganization being undertaken in the circumstances prevailing in the country and pointed out that there were more pressing problems such as defence, food, refugees, inflation, production, etc. The formation of provinces exclusively or even mainly on linguistic considerations, they argued, would be inadvisable and the emphasis should primarily be on administrative convenience. The Congress Working Committee adopted the report of the JVP Committee in April 1948, and it remained the position of the party as seen in its election manifesto of 1951.[4]

By the early 1950s, the demand for linguistic provinces had become strong and politicized. Various political groups were interested in their formation as they hoped to gain control over the administrative machinery in the new political set-up. The Congress party itself was badly divided, the national leadership being opposed to linguistic states while the state-level leadership and cadres were keen to form them. The reports of both the Dar commission and the JVP Commission were hence received with general disappointment throughout the country, particularly the south, where the demand for linguistic reorganization was the strongest. Between 1951 and 1953 the agitation for the formation of a separate state of Andhra became acute, and its formation in 1953 following the death of Potti Sriramulu, led to strident demands by people in other regions. There were demands for a Greater Gujarat, Maha Punjab, United Maharashtra, Maha Vidharbha, and a separate Karnataka etc., many of which conflicted with each other. Moreover, the demand for a Vishalandhra, which would include the Telugu-speaking areas of Hyderabad, was still going on.[5]

By the time the State Reorganization Commission (SRC) was appointed by the government in 1953 to study the issue of reorganization in its entirety, the idea of reconstituting states along linguistic lines was fairly well accepted. The Commission discussed four governing principles that will structure its recommendations:

(i) preservation and strengthening of the unity and security of India;
(ii) linguistic and cultural homogeneity;
(iii) financial and administrative considerations; and
(iv) successful working of the five-year national economic plan.

Overall, however, the SRC underlined the primacy of the linguistic factor in the demarcation of state boundaries. It conceded that the demand for linguistic reorganization had gathered momentum and in some cases assumed the form of a "separate political programme".[6]

Hence, the main task of the Commission became the creation of linguistic states while keeping in mind the paramount factor of security and unity of the country. It attempted equilibrium between discouragement of disruptive sentiments such as provincialism or linguistic fanaticism, and full scope for the unhampered growth of the genius of each group.[7] The Commission reviewed in some detail suggestions other than those made along linguistic lines for the redrawing of state boundaries. The principle of natural economic regions was considered in several alternative patterns: that arising out of the desire for unified river valley control; that based upon the 'nodal' concept in which important cities/towns could form the nucleus of regions; division into regions based upon levels of per capita income, etc. In each of these, the commission not only found some merit, but also some difficulties. It also discussed the question of smaller versus larger states, and was of the view that Indian experience had not shown that "in large states standards of administration deteriorate ... some of the larger states have proved to be the best administered".[8] In fact, it argued that size and efficiency were not related.

Discussing the seminal issue of linguistic reorganization the SRC pointed out its advantages. It was of the view that in a federal system each unit must be homogeneous and in India, "language provides the only rational basis for reconstructing the states, for it reflects the social and cultural pattern of living obtaining in well-defined regions of the country".[9] Each state could use its own language for purposes of administration and education. This would encourage the people's participation in decision-making and welfare programmes, and all linguistic groups would gain "political and economic justice". In contrast, in multi-lingual states, all the benefits of government policies would go to the majority community, creating animosities. The Commission argued that unilingual rather than composite states would be better, particularly as many states were already unilingual, and such a promise had already been made during the national movement.

At the same time, the SRC pointed out the dangers inherent in unilingual states and suggested means to overcome them. Unilingual states could encourage exclusivism and weaken the unity of the nation, which was already fragile. The use of regional languages would mean lack of a common language of administration and common educational standard. Also, national planning would be hampered and maximum utilization of resources would not be possible leading to uneven economic development. The Commission also warned against the consequences of the notion of a 'homeland' for each language group, and overemphasis on state autonomy, which could lead to regional loyalties. While agreeing that the wishes of the people were important, it held that the concept of 'self-determination' should not be conceded. Finally, while agreeing that historical factors were important, it pointed out that these could be interpreted in various ways and to support different positions, hence, the present was of greater importance.[10]

Finally, the SRC recommended that the linguistic factor should not be deciding but the other factors, such as financial viability, size, etc., should also be considered, and each case separately considered on its own merit. When the evidence had been examined, the Commission recommended a redrawing of India's political geography along lines, which more or less coincided, with many of the linguistically based demands. On the basis of these factors, the Commission recommended the break-up of the three categories of states (A, B and C) and the creation of only two types, namely, states and union territories, the latter being centrally governed. While part A states provided the standard and were to be maintained with some changes, the other two categories would be integrated into the nearby part A states on the basis of language. Sixteen states on the basis of language were to be formed, with the exception of the bilingual states of Bombay and Punjab, and all remaining minorities in them, linguistic or otherwise, were to be granted safeguards within the Constitution. The Commission also went into the specific problem of each of the major states created. Madras city would remain within the state, and two states of Andhra and Hyderabad, consisting of the Telengana region, were to be created, which could be merged later, if the people so desired. A composite state of Bombay, in which the Marathi and Gujarati areas would remain together, and a separate state of Vidarbha were to be created. Most of the problems lay in the south. In the north, the Commission, in spite of much difference of opinion, decided to keep the large state of Uttar Pradesh intact. Thus, the Commission recommended large unilingual states, which it felt, would satisfy the people and be of advantage in governance.[11]

The interval between the submission of the SRC's report in December 1955 and the official demarcation of states on 1 November 1956, was marked by demands and counter-demands by various groups based upon the linguistic principle, which forced the government to modify some recommendations of the Commission. Congress leaders also had to exert pressure on their members in various states to agree to the Commission's recommendations. The problems of Bombay state in the west, border disputes between West Bengal and Bihar in the east, and the rival claims made in the Punjab in the north, were some of the most troublesome and dangerous developments.[12]

The recommendation of the SRC for a bilingual state of Bombay, consisting of both Gujarati and Marathi speakers, and a separate state of Vidarbha, was rejected by Congress members and even by the Congress Working Committee. After many debates within the party and the Bombay Assembly, a bilingual state of Bombay, including Vidarbha and Bombay city, was agreed upon, but it was not acceptable in Gujarat, which witnessed violent demonstrations. The Congress was caught between the demands of the Samyukta Maharashtra and Maha Gujarat emanating largely from within its own party ranks, and ultimately two states had to be created. The proposal to merge the two states of Bihar and Bengal, which ran counter to the SRC's recommendations, but had the approval of the two Chief Ministers of these states and the Prime Minister, also met a similar fate. It was violently opposed by the West Bengal Linguistic States Reorganization Committee, a united front of the leftist parties of the state, and by political groups within the Congress and outside. The left parties argued that distinct linguistic nationalities existed on the sub-continent and must be recognized. The national government had hoped that if the merger of Bihar and Bengal could be effective, similar moves could be instituted for merging many other regions, such as parts of Gujarat and Rajasthan, a Dakshina Pradesh in the south by merging the three, or if possible four states, to create large economic regions, thereby underplaying the linguistic issue. Finally, due to massive demonstrations in many parts of the country, the proposals had to be withdrawn and the linguistic principle triumphed.[13]

Thus, the reorganization of the states as it was carried out in 1956 was in response to the strident and often violent and popular pressures of the time. Members of the Congress party in the states, particularly Maharashtra, Karnataka and Andhra, also were insistent and made representations before the SRC for linguistic reconstitution. The pressures arising from profound attachments to provincial, cultural, linguistic and historical groupings were such that regions based upon economic and administrative considerations had little chance for serious consideration as the basic political unit. Many and varied groups competed for recognition as units of the newly designed Union. While some felt that Nehru had bowed to pressures, others believed that he had bowed to democracy.

Ambedkar's Views Examined

While both the report of the States Reorganization Commission (SRC) and the principles on which the government took action are fairly well known, the position of Ambedkar, one of the makers of the Constitution of India and leader of the Scheduled Castes (SCs), has not received adequate attention. His views were outlined in his *Statement to the Linguistic Committee* in 1948,[14] in which although his primary focus was on the state of Maharashtra,[15] general principles pertaining to all states were also outlined.

In keeping with other political leaders of his time Ambedkar agreed that the popular demand for linguistic states had to be recognized and examined. He argued that the provinces have all the elements of a distinct nationality, and should be allowed the freedom to grow to their fullest in nationhood. However, unlike the SRC, for him, the most important justification for reorganization on linguistic lines was the 'definite political advantages' that would accrue for the functioning of a democratic polity in India. Democracy would work better in linguistic provinces, rather than in mixed provinces, as social homogeneity, i.e., the position of a common language and culture would promote unity; whereas heterogeneity would result in division into hostile groups, and power would be used to promote the interests of a particular group which would then dominate the others.

A unilingual state would be more stable than a multilingual state, which he felt was also borne out by an examination of other states such as Germany, France or Italy, which are homogeneous states with a single language. Based on this principle Ambedkar was critical of the retention of a mixed state of Bombay as advocated by the SRC. He pointed out that the intense enmity between Maharashtrians and

Gujaratis or Andhrites and Tamilians was well known. Separate linguistic states would therefore remove cultural tension and strengthen democracy. He also agreed with other leaders that the issue of reconstruction into linguistic states could not be postponed. First, the principle had in fact been accepted in the case of six provinces whose administrative boundaries coincided with those of a linguistic group – Assam, Bengal, Bihar, Madras, Punjab and Orissa. Second, the demand in the remaining provinces had reached emotional and violent levels.[16]

Ambedkar was nevertheless aware of the dangers inherent in the creation of linguistic states. First, a linguistic state with its own language could in time develop into an 'independent nationality' and India could become a 'medieval' society consisting of warring states. Second, within the states, castes are so distributed that in any given area one or two castes are dominant, and others are subservient to it. This subservience arises from their smaller numbers and economic dependence on the dominant castes as the latter own not only most of the land in the villages, but also businesses, jobs, etc., in the urban areas. This could happen, Ambedkar argued, for example, in Punjab where Jats, in Andhra Pradesh the Kammas and Reddys, in Karnataka the Lingayats and Vokkaligas, and in Maharashtra the Marathas are dominant. It would have important repercussions on the system of single-member constituencies adopted under the Constitution, as voting is always community based, and the candidate of the majority community would win due to support of sheer numbers, and not competence. Moreover, there is not only a hierarchical status system, but each caste has all the exclusiveness and pride, which a nation has, leading to a collection of "major and minor nations" on the sub-continent. With the creation of linguistic states, Ambedkar opined, these rivalries would be sharpened, and the minorities would be crushed.[17]

Ambedkar differentiated between a *political* majority that constantly undergoes change in a democratic system, and a *communal* majority, which remains fixed even in democratic societies.[18] As the area of a state increases, the proportion of the minority to majority decreases, rendering the minority position precarious and providing opportunities for the majority to practise greater tyranny. He illustrated this with reference to Maharashtra where he pointed out the proportion of caste Hindus to untouchables would be fourteen to one. The creation of smaller states would make the burden on the minorities much smaller enabling them to bear it and fight against it politically. To protect the minorities the Constitution would need to be amended to make provision for a system of plural-member constituencies with cumulative voting. As the leader of the SCs, an underprivileged section who were already experiencing exploitation in many states, Ambedkar was able to visualize such a situation. Thus, he saw clearly the pitfalls of linguistic states and the consequences for democracy, which was his primary concern. Where Ambedkar disagreed with the SRC and leaders of the Congress was in advocating a number of 'checks and balances' which he felt would remove the dangers inherent in such a reconstruction.[19]

The first was to provide in the Constitution that the regional language would not be the language of the state. He argued that the official language of the entire country should be Hindi, and until it was accepted and learnt by all, English could continue. This, he held, was essential as separate regional languages would lead to the centre having to communicate with every state in a different language, and separate regional languages would divide people, leading to regionalism. Second, and more important, people speaking the same language did not need to be grouped into only one state, but there could be more than one state with the same language. The formula of one state-one language, he pointed out, was not to be confused with that of one language-one state. The latter meant that all people speaking one language would be brought under one government, irrespective of area, population and dissimilarity of conditions among the people. Rather, people speaking one language might be divided into many states, depending upon (1) requirements of efficient administration, (2) needs of the different areas, (3) sentiments of the different areas, and (4) proportion between the majority and the minority. This would serve two purposes: it would lessen the importance of regional feelings and differences, and also remove the existing disparity in size.[20]

The question of size was important for Ambedkar not only from the point of administrative efficiency, which was the only aspect that the SRC had considered. He pointed out that equality of size of states in a federation, and the interrelationship among states were extremely important aspects in a democratic polity. The size of the states, as proposed by the Commission would be eight states with a population between 1 and 2 crore each (Rajasthan, Punjab, Orissa, Kerala, Karnataka, Vidarbha, Hyderabad and Andhra); four with a population between 2 and 4 crore (Madhya Pradesh, Bengal, Madras and Bihar); one with over 4 crore (Bombay); and one with over 6 crore (Uttar Pradesh). In fact, K.M. Pannikar, a member of the Commission, in his dissenting note on Uttar Pradesh, had argued that too great a disparity in size could lead to suspicion and resentment among states and generate forces likely to divisive of the federation.[21] In India, Ambedkar also pointed out, the fact that the powers of the two Houses are not equal as in the USA made the disparity of population even more important.[22]

A related aspect highlighted by Ambedkar was that the SRC, by creating big states, had introduced a new *political* problem of north versus south. No doubt, there were important differences between the two areas in terms of language and culture. Also, they disliked each other. The south did not want Hindi as the national language. In the circumstances, the recommendation of the Commission would lead to consolidation of the north into large states such as Uttar Pradesh, and balkanization of the south into a number of smaller Dravidian states. This, as many of those representing before the Commission had pointed out, had already created apprehensions of the domination of Uttar Pradesh, i.e., of the north, in national affairs.[23]

To meet these problems, Ambedkar recommended the division of the four large states of Uttar Pradesh, Madhya Pradesh, Bihar and Maharashtra. Uttar Pradesh, he held, could be divided into three states – western, eastern and central – with their capitals in Meerut, Allahabad and Kanpur respectively. Each would have a population of approximately 2 crore, which, he held, should be regarded as the standard size of population for a state to administer effectively. Similarly, the two states of north and south Bihar, with a population of approximately over one-and-a-half crore, could have their capitals at Patna and Ranchi respectively.

The new state of Madhya Pradesh, created by the SRC, which would have a population of 26.1 million and an area of about 1,71,200 sq. miles, could be divided into north and south Madhya Pradesh, making it more manageable. Maharashtra could be divided into four states coinciding with both economic regions and the demands of the people. In this way, the rule of one language-one state could be followed, and other considerations could also be kept in mind.[24]

Another means of removing the tension between the north and the south suggested by Ambedkar was to relocate the national capital. Delhi was too far from many parts of the country, particularly the south. Hyderabad in central India had a better climate than the extremes of Delhi, was far from the borders and hence could be easily defended, and would make the south feel closer to it. Hyderabad was equidistant from all major cities in the country, and had beautiful buildings, which could be used.[25]

Conclusion

In recent years there has been increasing recognition of the need to strengthen federalism by reorganizing the states, to accommodate the demands of people of various regions and groups. While fifty years have passed and many changes and new problems have arisen in the working of the federal system, some aspects of Ambedkar's ideas remain relevant in such an exercise. In this context, two aspects of Ambedkar's writings on the subject are discussed below: the size of states and reorganization on the basis of more than one state based on the same language.

The issue of size can be discussed in terms of the four principles, outlined by Ambedkar, of development, efficiency, equality and democracy. The creation of large states with unequal sub-regions has resulted in the creation of backward sub-regions, and their exploitation by the advanced sub-regions. This exploitation has been, as Ambedkar pointed out, by the dominant caste elite, who have been the major beneficiaries of the development, which has taken place since independence. Experience has shown that large states have a greater propensity to perpetuate the existing inequality between economic strata, expand the influence and power of dominant castes, and promote caste solidarity and political factionalism in the overall condition of the given economic disparities.

This has spawned movements for self-development, identity and ultimately separate states. Vidarbha, Marathwada, Saurashtra, Jharkhand, Telengana, Chattisgarh, etc. are good examples. Demands for the creation of these states were placed before the SRC but were rejected in favour of large consolidated states, ignoring any sub-regions within them.

Separated from Madhya Pradesh in 1956, the eight districts of Vidarbha, which were described by the SRC as a self-sufficient cotton-growing region and economically viable as a separate state, have been demanding separation from Maharashtra for a long time, their major grievance being neglect within the larger state. Similarly, there have been demands for the creation of Chattisgarh and Bundelkhand, based upon both ethnic and economic grounds. The genuine demands of unequal groups and minorities and spontaneous movements for progressive change are more satisfied than promoted in these states.

That the principle of language even in the 1950s/60s was only one of the grounds on which division was possible, is evident from the Telengana movement in which leaders from the region had demanded a separate state, and continue to do so. This is seen in the formation of the Telengana Juna Sabha in June 1998. Affected by Naxalite violence, poverty and deprivation, its supporters point out that Telengana is bigger than any of the three new states promised by the government in New Delhi of Uttaranchal, Vananchal and Pondicherry. In Karnataka too, the Kodagu Rajya Mukti Morcha is planning for an 'ethnic' state of Coorg under Article 371.

In terms of efficiency, large and unwieldy states such as Uttar Pradesh, Madhya Pradesh and Bihar have proved, as Ambedkar argued, to be less manageable or well governed than smaller states such as Haryana and Himachal Pradesh. The latter have shown faster development and are more responsive to the needs of the people. Smaller and medium states would help mass mobilization and greater participation in development by bringing government closer to the people and making it more responsive to local and specific sub-regional demands. The creation of many smaller states would also put them on a more equal footing in the Lok Sabha and Rajya Sabha, removing a grievance that a few large states have occupied important and influential positions in the central government. However, the creation of only a few small states, as the government in the New Delhi is attempting to do, even if justified in terms of people's long-standing demands, would give rise to a plethora of demands creating tension and divisions within the federal structure.

The principle of more than one state, based upon the same language, remains a useful and relevant principle on which states could be restructured. Within this larger principle factors such as equitable growth, geographical factors, administrative convenience, etc., could also be taken into consideration. Not only would this reduce the size of states, more importantly, it would correspond to the demands for statehood based upon ethno-cultural aspirations of some of the smaller sub-regions and minority groups in the country. This would also strengthen both democracy and the federal system.

Notes

1. Broomfield, *Mostly About Bengal., Essays is Modern South Asian History*, Manohar, Delhi, 1982.
2. Joan Bondurant, *Regionalism versus Provincialism: A Study in Problems of Indian National Unity,* Indian Press Digests Monograph Series, University of California, Berkeley, December 1958, pp. 20-22.
3. G. Ram Reddy and B.A.V. Sharma, *Regionalism in India: A Study of Telengana,* Concept Publishers, New Delhi, 1979.
4. For both the reports, see P.K. Sharma, *Political Aspects of States Reorganization in India*, Mohuni Publication, New Delhi, 1969.
5. Joan Bondurant, op. cit.
6. States Reorganization Commission, Manager of Publications, Government of India, 1955: 35.
7. Ibid., p. 32.
8. Ibid., p. 61.
9. Ibid., p. 35.

10. Ibid., p. 46.
11. Ibid., pp. 67-80.
12. Joan Bondurant, op. cit., pp. 71-76.
13. Ibid., pp. 76-104.
14. Later published as "Thoughts on Linguistic States" in *Speeches and Writings Baba Saheb Ambedkar,* Vol. 1, Education Department, Government of Maharashtra, 1979, pp. 99-128 (henceforth, cited as *Speeches & Writings).*
15. On Maharashtra see "Maharashtra as a Linguistic State", *Speeches & Writings.* n. 14.
16. Ibid., pp. 102-104.
17. "Thoughts on Linguistic States" n. 14, pp. 167-68.
18. Ibid., p. 169.
19. "Need for Checks and Balances", article on Linguistic States, first published in *Times of India,* 23 April, 1953, published in *Speeches & Writings,* pp. 132-35.
20. "Thoughts on Linguistic States", n. 14, p. 165.
21. Panikkar's plea was primarily based on political grounds rather than accepted principles of reorganization. He argued that the large size and number of seats in the Lok Sabha would make the position of Uttar Pradesh politically superior to the other states, a situation for which there was no check in the Indian Constitution. It could also exercise stronger political influence through the party machinery in the working of the Federation. See, P.K. Sharma, "A Reorganization of Uttar Pradesh", n. 5, Chapter VII, pp. 180-192.
22. "Thoughts on Linguistic States", n. 15, pp. 141-42.
23. Ambedkar mentions that Rajagopalachari, in a private conversation with him had expressed the fear that the prime minister would always be from the north. *Thoughts on Linguistic States,* n. 15, p. 149.
24. Ibid., pp. 150-52.

12 Contesting Views on Panchayati Raj

NARENDER KUMAR

Panchayat has come to occupy an important place in post-independence India, indicating the trend towards decentralization of powers to the local authorities. The pattern of decentralization involves both the delegation or devolution or transfer of political and administrative powers.[1] It also implies the extension of democracy to the grassroots level for people's participation. Panchayati Raj seeks to link the units of administration in the most remote villages. While its proponents see it as promoting local autonomy and minimizing supervision and control by the higher authorities, its detractors see it as the beginning of the ruin of the country by strengthening deleterious norms, ties and institutions.

In British times, there was a spate of legislations relating to the establishment of panchayats covering major parts of the country, including the princely states. After independence, the Constitution made a provision for panchayati raj institutions (PRIs) in the Directive Principles of State Policy. According to Article 40, "The State shall take steps to organize village panchayats and endow them with such powers as may be necessary to enable them to function as units of self-government". The idea gained further impetus in 1952, wherein community development programmes were launched in some selected localities of various states. Again, in 1956, the National Extension Service (NES) scheme covered the whole country for village development. The unsatisfactory results of the scheme forced the Government of India to appoint a committee headed by Balwant Rai Mehta to study the problem and suggest remedies by way of implementing the scheme uniformly throughout the country.

Gandhi, Ambedkar and Jayaprakash Narayan have been among the pre-eminent Indian thinkers who have expressed themselves on the issue of panchayats. The present paper seeks to analyze their thinking in terms of gram panchayat in the context of the village system, panchayat as judiciary, as representative body and finally examine the preconditions for the success of Panchayati Raj.

Gandhiji viewed the village system as self-sufficient, independent of its neighbours for vital needs and yet interdependent for many others. He believed in the innate mutual goodness and understanding capacity of villagers to run the affairs of the community. Panchayats, being engaged in the legislative, executive and judicial functions of the village, were handy for quick decision-making and implementation.[2]

Ambedkar differed in his view on the matter. Castes being a predominant factor in the affairs of the village, he said, the village republics spelled ruination for the country and played no part in its affairs and destiny. He described village panchayats as a sink of localism and den of ignorance, narrow-mindedness and communalism.[3] India could not build up a national spirit because of its village system, saturating the people with local particularism and local patriotism. Because he was unequivocal in this view in the Constituent Assembly, even the members in favour of Panchayati Raj system failed to have it included in the Constitution.

Jayaprakash Narayan, although an ardent supporter of Panchayati Raj, was not satisfied with the traditional village system based on the premises of monopoly of landed property in the hands of a few, absence of social security and lack of a system that could provide weaker sections economic support. He rejected the idea that democracy prevailed in village republics in ancient India. His preference for Panchayati Raj system was not because of panchayat as executive and its deliverance of goods to the masses but for people's collective decisions based on consensus. Gram Sabha for him was the ideal decision-making body and not the five members of panchayat deciding the destiny of the whole village community.[4] He hailed the idea of decentralization of power in the hands of people but with alterations in the traditional village structure.

Panchayat as Judiciary

Gandhiji favoured the transfer of judicial powers to the panchayats in order to make justice available to the people quickly.[5] For him, panchayat being represented by the *Panch Parmeshwar* (five gods) reflected the spiritual sacredness. He advocated making justice inexpensive, limiting the number of courts with simple procedure. Village-level disputes, in his view, were quite simple and there was no need of complex judicial provisions to run the affairs of the village. The decisions of the panchayats were to be final except in cases of corruption and obvious misinterpretation of law.[6]

In Ambedkar's view, to deliver efficient and correct judicial decisions, a person had to be (a) trained in law, (b) have an impartial outlook, and (c) his role had to be independent. Panchayat, being an elected body, could have illiterates or literates but not necessarily with the qualifications needed to adjudicate. Nowhere in the world he found an elected judiciary, he observed.[7] An illiterate population, deep in poverty and wallowing in superstitions could not produce even a single person who could understand the complexities of the judicial process and deliver justice to the people. Citing an instance of caste cleavages during a debate in Bombay Legislative Council, he said: "In a certain village of Satara district in which non-Brahmins boycotted the Brahmins, the Brahmins could not get a barber to shave them, they could not get the village *Bania* to sell them provisions and they could not get people to do any service for them. The Brahmins had either to grow a beard or to walk seven miles to Satara to have a shave."[8] This kind of trends being common in village, it was impossible for him to believe that justice could be distributed between men of different castes and creeds. The pragmatic compulsion for any elected member of panchayat as judicial functionary acted against their being impartial. Ambedkar was all for the extension to villages of honorary bench magistrates in towns or for division of each district into judicial circles to discharge their duties towards the people in villages.[9]

Jayaprakash Narayan (popularly called as J.P.) argued that jurisprudence must grow out of history and heritage, pride and prudence taking the needs and value system of our own culture into consideration. The equilibrium of social relations was a continuous process of change for many reasons and the system needed to be adjusted accordingly. He termed centralized justice capitalist in nature and beneficial for a few. The common man could seek justice through panchayats. Roving courts should be constituted and panchayat members could be the assessors to these courts. He maintained the role of panchayats to be superior to the legal courts, since the panchayat members were to be real judges assessing the rulings of higher courts.[10]

Representation and Elections to Panchayats

The electoral process of panchayat is another aspect of debate. Who should represent the people in the panchayats? How many members ought to be elected? Should the election be direct or indirect?

Gandhiji argued, "there should be election of five persons with required authority and jurisdiction".[11] These members should have the prescribed qualifications like selflessness, ability and integrity. Election to the village panchayat was to be direct. These elected members, in turn, would represent at taluq level. The taluq-level elected members would elect members of the district panchayats. The district panchayats would elect the *prant* (provincial) panchayat and the provincial panchayat would constitute the *rashtriya (national) panchayat*. In this scheme, there were to be no special provisions for the representation of depressed classes, women or other disadvantaged groups. The qualification for an adult to be a voter in the panchayat would be in the form of manual labour, and not a position in terms of ownership of property.[12]

Ambedkar, being opposed to the traditional village system, did not speak much about panchayats in the Constituent Assembly debates. He expressed his views earlier during the Bombay Legislative Council debates in 1932-33. His prime concern was the status of the depressed classes in the new panchayat legislation. He demanded representation of the marginalized sections in the panchayats, with adult franchise for the whole village community. Responding to a charge that demanding special representation for minorities (depressed classes) amounted communalism, he said, "without communalism there can be no self-government in India". Without knowing who was their representative or was there any representative at all to assert for the protection of the rights of the depressed classes, going to the ballot box will not mean much for them. Their representatives' participation in the proceedings was not enough. What was important was deciding the matters. He asserted, "communal representation is not a vicious proposition but a necessity for the safety and security of different classes in the country."[13]

J.P. suggested the panchayat elections to be without contest among individuals as the village community was divided not only on caste-class and family factions but also lacked collective will in the village and "self-government through faction fighting will not be a self-government but self-ruination".[14] The entire village adults were to constitute a stationary collective body called Gram Sabha with the panchayat to work as its executive.

Thus, both Gandhi and J.P. wanted the participation of whole village community but in their scheme of things there was no place for special representation. J.P. expressed his ideas for consensual politics, whereas Ambedkar asserted for special representation to the underprivileged to influence the decisions of panchayats through participation.

Preconditions for the Success of Panchayati Raj

All the three thinkers talked of preconditions for making the dream of the powers to the people a reality. Gandhi's emphasis was basically on development of mutual trust and self-help and election of selfless and incorruptible people.[15]

Ambedkar, on the other hand, being not against the objective of devolution of power to the people in principle, advocated special representation for the minorities on communal lines, extension of judicial circles, expertise to the villages instead of village panchayats working as judiciary, social and economic equality in the village to be the essential prerequisites for transferring powers to the local bodies.[16]

For J.P., there was a need of both structural and functional alterations in making the Panchayati Raj a success. He expressed the view that the power should be vested in the people, not among, five representatives of the village community for the execution of developmental programmes, thus making the Gram Sabha the tier at the bottom instead of Gram Panchayat. The elections to the panchayats had to be with contest, based on consensus among the villagers. Not only a procedural reform of the administration but a political revolution for the people was needed. J.P. emphasized the ownership and management of all village land in the hands of the Gram Sabha and its equal distribution among all members of the community and to provide minimum social security and welfare measures for the weaker sections of society. J.P. also stressed the need for the social education of the masses to make Panchayati Raj real democracy.[17] In terms of transferring the powers to the panchayat, he was closer to Ambedkar. The Gandhian approach was an ideal, whereas Ambedkar and J.P. were more realistic.

J.P. believed that Panchayati Raj could become the base for participatory democracy only when certain conditions were fulfilled, namely, social education, abolition of traditional prejudices, land reforms, etc. Such measures could transform the rural society. In their absence, power to the people would be a distant dream. Thus, J.P. was much closer to Ambedkar than Gandhi in his formulations of Panchayati Raj. He was something of a reformist Gandhian. Ambedkar, on the other hand, wanted to radically transform the society before introducing the decentralization of power.

Ambedkar's Views in the Context of the 73rd Amendment Act

Ambedkar first time expressed his opinions on Panchayati Raj in the Bombay Legislative Assembly debates and then in the Constituent Assembly. Born and brought up in the untouchable community, his experiences with the social phenomenon left lasting imprints on his ideas and vision regarding the whole Indian society that primarily lived in the villages.

Though not opposed to the principle of decentralization of power to the people, Ambedkar questioned the predispositions that structured the celebrated village community and then the benefit of such provisions will also align themselves according to the existing divisions within the village community. Village community had sharp social, economic, cultural and political differences marked by divisions between touchables-untouchables caste Hindus-minorities, landlords-landless labourers, great traditions-little traditions, ruling class-ruled class, etc. In his view, it was impractical to expect that caste Hindus would willingly accept untouchables as their representatives and implement their decisions. Gandhi, on the other hand, envisaged complete political and administrative decentralization at the village level, with an indirectly elected government at the top. He enunciated his views on the structural content of the people's democracy and sovereignty at the grassroots level, which he described as Panchayati Raj, in 1946-47.[18]

Influenced by these observations of Gandhi several members of the Constituent Assembly pressed for the inclusion of village panchayats in the new Constitution, where the attitude of the drafting committee and especially of Ambedkar was that village panchayats could not be the basis of new democracy. Ambedkar pointed out that the principal aim of village communities was somehow to retain their existence, and as such they had played little role in affairs and destiny of the country. He opposed the introduction of Panchayati Raj on the ground that in the prevailing conditions, where rural society was conservative and dominated by the traditionally privileged class, village democracy would become exceedingly conservative, reactionary and illiberal. The traditionally dominating class would use the political institutions of Panchayati Raj to perpetuate their privileged position. Unless power was concentrated in the hands of socially suppressed section of society, it was not possible to wipe out the social, legal and cultural disabilities affecting that section.

The central government needed to act as a powerful curb on the local majority to save the minorities from the tyranny of the majority. His forceful arguments in the Constituent Assembly led it to adopt a middle path for the introduction of Panchayati Raj kind of arrangement in the Directive Principles of State Policy that depended on the will of the regimes in power.

Experience has justified Ambedkar's criticism. Wherever village panchayats have been established following the Balwantrai Mehta Committee recommendations, the persons in seats of authority belong to the upper classes of the rural society.[19] L.M. Singhvi observed in 1972 that "two decades or more of panchayat raj institutions premised on the philosophy and institutional approach of Mehta Committee have not brought about a political or psychological revolution ... there is an erosion in the commitment to the philosophy of panchayati Raj".[20]

For the successful functioning of Panchayati Raj, Ambedkar primarily talked of (1) reservation for minorities, i.e., the present-day SCs/STs, (2) extension of judicial expertise to panchayats, and (3) reform of caste. The 73rd Amendment Act provides, among other things, (1) reservation of seats for SCs/STs at the village level not only as members but also as sarpanchas, chairpersons of panchayat samitis at block level and zilla parishads in the districts according to their population, (2) preparation of plans for economic development and social justice and its implementation by the elected persons, and (3) implementation of land reforms, poverty alleviation programmes, welfare of weaker sections, particularly of the SCs/STs. The 73rd Amendment Act provides reservation for SCs/STs not only as members but also as heads in PRIs at different levels, fulfilling Ambedkar's first prerequisite. Land reforms have been the continuous objective in Panchayati Raj legislation that has now been included in the 11th schedule of the Constitution. The process of annihilation of caste and extension of judicial expertise remains untouched by this Act also.

The experience of reservation for SCs/STs as representatives needs emphasis. As the co-option in early days could not put SCs/STs in the decision-making places, so reservation at every level has been proposed in the new Act. A study conducted for an M.Phil dissertation on Haryana[21] reveals that leadership among the marginalized section that is primarily illiterate and working as labours either in the fields or in towns is emerging. A new enthusiasm prevails in the community after the implementation of the Act. A field study conducted by P. Sainath[22] reports that when an SC woman sarpanch in a village of Tikamgarh district of Madhya Pradesh tried to unfurl the national flag on the occasion of Independence Day, there was a protest by another sarpanch, who belonged to a dominant caste that led to social tension in the village and subsequent social boycott of the SC community. Such incidents are common wherever Dalits assert their right.

The extension of judicial expertise to the panchayats and a policy for the annihilation of caste, as suggested by Ambedkar, finds no place in the new Panchayati Raj Act. There is a mention of social justice, primarily having economic connotations. This could be an indirect step but not concrete enough for the objective of annihilating caste. Caste prejudices are sharper in the villages and still remain entrenched.

In spite of its shortcomings, the Act is expected to provide better chances of organizing SCs/STs and resisting the dominant sections in panchayat elections. The regulation of elections by the Election Commission may minimize booth-capturing and similar strong-arm tactics. This could enable the weaker sections to mobilize freely during elections and exercise their franchise without any hindrance.[23] Given the kind of socio-economic power structure that prevails in Indian society, their participation may not necessarily entail mass participation. Decentralization has to be preceded by series of measures like land reforms, reduction in concentration of wealth and removal of social inequality. For the success of Panchayati Raj, and to fulfill the dreams of Ambedkar and other architects of the constitution of India, the central and state governments will have to meet the aspirations of the underprivileged lot of the society.

Notes

1. *B.R. Mehta Committee Report,* 1958, Government of India Publication, p. 1.
2. *Harijan*, 29 July 1938.
3. *Constituent Assembly Debates*, Government of India publication, Vol. VII, p. 39.
4. J.P. Narayan, *Swaraj for the People*, Akhil Bharatiya Sarva Seva Sangh, Banaras, p. 1216, 1961.
5. *Young India*, II, p. 436.

6. *Harijan*, 30 August 1938.
7. B.R. Ambedkar, *Writings and Speeches,* Vol. II, p. 108.
8. Ibid., p. 110.
9. Ibid.
10. J.K. Sharma, *Total Revolution*, Janhit Prakashan, Delhi, p. 245.
11. *Harijan*, 26 July 1942.
12. *Young India*, II, p. 35.
13. B.R. Ambedkar, *Writings and Speeches,* Vol. II, p. 115.
14. Quoted by S.N. Mishra and Sweta Mishra, in 'Future of Panchayati Raj after 73rd Constitutional Amendment Act', *Kurukshetra*, April 1995.
15. M.L. Sharma, *Gandhi and Democratic Decentralisation in India*, pp. 16-17.
16. B.R. Ambedkar, *Writings and Speeches*, Vol. II, pp. 106-8.
17. *Swaraj for the People*, p. 4-7.
18. B.N. Gandhi, *Gandhi's Social Philosophy*, Vikas Publications, Delhi, 1973, pp. 175-76.
19. Vraj Mohan Sinha, "Democratic Decentralization" in Mathur and Iqbal Narain (eds.), *Administrative Decentralization,* Asia, Bombay, 1969, p. 68.
20. L.M. Singhvi, "The Dilemmas" *Seminar,* August 1972, p. 33.
21. Narender Kumar, "Political Participation of Scheduled Castes: A Case Study of Three Gram Panchayat Elections in Haryana", 1994.
22. P. Sainath, *The Hindu,* 26 June 1998.
23. Naravana, "Panchayati Raj and SCs/STs/OBCs" in R.P. Joshi (ed.), *Conceptualization of Panchayati Raj: A Reassessment*, Rawat Publications, 1998, p. 78.

Part Four

Caste System and Untouchability

13 Caste and Untouchability: Theory and Practice

GHANSHYAM SHAH

Ambedkar was not an armchair academic philosopher. He was a political leader whose primary concern was to liberate Dalits from the shackles of social oppression and translate his philosophy into action so as to build a new social order. For that, abolition of the caste system was his target. This paper aims at examining Ambedkar's thought on the caste system in general and untouchability in particular and his prescription for its abolition. What is the relevance of his theory in practice? We examine this question in the context of empirical evidences on the situation of untouchability in contemporary India.

At the outset, four points need to be noted. *First,* whatever Ambedkar spoke and wrote has to be seen in the context of the time in which he worked. The colonial state, by and large, did not wish to disturb the social status quo and hence it legitimized the caste system through various ways. On the other hand, the Congress party, dominated by the upper castes, particularly Brahmins, challenged the caste system but it initially was not willing to take up the problem of untouchability. It recognized caste as a social problem for the first time in 1917 when the leaders realized that with separate electorate to the depressed classes, they (caste Hindus) would be in minority. The problem was taken up because of political exigency. During this period, Hindu orthodoxy was in the dominant position. *Second*, it was a time when industrialization and urbanization had limited scope and extent. *Third*, Ambedkar more often than not responded to the questions posed to him by opponents through deeds and speeches. In such a situation polemical discussion was inevitable. *Fourth,* his views on caste and untouchability have to be seen in relationship with his vision for the future social order and the role of the state.

Caste and Untouchability

Ambedkar has spelled out his main thesis on caste and untouchability in *Castes in India, The Hindu Social Order: It's Essential Principles, Annihilation of Caste* and *Who Were The Shudras?* According to Ambedkar, caste is the central core of the Hindu social order. There is nothing like 'Hindu society'; it is only a collection of castes. "Each caste is conscious of its existence. Its survival is the be all and end all of its existence.... There is no Hindu consciousness of any kind. In every Hindu the consciousness that exists is the consciousness of his caste" (WAS I.50).

Ambedkar does not subscribe to the racial theory of the origin of caste. According to him, the caste system did not come into existence as a means of preventing the admixture of races or as a means of maintaining the purity of blood. Before the origin of caste, the Hindu society, "in common with other societies, was composed of classes and the earliest known are the (1) Brahmins, or the priestly class; (2) the Kshatriyas, or the military class; (3) the Vaishyas, or the merchant class and (4) the Shudras, or the artisan and menial class (WAS I.18)". There was then mobility across the classes, hence "classes did change their personnel". The Shudra "though belonging to a lower class nonetheless was a free citizen in days before Manu"... (WAS III.424).

Later in history, "the priestly class socially detached itself from the rest of the body of people and through a closed-door policy became a caste itself". In course of time the other classes got sub-divided. Endogamy was institutionalized which closed the door for social intercourse. A caste became "an enclosed class". Caste originated with endogamy (WAS I.14). Brahmins originated this 'unnatural institution'. The system was "imitated by all the non-Brahmin sub-divisions or classes, who in their turn became endogamous castes" (WAS I.18). Such imitation occurred because "the Brahmin is a semi-god and very nearly a demi-god. He sets up a mode and moulds the rest. His prestige is unquestionable and is the fountainhead of bliss and good" (WAS I.19).

In Ambedkar's view there was no separate Shudra *varna* in the early (Vedic?) Indo-Aryan society. The Shudras then ranked as part of the Kshatriya *varna*.

There was continuous feud between the Shudra kings and the Brahmins in which the Brahmins were subjected to many tyrannies and indignities. As a result of hatred towards the Shudras generated by their tyrannies and oppression, the Brahmins refused to perform the *Upanayana* of the Shudras. Owing to the denial of *Upanayana*, the Shudras who were Kshatriyas became socially degraded, fell below the rank of the Vaishyas and thus came to form the fourth *varna* (WAS VII.12).

Later, the Brahminical Hindu religion, by evolving the purity-pollution concept, treated some sections of Shudras as untouchables who were competing with Brahmins. By the fourth century, as the Brahminical orthodoxy took firm stand, cow slaughter became a punishable offence. This was a reaction against Buddhism. From stopping cow slaughter, the Brahmins went a step further; they went against eating beef. Cows were now held sacred, and beef eating was considered profane. Consequently, beefeaters came to be regarded with scorn in society. According to Ambedkar, hatred for Buddhism, coupled with contempt for beef eating, were the reasons for making these people untouchables.

Caste was legitimized with divine basis and religious sanction through 'Shastras'. It is based on the doctrine that men are created from different parts of the divinity. Such doctrine generated "the belief that it must be divine will that they should remain separate and distinct. It is this belief which has created in the Hindu an instinct to be different, to be separate and to be distinct from the rest of his fellow Hindus" (WAS III.100). Caste has 'fissiparous' character. Caste does not tolerate "any innovation that seriously antagonizes the ethical, religious and social code.... Castes have no mercy for a sinner who has the courage to violate the code. The penalty is excommunication and the result is a new caste" (WAS I.21). Graded inequality is a fundamental principle of the caste system.

The four classes are not, on horizontal plane, different but equal. They are on vertical plane not only different but also unequal in status, one standing above the other. In the scheme of Manu, the Brahmin is placed at the first in rank. Below him is the Kshatriya. Below the Kshatriya is the Vaishya. Below Vaishya is these Shudra and below Shudra is the ati-Shudra or the untouchable. This order of precedence among the classes is not merely conventional. It is spiritual, moral and legal. There is no sphere of life that is not regulated by this principle of graded inequality (WAS III.107).

The principle of graded inequality has been carried into the economic field. It does not "recognize equal need, equal work or equal ability as the basis of reward for labour. Its motto is that in regard to the distribution of the good things of life those who are reckoned as the highest must get the most and the best and those who are classed as the lowest must accept the least and the worst" (WAS III.111).

Fixity of occupations based on heredity is another principle of the caste system. Caste system is not merely division of labour. It is also a division of labourers. In this system the labourers are graded one above the other.

The gradation of castes "makes it impossible to organize a common front against the caste system.... Castes form a graded system of sovereignties, high and low, which are jealous of their status and which know that if a general dissolution came, some of them stand to lose more of their prestige and power than others do" (WAS I.72). Therefore general mobilization of Hindus against the caste system is impossible.

Ideal Social Order

Ambedkar's ideal society is based on the principles of liberty, equality and fraternity. An ideal society should be varied, mobile, should be full of channels for conveying a change taking place in one part to other parts. In an ideal society there should be many interests consciously communicated and shared. There should be varied and free points of contact with other modes of association. In other words, there must be social endosmosis. This is fraternity, which is only another name of democracy. Democracy is not merely a form of government. It is primarily a mode of associated living, of conjoint communicated experience (WAS I.57).

Annihilation of Caste

The big question is how to annihilate caste? First of all, Ambedkar pleaded for "a moral regeneration" of Hindu society. It had to be given "a new doctrinal" basis "that will be in consonance with liberty, equality and fraternity, in short, democracy". Ambedkar argued: "The real method of breaking up the caste system is not to bring about intercaste dinners and intercaste marriages but to destroy the religious notions on which caste is founded"...(WAS I.32). He strongly advocated destruction of the belief in the sanctity of the Shastras. "It is no use telling people that the Shastras do not say what they are believed to say, grammatically read or logically interpreted. What matters is how the Shastras have been understood by the people" (WAS I.68-69). "Religion is the source of power" (WAS I.44). However, he did not mean that it is the only source of power. In the same essay he maintained, "religion, social status and property are all sources of power and authority, which one man has, to control the liberty of another" (WAS I.45).

In polemical argument he did maintain that social and religious revolutions are a precondition for political revolution. He argued: "The emancipation of the mind and the soul is a necessary preliminary for the political expansion of the people." But that does not mean that he believed that political power and transformation had no meaning till social and religious transformation was attained. What he emphasized is that the processes of social and religious transformation needed to be initiated and be on agenda along with the process of political revolution. While arguing with socialists, he maintained that 'the social order prevalent in India is a matter which a Socialist must deal with, that unless he does so he cannot achieve his revolution and that if he does achieve it as a result of good fortune he will have to grapple with it if he wishes to realize his ideal, is a proposition which in my opinion is incontrovertible. He will be compelled to take account of caste after revolution if he does not take account of it before revolution. This is only another way of saying that, turn in any direction you like, caste is the monster that crosses your path. You cannot have political reform; you cannot have economic reform, unless you kill this monster' (WAS I.47).

Ambedkar was aware that the Brahmins, who had a vested interest in the caste system, would not accept his suggestions and bring moral regeneration in Hinduism, based on the principles of liberty, equality and fraternity. He asked the Dalits to abandon Hindu religion and adopt Buddhism. He admitted that there was caste among Muslims, Sikhs and Christians also, but this has no religious consecration; but among the Hindus most decidedly it has. Among the non-Hindus, caste is only a practice, not a sacred institution. They did not originate it. With them it is only a survival. They do not regard caste as a religious dogma. Religion compels the Hindus to treat isolation and segregation of castes as virtue. Religion does not compel the non-Hindus to take the same attitude towards caste. If Hindus wish to break caste, their religion will come in their way. But it will not be the case of non-Hindus (WAS I.65).

To Ambedkar annihilation of untouchability and emancipation of untouchables was basically a problem of social, political and economic equality. He frequently asked untouchables to organize, educate and agitate for political power. In 1933, he asked his fellow untouchables:

> You have now a way of bringing about change, an improvement in your life conditions. That way is through political action, through appropriate laws.... you can make government provide for you what you are now denied – food, clothing, shelter, education.... Hence, instead of resorting to rosary counting or prayer, you should now depend on the political path; that will bring you liberation.... The conflict, hereafter, will not be between the British and the Indians, but between the advanced classes of India and backward classes. No borrowed or hired person who does not belong to your class can further your welfare by the least degree. You must rid yourselves of internal divisions and organize strongly... (quoted by Gore, 1993: 213).

There can be no gainsaying as political power in this country has for too long been a monopoly of a few and that many are not only beasts of burden, but also beasts of prey. This monopoly has not merely deprived them of their chance of betterment; it has snapped them of what may be called the significance of the life. These downtrodden people are tired of being governed. They are impatient to govern themselves. The urge for self-realization in the downtrodden classes must not be allowed to devolve into a class struggle or class war... this can only be done by the establishment of equality and fraternity in all walks of life (cited in Rajasekhar, 1989: 225).

Ambedkar was concerned not only with formal political power and democracy. Political democracy – the right to vote and hold office – cannot be sustained for long without social democracy and economic equality. He observed in his final address to the Constituent Assembly:

> We must make our political democracy a social democracy as well. Political democracy cannot last unless there lies at the base of it social democracy. What does social democracy mean? It means a way of life, which recognizes liberty, equality and fraternity as the principles of life. These principles of liberty, equality and fraternity are not to be treated as separate items in a trinity. They form a union of trinity in the sense that to divorce one from the other is to defeat the very purpose of democracy. ... On the 26th January 1950, we are going to enter into a life of contradictions. In politics we will be recognizing the principle of one man one vote one value. In our social and economic life, we shall, by reason of our social and economic structure, continue to deny the principle of one man one value. How long shall we continue to deny equality in our social and economic life? If we continue to deny it for long, we will do so only by putting our political democracy in peril. We must remove this contradiction at the earliest possible moment or else those who suffer from inequality will blow up the structure of political democracy, which this Assembly has so laboriously built up. (WAS XIII.1216)

In order to attain economic equality he stood for industrialization and state socialism. He advocated nationalization of key industries and collective farming. In the memorandum – A Scheme of Political Safeguards for the Protection of Depressed Classes in the Future Constitutions of a Self-governing India – submitted to the First Round Table Conference, he laid down model articles on fundamental rights. The memorandum demanded: (1) equal citizenship, and fundamental rights declaring the practice of 'untouchability' as illegal; (2) free enjoyment of 'equal rights' protected by adequate constitutional remedies; (3) protection against discrimination; (4) adequate representation to the depressed classes in the legislatures; adult suffrage and separate electorates to the depressed classes for ten years; (5) adequate representation in services; (6) redress against prejudicial action or neglect of interest – facilities for education, etc.; (7) special departmental care, special minister and welfare bureaus; and (8) seat in the cabinet.

Ambedkar saw the root of untouchability in Hindu religion and therefore he was bent upon abolishing it. He pleaded that the Dalits should abandon Hinduism and adopt Buddhism, which stood on the principles of equality. Though he gave greater emphasis to the religious aspect of the problem, he did not ignore the political and economic dimensions of the problem. He emphasized that untouchables needed to get organized and get political power through struggles and available institutional channels to build a social order based on equality, liberty and fraternity.

Untouchability in the Contemporary India

Ambedkar and his followers embraced Buddhism in 1956. The path of conversion, he hoped, would lead to equality. The number of converts to Buddhism however, remained limited to less than 4 per cent of the Dalits, confined to certain untouchable social groups and geographic regions. A majority of them are found in Maharashtra. Of the total Buddhists, 86 per cent are in Maharashtra alone, and of the remaining 2 per cent in Madhya Pradesh, 1 per cent each in Uttar Pradesh and West Bengal and less than 1 per cent each in UP and West Bengal. The remaining less than 1 per cent are spread over Karnataka, Orissa, Delhi, Punjab and other states.

Though a small proportion of the untouchable changed their religion, the conversion brought momentum in the Dalit movement. It provided a "psychological freedom from the sense of being a polluting person" (Zelliot, 1998). Namdev Dhasal, a Dalit leader and poet observes, "conversion to Buddhism... freed the scheduled castes from mental and psychological enslavement.... Religion (has) an attraction for the common man and it was not easy to change his attitude toward it... (The Buddhists have) liberated themselves from old ideas of Karma and destiny and from worship of Hindu gods"... (ibid).

However, the position of the converted untouchables among the Buddhists and non-Buddhists has not improved substantially as far as equality is concerned. Internal social hierarchy among the converts persists. Many rituals of those converted to Christianity and Islam are closer to Hindu traditions (Fiske, 1972). C. Parvarthama (1967) observes:

> If people convert, but remain in the same village, follow the same occupation and eke out precarious living with no education or change in lifestyle, it would lead them nowhere. The neighbours would stick to status quo ante and recognize their verbal claims.... The primordial forces of caste, community, kinship and family continue to exert pressure on group life even after conversion.

The story of the Christian convert is not different. Lancy Lobo (1989) observes:

> In Tamil Nadu, within the Christian community in which Dalits have sought asylum, they continue to be considered untouchables or neo-Christians. In some places they are segregated inside the Church during the worship, are discouraged from serving at worship/ritual or be part of the Church choir. Their dead cannot be buried in common cemeteries....

Buddhist or Christian Dalits continue to remain an endogamous group. Of course, their new religion gives them notional equality and it does not theoretically legitimize caste-based graded inequality, but the position of Buddhists or Christians of untouchable origin is substantially not different from that of their counterpart untouchables in Hindu fold.

On the other hand, though the caste system has not been abolished, caste has undergone changes and has acquired new political meaning. Many Hindu reformists and even communal parties have appropriated Ambedkar. For them Hinduism and nationalism are co-terminus. This new wave of Hindu nationalism, which projects non-Hindus as aliens and outsiders, reinforces Hindu identity of untouchables without rejecting their low social position. Even the RSS has rejected Manu's authority on social order. In this process, many untouchables, particularly the educated middle class, feel that their struggle for equality and Hindu identity are not antagonistic. An associate of Ambedkar, Bhimsen Kardak argued against conversion, that they should fight within Hinduism for equality. He said:

> Even though I consider myself a follower of Ambedkar, I must confess that I do not agree with his call for conversion. Look, our fathers and ancestors lived and finally died as Hindus, but they did not leave the dharma. Of what use is it to leave our ancestral dharma and embrace some alien religion? What's wrong with our staying Hindus and continuing our struggle for equality? If not tomorrow, eventually, we will surely get our rights... we must keep our social movement alive, and together with caste Hindus, fight for our human rights (quoted by Gokhale, 1990).

The Indian State does not legitimize the caste system and discrimination in any form. The Indian Constitution has incorporated all the demands Ambedkar made in his memoranda, submitted in the First Round Table Conference. The Constitution has made a number of provisions under various articles to categorize the practice of untouchability as an offence. For example, Article 15(2) proclaims: "No citizen shall, on grounds only of religion, race, caste, place of birth or any of them, be subject to any disability, liability, restriction or condition with regard to:

(a) access to shops, public restaurants, hotels;
(b) the use of wells, tanks, bathing ghats, roads and places of public resort maintained wholly or partly out of state funds or dedicated to the use of the general public."

Similarly, Article 17 deals specifically with the issue of untouchability as an offence. It declares: "Untouchability is abolished and its practice in any form is forbidden. The enforcement of any disability arising out of untouchability shall be an offence punishable with law."

The Indian State follows two approaches to attain the objective of annihilation of caste-based discrimination. One is economic development in general and also special measures for economic development of Scheduled Castes (SCs) and other deprived groups in particular. It had been more or less assumed in the 1950s that economic development would provide the base and generate forces, which would automatically resolve social and cultural problems, including untouchability. Since independence the government has followed various strategies for economic development. The second approach is punitive action against those who observe discrimination in general and untouchability in particular. The Indian Parliament passed the Untouchability (Offences) Act in 1955. The Act outlaws the enforcement of disabilities 'on the ground of untouchability' in regard to, *inter alia*, the entrance and worship at temples, access to shops and restaurants, the practice of occupations and trades, the use of water sources, places of public resort and accommodation, public conveyances, hospitals, educational institutions, construction and occupation of residential premises, holding of religious ceremonies and processions, use of jewellery and finery. The imposition of disabilities is made a crime punishable by a fine of up to Rs. 500 and imprisonment for up to six months, cancellation or suspension of licences and of public grants. Later, on the basis of the recommendations of the Elayaperumal Committee (1969), the penal provisions of the Act were made more stringent. The Untouchability (Offences) Amendment Bill, 1972, renamed as the Protection of Civil Rights

(Amendment) Act, 1976, came into force in 1976. The Act provides for enhanced and stringent punishment, including collective fines for offences relating to untouchability. Later, the Scheduled Castes and Scheduled Tribes (Protection from Atrocities) Act, 1989 was enacted.

To what extent and in which spheres has untouchability been abolished and in which spheres is it still observed? It is by and large agreed that blatant untouchability is hardly practised in urban areas. We do occasionally come across exceptions. Several micro-studies show that untouchability is still observed in several spheres in rural areas. To give an instance, twenty-five years ago, I.P. Desai conducted an inquiry on "Untouchability in Rural Gujarat" (1976). The study covered 69 villages for observation. The villages were selected randomly according to the size of the district. We have revisited the same villages in 1996 to see the changes in the sphere of the practice of untouchability. Two investigators were trained in observation and interview method. They read the earlier village reports and the study. The sample villages were distributed between the two for fieldwork. They then visited the sample villages and stayed there for five to seven days. During the stay the researchers talked to untouchables and others (the latter called 'Savarnas' in villages), visited untouchability localities, school, temple and observed the behaviour of the villagers in shops, panchayat office, temple, hotel, near the well, etc.

The study does not address the question by dichotomizing the situation, whether untouchability exists or not. Instead, the initial study looks into the practice of untouchability in seventeen spheres of village life, which includes the private and public domain. The public domain is divided into two spheres. One is those of institutions and places, which are managed through funds provided by the state and/or local community from common resources like land, forest, pond or river. The other sphere of public life is managed by the market in which the relationship is contractual of buying and selling services, panchayat, common source of water and temple. The latter includes shops, commodities and/or services. The former includes public transport, public roads, school, postal selling goods, and services such as hair cutting, tailoring, and paying wages. The private sphere is confined to allowing members of untouchable castes inside one's house without discrimination. There are some quasi-public spheres, which involve personal preference in public places. We have specifically observed interaction between labourers while carrying out the work in farm or other places.

Table 1

Observance and Non-observance of Untouchability in Different Behavioural Situations in 1996 and 1971

Behaviour	*1996*			*1971*		
	Untouchablity observed	*Nebulous*	*Untouchability not observed*	*Untouchability observed*	*Nebulous*	*Untouchability not observed*
Public Transport	1 (1)	4 (6)	64 (93)	3 (4)	-	65 (96)
School	-	-	69 (100)	4 (6)	1(2)	57 (92)
Post-office, while buying stamps	2 (4)	2 (4)	47 (92)	1 (4)		24 (96)
Delivery of letters by postman	4 (6)	2 (3)	62 (91)	10 (17)	-	49 (83)
Panchayat sitting arrangement	12 (18)	8 (12)	46 (70)	23 (47)	-	26 (53)
Savarna and untouchable workers in the field	17 (26)	11 (17)	38 (57)	23 (42)	-	32 (58)
Paying wages to untouchable workers	20 (29)	9 (13)	40 (58)	38 (69)	-	17 (31)
Giving things and receiving money in shop	14 (22)	4 (6)	47 (71)	35 (67)	-	17 (33)
Entry into private shop	14 (21)	5 (8)	46 (71)	46 (85)	-	8 (15)
Entry into private house	55 (80)	10 (14)	4 (6)	62 (90)	-	7 (10)
Entry into temple	44 (69)	4 (6)	16 (25)	57 (89)	2 (3)	5 (8)
Barber serving SCs	39 (68)	5 (9)	13 (23)	48 (94)	-	3 (6)
Potter selling pots to SCs	10 (22)	5 (11)	31 (67)	26 (72)	-	10 (27)
Tailor giving service to SCs	1 (2)	-	42 (98)	11 (31)	2 (5)	23 (64)
Restrictions on roads	3 (4)	13 (19)	53 (77)	41 (60)	-	27 (40)
Common source of water	14 (61)	6 (26)	3 (13)	7 (28)	13 (52)	5 (20)

Note: Figures in the bracket are percentage to total.

Table 1 reports our observations regarding the practice of untouchability in different spheres. Though we have tried to present the observations objectively, an element of subjectivity cannot be ruled out. Bias of the respondents who narrated their views on untouchability and the bias of the investigators may have coloured the observations. Moreover, when we are told that some members of the village observe untouchability and some do not, we have treated such a view as practice of untouchability in the village. Similarly, though untouchability is not actually observed, some members of the untouchable castes expressed to us that they are made to feel that they are not supposed to touch the Savarnas and should keep their distance. Hence, untouchable members avoid possible touch, such as when moving about on roads and travelling in public transport. Such a situation is treated as the practice of untouchability. We have relied more on the opinion of the SC untouchables than others.

The practice of untouchability in the sitting arrangement of the students in village schools was negligible in 1971. It has disappeared completely in 1996. SC and non-SC students intermingle in the school freely. However, their friendship in many villages does not extend after school hours. They hardly visit each other's house. Non-SC teachers do not discriminate against SC students but they are not easily accessible to SC students outside the school boundary. All the schools do not have the facility of drinking water for students. Wherever it exists, all students take water from the common vessel. Neither SC students nor their parents complained of discrimination by Savarna teachers. There was no conspicuous discrimination in sitting arrangement while distributing the mid-day meal. In a few villages some Savarna students do not take the mid-day meal partly because their parents do not wish them to take cooked food along with SC students in school. They also come from well off families who do not care for the mid-day meal.

Nearly 10 per cent of the village schools have teachers belonging to SCs. None of them complain that their colleagues discriminate against them in school. They take water from the same source in the school and also occasionally take snacks and tea together. However, except in south Gujarat, these teachers do not get accommodation in Savarna locality of the village. They either commute from their village or from nearby town or they get house on rent from SC in Dalit locality. A teacher from the north Gujarat village stated: "They do not say that they would not give house on rent to us, but they would give excuses indicating that we were not wanted in the Savarna locality.

Even if we get one we would not prefer to live there because we fear that neighbours would not help when we need help in sickness and other crises. Also, we fear that they may insult us if something goes wrong." Another teacher said: "Our relatives from villages visit us. They are not well clothed and do not know the etiquette of the upper caste, hence we get embarrassed if we live in Patidar or Baniya locality. It is better to live with one's own caste fellows. You get intimacy with them, whereas in the Savarna locality you are alien."

All villages are more or less covered by state bus transport in the fair season. Untouchability is not observed while boarding and sitting in the bus in 93 per cent of the villages. Crude discrimination against SCs is observed in only per cent of the villages, where they are almost disallowed to sit with Savarnas. In the remaining 6 per cent of the villages, the practice of untouchability is nebulous. That is, a member of the SC is expected to stand up and give his seat to a Savarna passenger; or the latter is allowed to board the bus first. Quarrels occur if a member of the SC does not vacate the seat for Savarna passenger. "They [SCs], particularly the youth, have become arrogant and do not show respect to us and do not give seat," a member from the upper caste complained.

The 1971 study found that there were certain restrictions on the free movement of the SCs on some roads in as many as 60 per cent of the villages. Though the numbers of such villages have declined considerably, but the SCs still encounter some restrictions on their movement in 23 per cent of the villages. There is no explicit ban on their using certain village roads, but they are subjected to abuse and even physical assault if they enter certain *khadaki*, i.e., streets of the upper castes. They have to stop and give way to members of the upper castes, particularly Brahmins and Rajputs in general and elderly persons of the dominant upper castes in particular. An elderly Dalit from Sarangpur village in the Panchmahal district said: "Savarnas do not freely touch us, we also observe our *maryada* [boundary] and accordingly use the road for our movement." The SCs do not take out *Varghoda* (marriage procession) on the main roads of these villages, for fear of ridicule by the dominant caste. R.K. Hazari, a leading economist, recalls this humiliating experience of his younger days:

> One morning, as I was going through this very narrow street, I saw a few high-caste Hindu children coming toward me; but, as soon as they saw me, they stood up against the wall, and one of them shouted to the others to keep clear of the Untouchable. This distressed me deeply, perhaps because I was weak from illness, and, for the first time, I became aware of real anger within myself (1969:91).

Untouchables of any villages must be mentally prepared for such distressing experience once in a while.

Most village post offices and postmen do not practise untouchability while giving stamps and taking money as well as delivering mail. The postmen go to the Dalit localities and hand over the mail to the addressee. But postal employees observe untouchability in 8 to 9 per cent villages. They do not give postal stationery and mail in hand of the SC addressee. There is a slight decline in the practice of untouchability during the last twenty-five years in delivering mail, but there is no change in selling postal stationery. In fact, the proportion of villages in this category has increased. One may argue that postal facility has expanded during this period from 24 to 51 villages. In many villages postal stationery is sold from the private residence of the postal employee.

Open or subtle untouchability is practised in panchayat meetings in 30 per cent of the villages. The proportion was 47 per cent in 1971. There is not only reservation of seats for the SCs, but since 1976 the Gujarat government has constituted Social Justice Committee (SJC) in panchayat institutions composed of the SC and ST members to protect the interests of the deprived communities. However, SJC is either not formed or remains on paper in 60 per cent of the villages; in the rest, they hardly function. The sitting arrangement in panchayat offices – thanks to legal provisions – is common for all members. But, there is a tacit convention whereby certain seats are marked for SC members. One SC member from the village in Sabarkantha district reported: "The sitting arrangement is the same for all the members, but the SC ['untouchable' expression used by the respondent] member knows his boundary and occupies a seat accordingly. Though tea and snacks are served to everyone, SC members are given in the separate plates and cups meant for them. Water is also served in a glass meant for them only. Cups, glasses and plates meant for the SCs are kept separately in the cupboard. In the past the members used to wash their used utensils. But now it is not done. They are washed by the panchayat peon." In another village in Ahmedabad district, an SC youth reported: "Though as such there is no discrimination for members in the sitting arrangement in panchayat meetings, tea, water and snacks are not offered to Jagdish Parmar, SC member. Whenever the eatables are to be served, the upper caste members manage to see that Parmar leaves the panchayat office."

In most villages, three out of four SCs are not allowed to enter beyond the threshold of the village temples. At most they could have *darshan,* i.e., worship from a distance. There is variation in some villages, with one temple open for the SCs and restrictions observed in another. For instance, in the village Kothamba Pella, in Panchamahal district, the SCs are not allowed to enter the Mahadeo temple, but they can enter the temple of Goddess Kodiyar, who is considered to be the goddess of the lower castes. Because of the restriction on temple entry, Dalits in many villages where they are in a large number have constructed their own temples in their localities to avoid confrontation. In three villages the SC youths insisted on temple entry. There was initial resistance but they were not stopped. But in one case such Dalit youths were beaten for violating the custom. They were told that they should maintain their *maryada* (social limits). "Law cannot help them in the village", an upper caste person told us. In village Eklera, in Junagadh district, we witnessed that Dalit girls were not allowed by the temple priest to perform *puja*, worship the Lord Mahadeo, which was a part of Shankar-Parvati *Varta*, i.e., celebration. While the investigator was talking to the girls, a Dalit leader of the locality stopped the girls to discuss the matter. He said: "Let us not discuss and precipitate matter. After all, we have to live in the village and we cannot afford to have conflict with the upper castes. If the conflict accentuates, we would not get work. We depend on them for our livelihood." In village Sokhada, in Vadodara district, the Dalits were not allowed to play Holi in 1995 by upper caste youths. The later asserted that the land on which the Holi was arranged did not belong to the SCs, it was village common land. The Dalits had to seek protection from the police.

In 1971, 44 villages had separate water facility for the SCs near their localities. Two villages have been added in twenty-five years in providing this facility in SC localities. Since there is a separate source of water, the problem of untouchability in normal times does not arise. But, during a water crisis, the SCs experience difficulties and discrimination in taking water from Savarna localities. From the remaining 23 villages, in which the untouchables take water from the common source, untouchability is practised in 61 per cent of the villages. In most such villages SC women take water only after the upper caste women; or their tap or position at the well is separately marked so that they do not touch the SCs. But, in seven villages (that is 11 per cent of the sample villages), the SC women are not allowed to fetch water from the well. They have to wait till the Savarna women pour water in their pots. The Dalit women are humiliated by the upper caste women who shout at them: "Keep distance, do not pollute us." We asked a caste Hindu leader in one such village in Kheda district: why the SC women were not allowed to fetch water from the village well. He replied: "There is no one in the country who is more *sukhi* [happy] than them [SCs]. When they ask the villagers for *rotalo* [bread], when they ask for other eatables and foodgrain, they get it. If I go like them I would not get even a single food grain. When they go to the well to get water, our women folk pour water in their pots; they have to do nothing. What a great life they have! Are they not happier than you and me?"

The practice of untouchability has strikingly declined in occupational activities – in buying and selling commodities. In 1971, in as many as 85 per cent of the villages, SC members had no permission to enter shops. Such restriction has been reduced to 30 per cent villages. Similarly, the practice of untouchability in giving things and receiving money has been reduced from 67 per cent to 28 per cent. A Baniya grocer said: "We do not observe untouchability in the shop. Like other clients they too enter the shop. We do not mind giving things in their hands. If we observe untouchability, we would not get SC customers and our income will go down. We cannot afford that." However, one-fourth of the shopowners still do not feel the need to adopt such an approach. One of them bluntly asked, "Where also they will go?" Also, shopowners who do not discriminate against SC customers may not always treat them at par with non-SC customers. In village Kadi, in Mehsana district, when a Dalit bargained with the shopowner over the price of a battery cell not only he but other Dalits of the village were severely beaten up by the members of the dominant caste in 1995 (Desai and Parmar, 1995). An SC teacher in village Nigala in Sabarkantha district said: "Last year [1995] there was scarcity of kerosene, hence whenever the supply of the kerosene used to come to the village, there was a queue to get it. I was in the queue. When my turn came, the seller, Vaghari by caste, asked me to get out of the queue. I asked him why? He replied, 'don't you feel ashamed physically touching others? These *dhedas* [derogative word for untouchables] are shameless'. Other caste Hindus supported him and I was watching the scene helplessly..." In this case, the shopowner had no need of a customer.

The status of being untouchable comes in the way of SC entrepreneurs in starting a shop in a village. They fear that upper caste members would not patronize their shop or might harass them. In a village in Ahmedabad district, when a Dalit auto-rickshaw driver asked for the fare from a sarpanch belonging to middle caste, he was severely beaten. Such cases are not rare. They haunt the Dalits and prevent them from practicing an occupation, which might compete with the dominant castes.

Most tailors do not observe untouchability. They touch the SC clients to take measure. However, most of them do not repair used clothes of the Dalits. Nearly one-third of the potters observe untouchability while selling pots to SC clients. Nearly 70 per cent of the barbers refuse to attend SC males. Muslim barbers do not practise untouchability. Traditional patron-client relationship still continues, though the client pays in cash for the service. Whereas, in few large villages barbers have set up shops, many do not mind attending SC clients. But, in Kalamasa in Kheda district, the barber refused to serve an untouchable. When the untouchables complained to the collector in 1985 that the barbers were refusing to attend them, the police came and sealed the shops. The barbers then gave in writing that they would serve SC customers, but have not opened their shops.

I.P. Desai observed that "there may be less untouchability between the Savarna and the untouchable workers engaged in activity of similar or same social status and working in same or the common situation". (1976:261) Facts do not bear out this observation. Untouchability between SC and non-SC workers is observed in as many as 58 per cent villages, about the same as twenty-five years ago. Meanwhile, the conflict between SC and other backward castes (OBCs) has increased in Gujarat. It is observed in the villages that members of the OBCs, particularly in central and north Gujarat and Saurashtra, observe relatively more untouchability than Baniyas and Brahmins. These are castes that have not been able to improve their economic condition.

In the sphere of house entry, the extent of untouchability has remained almost intact between 1972 and 1996. Except a few villages, SC members do not get entry beyond the outer-room of the Savarnas. Even in the villages where younger persons do not believe in physical untouchability, and who serve tea to SC guests in their houses, entry into the dining room is generally not encouraged. "I do not believe in untouchability. I have good friendship with SC members. We eat and drink together, but in the house we have to be somewhat careful because of elderly persons", a Patidar youth said.

There is no striking change in occupation and economic condition of the SCs in the sample villages since 1971. A majority still work as agricultural labour. A few received land from the government under various pieces of land reform legislation, the land is small, infra-structure almost non-existent, and on the whole they do not produce marketable surplus. SCs continue in their traditional occupations such as removing carcasses of dead animals and night soil, scavenging and sweeping, tanning, selling skills and bones. In few villages, a few SC families still collect *varu,* i.e., left over food, from Savarnas. A tiny number of SCs, i.e., 17, has taken up high school and college education. A few have got government employment. Such occupational diversity however, is marginal in rural areas.

Legal punitive measures, economic development, both of the SCs and the rest of the population in terms of diversity of occupations, competitive polity and liberal secular values have certainly affected inter-caste relationship in general and SC-non-SC relationship in particular. The practice of untouchability has been considerably reduced in some public spheres, which are directly managed by state laws and which have a relatively non-traditional character like schools, postal services and elected panchayats. The number of villages observing untouchability on public roads, restricting free movements of the SCs, has considerably declined from 60 per cent in 1971 to 23 per cent in 1996. But, it would seem to have jumped the gun when the I.P. Desai observed in 1972 that "it is nearly the established practice that the untouchable is not discriminated against in the public sphere" (1976: 259). They are certainly not discriminated against in all villages, but as many as 30 per cent of the village panchayats still observe open or subtle discrimination with their elected members belonging to SCs. Untouchability in public transport and post offices, which was not widespread in 1971, still persists, with the proportion of villages observing untouchability in these spheres, in fact, have slightly increased.

The days have gone when some untouchables imbibed Brahminical values of *dharma* and *karma*, accepting their station in life with resignation. We did not come across even one old man who said: "You may have given up your religion,... but we have not given up ours" (Hazari, 1969: 153-54). There might be such a thing as what Barrington Moore (1978) calls "pride in resignation" it is hardly found now. They do revolt occasionally. Many of them assert their rights, which is the reason for rising cases of atrocities against them. At the same time, all of them do not confront the dominant castes and classes because they are in a minority and fear failure. Some explain that after all "we have to live in the village and we are dependent on them". But they may still resort to various tactics that the weak use, when they cannot openly revolt.

Discussion

Untouchability, though rooted in the notion of purity and pollution of the caste system, is not just an ideological and cultural phenomenon. Whatever its origin, traditionally, it has been closely related with the material condition – division of labour, economic status and occupation. In course of centuries, religious ideology and culture – value system, lifestyle, interpersonal relationship etc., dominated by the ruling class Brahmins, reinforced economic and social divisions in the form of segregation of residence, economic returns, rituals in the form of customs camouflaging economic returns and security. In the process ideology and culture have also become a part of production relationship.

Like all societies, caste society also is not stagnant. With the changes in production relations, particularly in the capitalist system, though weak in India, with feudal attributes, in the colonial and post-colonial period, the ideological base of caste has been weakened and its material base, though not uprooted, has been eroded. The caste system in contemporary India has no relation to pre-capitalist production relations. Caste-based discrimination and hierarchy do exist, but their nature is different from the past.

Caste is no longer homogeneous in terms of occupation and wealth. Stratification within most castes has developed during the last fifty years. Its endogamous character is changing in different clusters of castes though not at the same speed as that of economic differentiations. The political meaning of caste has changed traditional social boundaries and new formations are taking shape.

The state does not legitimize caste-based discrimination in general and untouchability in particular, though the measures it has taken against the practice of untouchability and for the welfare of the deprived castes are half-hearted and inadequate. At the same time, these measures, which are in response to the Dalit movements, capitalist economic structure and competitive politics, have changed the nature of the caste system and untouchability.

References

Ambedkar, B.R., *Writings and Speeches*, Vol. I, Mumbai, Government of Maharashtra, 1989.

—, *Writings and Speeches*, Vol. III, Mumbai, Government of Maharashtra, 1987.

—, *Writings and Speeches*, Vol. VII, Mumbai, Government of Maharashtra, 1989.

—, *Writings and Speeches*, Vol. XIII, Mumbai, Government of Maharashtra, 1994.

Desai, I.P., *Untouchability in Rural Gujarat*, Bombay, Popular Prakashan, 1976.

Desai, K. and R. Paramar, "Kadi: Signs of Dalit Assertion", *Economic and Political Weekly*, July 1, 1995.

Elayaperumal, L., *Committee on Untouchability, Economic and Educational Development of Scheduled Castes*, New Delhi: Government of India, 1969.

Fiske, A., 'Scheduled Caste Buddhist Organisation' in M. Mahar (ed.) *Untouchables in Contemporary India*, Tuscon: University of Arizona Press, 1972.

Gokhale, J., "Evolution of Counter Ideology: Dalit Consciousness in Maharashtra" in Frankel F. and M.S.A. Rao (ed.) *Dominance and State Power in India: Decline of a Social Order*, Two Volumes, OUP, New Delhi, 1990.

Gore, M.S., *The Social Context of an Ideology: Ambedkar's Political and Social Thought*, New Delhi, Sage, 1993.

Hazari, R.K., *Untouchable: Autobiography of an Indian Outcaste*, New York, Fredrick A Prapger Publishers, 1969.

Lobo, Lancy, Conversion, Immigration and Social Mobility of an Ex-Scheduled Caste from Central Gujarat, *Social Action*, 39, Oct-Dec, 1989.

Moore, Barrington, *Injustice: The Social Bases of Obedience and Revolt*, New York, ME Sharpe, 1978.

Parvarthama, C., *Politics and Religion*, New Delhi, Sterling Publishers, 1967.

Rajasekhar, V.T., "What is 'Dalit' and 'Dalitism'?", *Dalit Voice*, 8(2), December, 1989.

Zelliott, E., The Roots of Dalit Consciousness, *Seminar*, 471, Nov. 1998.

14 Towards a Theory of Caste and Class

GAIL OMVEDT

Ambedkar's writings on the class and caste came as a theoretical project from the time he described the fight of Indian dalits as being against "brahminism and capitalism".[1] However, he was an economist by training, not a sociologist, and though he did an immense amount of research on Indian social history, he wrote very little on the conceptual analysis of caste and therefore a complete theory of class and caste. What we have available are published writings that include an early essay on caste written as a student in 1916, books on *Who Were the Shudras* and *Untouchables*, and a large amount of unpublished writings and notebooks that provided the basis for these, most notably the essay on "Revolution and Counter-Revolution in Indian History".[2]

These writings not quite measure up to a full-fledged theory, but they do provide resources for one. Ambedkar did more than just take 'caste' as an important social structure in Indian history.[3] He had a theoretical perspective that gives a different vision and potential theory of society and history.

I would like to look at Ambedkar in the context of sociological theory. In fact, the majority of sociologists, even if not really Marxist, have been basically 'class'-oriented. Sociologists have disagreed about the definitions of class. Most American sociologists see it simply in terms of economically defined social stratification, giving upper, middle and lower class groupings. But they have been uncomfortable with race and also with caste. Functionalists as well as Marxists have in the end emphasized economic determinants of social class position.

Among classical sociologists, Max Weber was the one who offered the most consistent attempt to move beyond a simple economic class approach to understanding stratification. Weber's essay on "Class, Status and Party" made the major theoretical attempt to give a pluralistic theory. Groupings in the stratification system could be determined by economics (according to him, life chances within the market), prestige or relative honour, or power. His major examples from prestige as the basis of stratification, in which even poor members of high status groups retained a certain quality of 'honour' which wealth could not buy, come not from the caste system of India but from the estate system of medieval Europe.

The most interesting other example of an approach similar to Ambedkar's comes from W.E.B. Du Bois, the great African-American sociologist. (Interestingly, he took a course under Weber in Germany and Weber visited his conference at Atlanta during a US tour). Du Bois has only recently been recognized as a classical sociologist, but he did the first major study in urban sociology, *The Philadelphia Negro,* during 1897-99, and after that till 1910 carried out a series of monographs on Negro farmers, artisans, businessmen, college graduates and women. He wrote major works of historical sociology such as his *Black Reconstruction* as well as sensitive essays, including the notable ones published in *Souls of Black Folk*. Most significantly, he attempted to theorize 'race'.

Du Bois' concept of 'race' was put forward most strongly in his article "Conservation of Races" (Negro Academy, Occasional Papers 2, 1897), published about the time of Weber's visit. It is social, not a biological concept (it might be said that Du Bois' 'race' is related to biological race much as the concept of 'gender' and 'sex' are linked in feminist thinking). He argues:

> ... the history of the world is the history, not of individuals, not of nations, but of races, and he who ignores or seeks to override the race idea in human history ignores and overrides the central thought of all history. What then is a race? It is a vast family of human beings,

> generally of common blood and language, always of common history, traditions and impulses, who are both voluntarily and involuntarily striving together for the accomplishment of certain more of less vividly conceived ideals or life while race differences have followed mainly physical race lines, yet no physical distinctions would really define or explain the deeper differences – the cohesiveness and continuity of these groups. The deeper differences are spiritual, psychical differences, undoubtedly based on the physical but infinitely transcending them .... The whole process which has brought about these race differentiations has been the differentiation of the spiritual and mental differences between great races of mankind and the integration of physical differences (21-22).

Du Bois was seeking to identify a unit, different from and larger than a nation, affected by economic processes and exploitation, but by no means limited or explainable in terms of economics. His concept is close to what recently has been conceptualized by Samuel Huntingdon in terms of 'civilization' – and in his later work, as he grappled with Marxism and the traumas historically faced by African-Americans, he sought to use 'race' and 'class' as interacting categories. In many ways, as I have argued, he was a scholar-activist similar to Ambedkar, with similar theoretical and practical concerns.

The point is not that caste is race; Ambedkar himself specifically refuted the position that caste could be explained in terms of racial differences or racial conflicts. Rather, the point is that both 'caste' and 'race' represent non-class and fundamentally non-economic (though they have economic implications) forms of human groupings that are involved in various types of exploitation, domination and struggle. Ambedkar and Du Bois were theorist-activists, who sought a basis for understanding the society they lived in from the perspective of its most exploited section – and they sought to unite an emphasis on economic factors with the role of non-economic factors. In doing so, they moved in the direction of a Weberian type of pluralistic approach, though going beyond Weber in attempting to define the specific characteristics of race and caste. However, their contributions have been ignored within the social sciences. It is time to remedy this, and with this in mind I propose to look critically at Ambedkar's understanding of caste, and then make a few remarks about class.

There are various questions we might ask about caste as a social institution:

- What is the significance of caste within the general social order and how is it linked to other institutions?
- What type of social institution is it (i.e., is it in some ways mainly economic, mainly in the sphere of kinship, or politics or what) and what are its main characteristics?
- How did it arise in South Asia, that is, what were the socio-historical bases of its origin?
- What are its effects (economic, political, cultural etc.)?
- Can it be abolished (and should it be?) and if so, how?

To all these questions Ambedkar gave fairly clear answers, though not, I will argue, always satisfactory ones. He did not give us a theory of caste and class, but he laid some foundations for such a theory.

Significance of Caste

To Ambedkar, caste was the most important single aspect of Indian society and culture. It constituted, according to him, the cultural unity of India (and he insisted that India did have a cultural unity) and it exercised a major determinant role over political and economic life. Politically, it was not only a source of oppression for untouchables, and thus undemocratic in and of itself, it also was a barrier to achieving democratic unity ('national integration'). Caste prevented organization of the people, prevented unity, prevented the country from going ahead. Economically, it dragged down growth rates by segmenting the population in terms of their economic role, fostering acceptance of a pre-ordained traditional way of life, and discouraging innovation. (Ambedkar would have agreed fairly thoroughly with Weber's argument that the 'religion of India' was a barrier to economic development – capitalist or socialist). Caste, according to him, was linked to outmoded systems of thought; it was a thoroughly pre-modern and antique social order. And, by 'caste', Ambedkar meant not simply what the 'Hindu reformers' including Gandhi meant, the fragmentation of the multitude of *jatis*. By caste Ambedkar meant *chaturvarnya* linked to *swadharma* – the system of prescribing that an individual remain within the community of his birth and follow the occupation of his father.

On the question of caste, Ambedkar directly challenged both Gandhi and Nehru and other socialists. He saw Gandhi's project of reforming caste and eradicating untouchability but maintaining *swadharma* as illusory; 'Ram Rajya' was to him simply medieval backwardness. As for the socialists, who wanted to create a kind of managed socialist society while ignoring caste and treating it simply as a reflection of an economic base, he warned them:

> How can there be a revolution if the proletariat cannot present a united front? Suppose for the sake of argument that by some freak of fortune a revolution does take place and the Socialists come in power, will they not have to deal with the problems created by the particular social order prevalent in India? I don't see how a Socialist State in India can function for a second without having to grapple with the problems created by the prejudices which make Indian people observe the distinctions high and low, clean and unclean.

In order words, for Ambedkar, caste is an autonomous social institution that exercises an important determining influence on other social institutions. It is not simply a part of the 'superstructure' or a secondary, cultural institution, but a basic factor in social-historical development.

Essence of Caste

Caste involves economic exploitation and political domination, but it is not primarily an economic or political institution. Ambedkar was fairly insistent that the essence of caste was linked to endogamy, to the maintenance of a closed social group. Other characteristics, including a fixed profession, social status by birth, following the profession of one's parents, and social customs such as *sati*, child marriage, etc., could, he believed, be linked to this characteristic of closure. It was when the open *varna* system of the ancient Aryans became closed – when membership in any varna became limited by birth – that it really became a 'caste' system. In this sense, while the system is justified and backed up by religious ideology, it is basically a system with its roots in the sphere of kinship, a particular type of kinship structure. (Hierarchy is an aspect he more or less takes for granted.) This point Ambedkar makes in his first essay on the subject in 1916 and argues over two decades later in *Annihilation of Castes*.[4] Here, he argues that intermarriage is the only practice that will dissolve caste, and that the Hindu scriptures have to be given up because they provide the legitimizing sanctions that prevent this.

In other words, caste is a particular type of kinship system which gives closed (endogamous) groups that are hierarchically organized within a complex, agriculturally based surplus-producing society, philosophized and justified and thus maintained by Brahmanical religion and ideology.

Characterizing caste in this way seems to me a basically correct position. The more usual method of simply listing characteristics (endogamy, hierarchy, membership by birth, typical occupation, etc.) does not really give us a theoretical basis. Characterizing caste as a rigid form of division of labour is also not adequate, as Ambedkar pointed out, "caste is not a division of labour, it is a division of labourers". The fact is that extreme fragmentation linked to caste has its special features that go against the usual notion of division of labour.

Finally, while Ambedkar did not include hierarchy in his definition, he assumed it as a reality. Today, there are some sociologists such as Dipankar Gupta[5] who deny that hierarchy is a fundamental aspect of caste, while others would argue that Kshatriyas rather than Brahmans are the core of the system, given that the jajmani system basically involves all, including Brahmans, as dependants and clients of the Kshatriya 'yajman'. But evidence of caste origin stories cited by Gupta only shows that there is disagreement about hierarchy – and all the *jatis* which assert that their own 'real' or original position is higher in fact endorses hierarchy as such; the various arguments that they somehow descended from Brahmans also endorse and legitimize the superior position of Brahmans. From the point of view of untouchables (even if research shows them as not always accepting the legitimacy of the system) hierarchy is clear and quite unalterable. The complex relationship between Kshatriyas and Brahmans, with Kshatriyas (or the dominant castes/groups in their position) often able to keep Brahmans as dependent, does not really contest the superiority of Brahmans.

It may be noted that Ambedkar gives more stress to *varna*, as the guiding scheme/hierarchy within which *jatis* are fitted, than to the existence of innumerable *jatis*. Along with this he also described in various ways the lines of conflict generated by the *varna* hierarchy. In this, conflict is not simply a matter of innumerable *jatis* struggling for a place in hierarchy, but has its logic in the nature of the hierarchy itself. There are important struggles, which Ambedkar sometimes described as 'class wars' between Brahmans and Kshatriyas. Then, in a crucial way, Kshatriyas and Brahmans unite in a kind of alliance to repress, control and exploit Vaisyas and Shudras – basically all the productive groups. There is a major division between the twice-born (Brahmans, Kshatriyas and Vaisyas) and the Shudras, and finally another major division between all *savarnas* and the *avarnas,* the outsiders, including dalits, adivasis and nomadic tribes. All of these lines of conflict, like Mao's shifting contradictions, become salient at various periods of time.

Origin and Development of Caste

In the historical context, in which Ambedkar was working, anti-caste movement activists and intellectuals were generally propagating a modified racial theory of caste origins. The basis of this approach was laid by European thinkers who argued, from linguistic and other evidence, that the 'Aryans' or Indo-Europeans of India were basically similar to the originators of white Europe: these were said to have invaded and conquered the indigenous inhabitants of India and in the process laid the foundation for all of Indian civilization (in the nineteenth century, of course, the Indus civilization was not known to have existed); the high-caste or 'twice-born' were descended from Aryans and the Shudras, dalits, adivasis and others from non-Aryans. This theory proved handy not only for the British but also for the Indian elite, who accepted the Aryan theory themselves (Lokmanya

Tilak's *Arctic Home of the Vedas* provides an illustration).[6] Then, Phule and after him Periyar and others used the same very broad racial approach but stood it on its head: the Shudras and ati-Shudras, argued Phule, were descendants of original inhabitants, who had an egalitarian prosperous civilization until they were conquered by Aryan invaders, who used religion to dull their minds and caste to divide them.

It is important to note that Ambedkar rejected this approach. Time and again, he asserted that "caste is not a racial division but a division of people of the same race". Punjabi Brahmans and dalits were racially alike; Tamil Brahmans and Tamil dalits were racially alike. Ambedkar saw India, in other words, as created out of the intermingling of many races and there was no way in which Brahmans, Shudras or others could be easily characterized in racial terms.

But, if caste did not originate in the racial divisions created by Aryan conquest or as crystallized from the division of labour how did it originate? Ambedkar goes into this briefly in his 1916 essay.[7] He argues that caste originates with endogamy, that is, when a group becomes closed-in on itself, forbidding outside contact and outside marriage. This, he believes, was first done by Brahmans who turned the varna system (which originally had been open to mobility and merit) into a close one for themselves, and then spread to the large section of non-Brahman masses – partly by imitation and partly by enforcement (once some groups became enclosed they automatically closed out others). Thus, while early Aryan varna society was primitive and in many ways barbaric, according to Ambedkar, it did not have caste in the full sense. Caste originated among Brahmins when they undertook to constitute themselves as a closed-off group and transformed varna, originally a system of open mobility, into one of a fixed, birth-ascriptive hierarchy. The inequality of the system received religious and philosophical endorsement from Brahmanic Hinduism, and then spread to non Brahmans. Caste is thus explained as a creation of Brahmans, through a conscious religious-political strategy.

This explanation was generally maintained by Ambedkar in later years; indeed in his "Revolution and Counter-Revolution in Ancient India" which seeks to give a longer historical account, he quotes from his early article. Many criticisms can be made of it. It is insufficient. It is North India-biased; it ignores the existence of Mohenjodaro (as did Dange, writing almost at the same time), and has too much the character of a conspiracy theory. Explaining the adoption by non-Brahmans of the originally Brahmanic closed system in terms of imitation relies on social theories of imitation that are no longer acceptable. Nevertheless, we can say that Ambedkar's approach is an important one of why in the particular case of emerging surplus and/or conquest in India an elaborate *jati* system should have emerged and has been consolidated: other societies, after all, experienced conquest and the emergence of surplus and division of labour, but did not have caste. The other side of 'conspiracy theory', we might say, is human agency, and Ambedkar's theory has the merit of very clearly emphasizing the role of agency in the formation of caste. The role of Brahmanism, which he stresses, was a crucial factor in providing legitimation for the system and in consolidating and crystallizing it.

However, a major fault is that he does not subscribe the same agency to non-Brahmans, specially the Shudra masses, and explain why they should have accepted a system that was so obviously destructive for them. It does not really explain why innumerable *jatis*, and not just a few *varnas*, existed.

Ambedkar, perhaps, cannot be blamed too much for not having a full theory of caste formation since few social scientists or historians have given an adequate explanation of how caste has come to exist in South Asia and not elsewhere. The most satisfactory account I know of this process of caste formation has been given by Morton Klass in *Caste: The Origin of the South Asian Social System*. He argues that the tendency to closure existed among the many loosely organized and interacting tribal communities in South Asia. Once agricultural production emerged (first in the Indus valley and later with the spread of iron and cultivation in the Gangetic plain) and surplus was produced, as inequality and hierarchy emerged, the tribes crystallized into distinct *jatis* occupying different places in the various hierarchies, rather than as in other cases of inequality, constituted a graded hierarchy with marriages up and down the line. Thus, it would appear that caste (as an enclosed group) did not originally come to exist among Brahmans and then spread among the masses by imitation; rather, it was emerging as characteristic among a broad population, and the Brahmans (who originated themselves from diverse groups, both Aryan and non-Aryan) seized the chance to define themselves at the top of it. Brahmanic theory endorsed, legitimized and used caste inequality. The various ways in which the innumerable *jatis* were 'explained' by arguing that they were the result of *pratiloma* or *anuloma* marriages shows not only that such marriages existed but that there were identifiable groups of communities, often occupying particular social and economic niches, whose existence had to be explained. It may be argued that Brahmanic theory and Brahmanic action was essential in choosing to legitimize and solidify the tendencies to enclosure and exclusiveness – but this does not mean it created them.

On the whole, Ambedkar's emphasis on political struggle, ideology and religious beliefs is a significant reminder about the role of human agency in the social process. We may argue that it is inadequate as it stands, that it needs to be supplemented with the kind of understanding of socio-economic processes that historical materialism provides.

Caste and Class: Political, Economic and Social Factors

Finally, what about 'class' and 'caste'? Most of those who use these two concepts today make two mistakes. First, they write as if Ambedkar (and Phule) can be taken as theorists of 'caste' and Marx can be taken as a theorist of 'class' and the two simply need to be combined. Second, they write as if class were purely an economic factor and caste was a social-cultural one. It is sometimes also implied that class is adequate to understand European society, while caste is needed for Indian society. In all of this, neither 'caste' nor 'class' is seriously investigated.

Marxism, it may be argued, is not basically a theory of class. Marx himself insisted that the concepts of 'class' and 'class struggle' were not his inventions or main contributions, and that the theory of historical materialism is much more than this. Historical materialism, in fact, is a theory that emphasizes production as the basis of social life. In this sense, the additions made by Phule and Ambedkar are not simply to emphasize 'caste' but to insist that political factors such as struggles, violence, conquest etc. and ideological-religious factors are equally crucial. In this sense, they provide a basic supplement to historical materialism, perhaps broadly, as I have argued, within a Weberian framework.

It is not only in Indian society that 'class' can be considered a typically capitalist social institution. Weber, for instance, argued that in feudal Europe 'estates' based on specific attributions of honour or prestiges, with birth ascription for the nobility versus commoners, were important. If we define 'classes' as those social groups formed around ownership/control and non-ownership of the means of production, then it is only in industrial capitalist society that economic features become open and dominant means of group formation. (Here also, of course, they are not the only ones, as gender, race, caste, ethnicity continue to operate.) This is why, the term 'class' itself takes on its specific meaning only from about the eighteenth century within European languages also.

It may be argued, however, that the existence of caste hierarchy and fragmentation makes class formation particularly difficult in India. In pre-capitalist Indian society, caste structured exploitation and surplus extraction uniquely and decisively in ways that have to be thoroughly investigated. Ambedkar pointed out this again and again by arguing that caste was not a division of labour but "a division of labourers". It is thus a historical fact that while aspects of revolt and resistance to exploitation and caste hierarchy can be pointed out, India does not have the massive peasant revolts as found in China, or the slave revolts as found in ancient Rome. These were ways in which the exploited sections, who were pushed together, came together in revolt – even if the process of revolt was not historically successful. Caste fragmentation made this kind of coming together impossible not only because of the influence of religious ideology but because *jatis* were fragmented within the process of production itself.

In contemporary Indian society, of course, both class and caste operate as important social structures, and caste continues to operate not simply as a mobilizing factor on its own but also as a means of often hindering class formation.

Annihilation of Caste

Finally, two types of social action can be defined in regard to the caste system. (This is apart from those positions that would see the ending of dominance by Brahmans and annihilation of caste as coming about only through class struggle.) First, action against dominance by Brahmans and caste hierarchy, and second, annihilation of caste and of the innumerable fragmented *jatis*.

Both are relevant today and both were a part of Ambedkar's socio-political concerns. This is probably important to stress, because there is a section of the dalit movement today that would stop at destroying Brahmanism and caste hierarchy, and seek to maintain *jati* identity and utilize it for this purpose but also in many movements of oppressed *jatis*. But Ambedkar sought both the destruction of dominance, and a movement to destroy and move beyond the system itself.

The fight against hierarchy and dominance is mainly an economic and political fight, involving access to jobs (through reservations), education, land (where he gave various programmes at various times) and finally and necessarily political power.

The fight for the *annihilation* of caste as such is another matter. Here, Ambedkar outlined the main points in his essay with that name: fighting against closure (endogamy) through inter-caste marriage, and fighting the ideology that maintained this through the rejection of Brahmanic Hinduism and the taking up of religion of equality. The problem that this fight has not been fully successful till the present, that in spite of gradually increasing intermarriages, and conversion to various religions including Buddhism and Christianity, shows the persistence of the system. Since it was not simply dalits that created the system, the conversion and rejection of Brahmanism only by dalits is probably insufficient. *Mukti Kon Pathe?* remains the burning question of the day.

Notes

1. At a conference of dalit railroad workers at Manmad in 1938.

2. "Castes in India: Their Mechanisms, Genesis and Development". Paper read at Anthropology Seminar, Columbia University, 9 May 1916; published in *Dr. Babasaheb Ambedkar: Writings and Speeches*, Vol. 1, Bombay: Government of Maharashtra, 1989, Revolution and Counter-Revolution in Ancient India (*Dr. Babasaheb Ambedkar: Writings and Speeches*).

3. This seems to be the sense in which Sharad Patil uses Ambedkar (as well as Phule) in suggesting his interpretation of "Marxism-Phule-Ambedkarism" as a basis for an analysis of caste and class in the Indian context. Patil in fact remains basically a Marxist, he continues to see production and economic way of life as the motive forces for change, uses conventional sociological definitions to differentiate 'class' and 'caste' and simply argues that his methodology is 'multilinear' as opposed to 'unilinear', i.e., different societies went through different versions of the Marxist stages of history. He does not like Weber and I will argue, Ambedkar, Du Bois and others have a 'multicausal' or pluralistic as opposed to a 'monocausal' theory.

4. "Annihilation of Caste", *Dr. Babasaheb Ambedkar: Writings and Speeches*, op. cit.

5. Dipankar Gupta, "Continuous Hierarchies and Discrete Jatis", in Dipankar Gupta (ed.), *Social Stratification*, Oxford University Press, New Delhi.

6. It was really only after the upsurge of the dalit and non-Brahman movement in the 1920s claiming origin among non-Aryans, that the Hindutva theorists reversed their position and began to argue that Aryans had originated in India and that all were of one blood after all.

7. "Castes in India", op. cit. (n.2).

Part Five

Perspective on Indian History

15 Historicism: Confrontations and Inquiries

Y.S. ALONE

Growing interest in the antiquities and further explorations in Sanskrit and other texts in India resulted in the systematic study of India's past.[1] Studies further progressed in collecting numerous data in the form of inscriptions, sculptures, coins and archaeological remains. Archaeological excavations have thrown light on many aspects of the past, which undoubtedly resulted in better understanding of the historical characteristics. But, nevertheless, the textual sources remained the main source for understanding the nature of ancient society. Studies in the field of different Sanskrit and even Pali texts have been used to reconstruct the history of the country. On one hand, the writings by westerners were dominated by the idea of a Indo-European's common heritage, i.e., Aryan culture, on the other hand, the Indian scholars, mainly the Brahmanical scholarships, were busy in defending the cultural practices of their ancestors and viewed Indian society as a homogeneous cultural group, i.e., all the Indian traditions having a common origin in the Vedic culture. Brahmanical scholarship defended the very essence of Indian society with notion of the spirituality of Indian cultural practices, which gained dominance as a philosophical justification against the material concept of western culture. How and why the interpreters, who largely were Sanskritists and happened to be Brahmins, took the refuge of spiritualism as the essence of Indian culture needs to be probed further because their 'intentionality' as a particular social group in the reconstruction of past constituted their own interpretations as it also involved and sustained their socially dominant intellectual power.

While making broad periodization of Indian history, the British followed the lines of religious history such as Buddhist period, Hindu period, Muslim period etc. Indians too followed the same periodization. The British, being the rulers, read India's history not only from the administrative perspective, some of them were genuinely interested in their endeavours to study the past. The imperial discourses limited its understanding to see oriental cultures as different from and inferior to the west. The most important factor in the imperial discourse theory was that of racial supremacy, which was identified with the Aryan race. It was argued that the element of refinement in Indian culture appeared due to the coming of the Aryans and later remained unchanged until the establishment of the colonial rule. Studies were mostly confined to chronology of political dynasties, and exploring and translating the texts.

On the other hand, the native hegemonic discourse theory in the form of the Brahmanical interpretations consistently maintained the common heritage, which was traced back to the *Vedas* and spiritual aspects of the past, but their main task has always been to locate Brahmanical society in supreme social order to retain their (Brahmins) own hegemony. Thus, their role was not only to situate their own position but also to define their supremacy along with the colonial rulers in the realm of historical past, in terms of their affinity with the Aryan race. For many, the Indian society was a homogeneous religious and social group, which has originated in the *Vedas*. Later, the notion of 'nationalism' dominated the understanding of historical past and gave rise to the concept of 'Golden Age'. There was a combination of two factors, Aryan theory of race and 'Golden Age' along with the general agreement of the sacredness of the Brahmanical texts and religious practices. Following the criticism of the Aryan theory of race and 'Golden Age', the Brahmanical scholarship shifted their focus on the proto-historic cultures to prove it as Vedic civilization. Moreover, in their overall studies, there is no scope of locating the 'others' in their discourse systems.

Other schools of historical writings come from Marxist historians. An attempt has been made to synthesize the textual data with archaeological data. The past was viewed as a successive development in the means and relations of production. The historical past was narrowed down to the forces of production. It indeed reduced the scope of ideological development and the role of innovations and improvizations in technological changes as thought by the human mind. The greatest drawback in the Marxian approach is that of viewing Indian society from the class perspective, where castes are equated with the class configurations. Material conditions are seen as the determining factors in the development of history. Even the emergence and rise of Buddhism has not been seen as ideological and social movement very different from the Brahmanical religion. Such single-minded theoretical assumptions resulted in misunderstanding the conflicts in the Indian society at ideological, social and economic levels. The concept of dialectical materialism is diligently followed in understanding India's past. The development of Indian society, in its strategic four-fold division and its further expansion in *jatis,* has been addressed within the concept of class and the means of production. But, it may be noted that a particular *jati* may be involved in a particular profession but when equated with the other *jati* of the same social category, there is a degree of difference in their living and subsistence pattern. This issue has never been part of Marxist historian's concepts. There has been hardly any attempt to see the ancient Indian past centred on the principal conflict between the Vedic and non-Vedic ideologies and their social manifestations. Polity played an important role in bringing about several changes in society, but the relationship between religion and polity has always remained within the Brahmanical discourse framework with the touch of dialectic materialism. Thus, in this context, Ambedkar's interpretations of Indian history assume considerable significance.

Ambedkar moved away from the imperial and Brahmanical hegemonic discourse theories. He analyzed the nature of textual sources with their intentional context to locate the non-Brahmanical society. He viewed Indian society as a conflict between the Brahmanic and non-Brahmanic (mainly the Buddhist) in which polity and economy were interrelated. This paper is an attempt to situate Ambedkar's interpretations of history in the context of Imperial, Brahmanical and Marxist discourses of Indian history and to show how he differed from them. By the time Ambedkar wrote on Indian history, many studies were conducted that deployed textual source material. Sanskrit literature had already become a major source for uncovering the nature of Indian past, especially its social and religious history. Undoubtedly, the cultural practices of any society can be read through the literature. Therefore, for the reconstruction of social and religious history, the study of textual sources assumes importance because each text in itself conceptualizes its own world, constructing its own narrative having numerous connotations, which needs to be understood in its own social context and in a historical situation.

But, what made Ambedkar to go into the historical past and critically evaluate the existing norms of understanding? This question takes us to the conditionality of that time. Ambedkar, through his practical experiences, abandoned the agitation of temple entry for untouchables, at the time of Mahad Tank agitation, he burnt *Manusmriti* in 1927. He was well aware of the after-effects of these agitations. The temple entries would not solve the untouchable's untouchability, whereas burning of *Manusmriti* was an act to demonstrate an outright rejection of Brahmanical values. His interest in Buddhism also prompted him to understand the nature of Indian society differently because of the fact that the Buddhist texts give a different picture of Indian society than the Brahmanical texts. Initially, Ambedkar made no attempt to go into the historicity of caste and untouchability. But he was well aware of the intellectual discourses that were being offered by the westerners as well as Brahmanical scholarship. This appears to be the factor, which led him to critique the two hegemonic discourses. To put the matter with precision, he diligently followed the law of dependent origin (of Buddhism).[2]

I

"Caste in India"[3] was the first attempt of Ambedkar to understand and analyze the nature of Indian society and its systematization through the caste structure. The approach in this attempt is anthropological, deeply rooted in understanding the contemporary realities. It may be observed that though he was pursuing research in the field of economics but his interest also grew in other social sciences. It is not known how far his interaction with the then well-known social scientists of Columbia University at New York had made significant impact to structure his own argument.[4] The analysis in this paper does not aim at the historicity of the caste system in India. The paper appears to be an analysis from the present perspective; observations are drawn from the very functioning of the system and its possible causal factors for prevalence of such system, like the practice of endogamous marriage. Therefore, the possible way to break the structure is an exogamous marriage system. According to Ambedkar, the observance of endogamy marriage strengthens the caste system. Furthermore, his analysis also noted the possible effects of the principle for *sati* and enforced widowhood as well as child marriage as a means to maintain the caste structure intact. He observed the notion of surplus man and surplus woman in the community and considered enforced widowhood and *sati* in the endogamy marriage system as an imposed solution to this problem. One may disagree with his propositions due to prevalence of polygamy marriages in the Hindu society[5], however, polygamy marriages have not been observed to solve the problem of a surplus man and woman in the community, rather they are directed more to gender domination in the community. It is because of this attitude that enforced widowhood and *sati* became the cultural practice than a remarriage arrangement within the community. Nevertheless, the problem of caste has not been seen as a divine origin but how a peculiar conditionality becomes an imposing factor to observe certain social codes of functioning. Another noteworthy proposition was an outright rejection/disapproval to the racial theory, which was dominant during that time to explain possible racial character of the caste structure. For a particular social group in India, the racial theory suited them as it was within the norms of imperial discourse as well as to get the preferential treatment from the '*Gora Sahib*'. The rejection of colonial discourse was rejection of hegemonic attitude.

II

It is not known exactly when Dr. Ambedkar read the writings of Mahatma Jotiba Phule. Two books of Phule are worth mentioning to understand the further development of Ambedkar's ideas of interpreting the Indian history, namely, (1) *Gulamgiri*, and (2) *Shetkaryacha Aasud*, in which he extensively dealt with the religious conditions and its visible effects on the Indian society. In the former, Phule used Brahmanical literature extensively and tried to give meaning to the myths, whereas the latter is based on the then existing condition of the society and how the religious practices were interpreted as the causal factors for the economic, social and cultural oppressions. He termed such oppressions as *Bhataji-Shethaji* nexus. The analysis in the latter is also purely from economical perspective where forces of control are instrumental in the typology of social actions. According to Phule's interpretations, the problem of the farmers in the feudal and imperial power led to more oppressive condition that resulted in the degeneration of the society. As far as the first book, viz., *Gulamgiri* is concerned, today, one may disagree with his interpretation of the *Puranic* myths but his treatment and narrative understanding of the *Puranic* and other Brahmanical textual tradition clearly shows an altogether different understanding than the prevailing normative interpretation. For Phule, the mythical tradition too has some historicity and by displacing it from its self-centred proclamations, it recovers a different set of meanings and also provides some historical value. As a matter of fact, Ambedkar understood this position of Mahatma Phule. The other important author who impressed Ambedkar was Swami Dharma Teertha, whose standpoint was considerably different than the others. Swami Dharma Teertha did not romanticize the past and tried to interpret Indian history as a conflict of religious and social systems. Ambedkar also agreed to his contentions and wrote that the book was different and he himself was working on same problems.[6] Thus, in 1941, Ambedkar was studying the historicity of the complex issue of *varna* and *jati* in the Indian society. It was a long journey from his "Caste in India" till 1946 when he published his *Who Were The Shudras* and its second part in 1948 as *Untouchables*.

By this time, researches in India's history have grown considerably. Broadly, the interpretations have been centred on two objectives: one persists with following the textual tradition and the other pertains to the interpretation of the archaeological data. The textual tradition again had a different motive: for westerners, India remained a land of mystic complexities; besides, westerners' interest was pursuance of the common heritage, i.e., Aryan heritage. On the other hand, for Indians, the task was not only to resist the onslaught of the westerners' criticism of Indian traditions but also to project the achievements of cultural tradition as fundamentally different from the west. Furthermore, the 'nationalistic discourses' overpowered the interpretations in the history. The Indian tradition was conceived as romantic and divine because the very learned section itself belongs to a particular class, thus, there was no space for critical analysis of past. The discourse theory was shifted from the western attitude of imperialism to the native hegemonic tradition where intellectual attitude was overpowered by the customs and belief systems. A great amount of literature on the Indian religious and social history emerged through such studies. Important among the historians were Kane, Sukhtankar, Jayaswal, Srinivas Iyenger, R.D. Bhandarkar etc. As stated earlier, as far as the social and religious history of India is concerned, efforts for its reconstruction has been made in accordance with the respective groups, which shows how power in the interpretation has been retained by the respective group. The homogeneity of the tradition as uni-centric, organic unity of the Indian society has been maintained in the Brahmanical scholarship. It has been regarded as the mainstay of the Indian mind and thought. Thus, all the prevalent traditions were traced back to the *Vedas* and the later developments have been more like an offshoot of the Vedic tradition.

The chief source material for these reconstructions is the Sanskrit texts. While studying Sanskrit texts as source material for the reconstruction of the past, attitude of the then Brahmanical scholarship has always been that of the sacred one, defining the notion of divinity and the very functioning of mind in the realm of historical past based on their conscious hegemonic behaviour in the society, because the Brahmins knew that the mythical tradition was their domain where no other person would dare to enter. The *chaturvarna*, as a social system in ancient India, has been viewed as an ideal and divine without any critical re-examinations because the learned class did not see *chaturvarna* as a problem. For them, it was a religious practice, which was sacred. The belief system imbibed in the faith and divinity, mind operating with and aligned with the attitude of the oppressor of the native land, thus, had no sensitivity for critical examination of the textual tradition. So, there lies the problem and therefore, the explanations in the social history of India remained in the hands of oppressors, one was colonizer whereas the other group was native oppressors in the form of a particular social group. It was also a politics of confrontation and hostility to the social realities. Few indeed realized the limitations and attempted to provide open-mindedness with the help of textual traditions itself to oppose certain social and religious codes. But, such attempts remained mere co-optation at the level of translating action into the larger practices of society.

Who Were the Shudras[7] is a historical work by Ambedkar. The book begins with a dedication to Mahatma Jotiba Phule. Ambedkar clarifies his position as a non-Brahmin scholar who is engaged in search of a natural explanation of a human problem.[8] At the same time, he knew that as he was a political leader, his interpretations were likely to be misread. Therefore, he wrote: "I have not made this book as a preface to the non-Brahmin politics."[9] But, nevertheless, he understood the political intentions of Brahmanical texts by saying that "sacred books contain fabrications which are political in their motive, partisan in their composition and fraudulent in their purpose".[10] As has been said earlier, sociological problem of *chaturvarna* was approached on the two premises: one was a racial theory of Aryan invasion and the other was a theory of divine origin. Ambedkar shifted the premises to the more natural explanation of human problems. Hence, he questioned a corpus of textual data with 'why' and 'how'. For getting answer to 'why', Ambedkar very consciously noticed the 'intentions' as recorded in the textual tradition itself along with translating action into social practice, whereas to analyze 'how', nature of narrative account in the text itself is treated as an element of crucial evidence as the narrative account itself has deep-rooted meanings related with social practices. He was well aware of the fact that without disproving the western scholarship's Aryan invasion theory, and the Brahmanical theory of divine origin, his explanation of the nature of the complex historical process would serve no purpose. So, Ambedkar critically examined the Aryan invasion theory. He, however, did not go into the archaeological evidences but relied more on the textual sources.

The context and meaning of the word 'Aryan' assumed importance for him. It is the context of the signifier, i.e., a specific word (Aryan), which is used to establish the identity of the term and its application in the text itself and then verify with the interpretations of different scholars, a method adopted at generic and specific levels. While rejecting the Aryan invasion theory, he quoted several instances where the connotation of word 'Aryan' does not have racial characteristics but can best be understood by the prevalence of different religions among the different social groups.[11] He observed that "the theory of Aryan race was based on philological proposition put forth by Dr. Bopp in his epoch-making book called *Comparative Grammar* in 1835, and accordingly people had common habitat permitting close communion. The contention is based on the assumption that the Indo-Germanic are the purest of the modern representatives of the original Aryan race, and how could Aryan speech have come to India, this question can be answered only by the supposition that the Aryans must have come to India from outside hence the necessity for inventing the theory of invasion."[12] The Brahmins, in order to prove their supremacy, also believed in this theory due to affinity with the Sanskrit language.

The next is the critique of the origin of the Shudras as a divine concept and believed to have its origin be in the *Vedas*, which indicates the intellectual attitude perpetuated by the Brahmanical scholarship. This has amounted to the distortion of social and cultural life of Indians. The cultural practices that have been both current and centuries old have a definite bearing in shaping the intellectual attitude of people, which is hegemonic and based in graded inequalities. To move away from the distortions created by Brahmanical scholarship, Ambedkar again went into the origin of the argument. He is very apt in presenting a critique of Max Muller. According to Muller, the order of the literature is first the *Vedas* and then the *Brahmanas* and *Sutras*[13], which would indicate that the *Purushsukta* of the *Rigveda* is as old as the *Vedas* itself. It is this opinion, which received full sanction from the other scholars including the Brahmanical scholars as it would explain the belief that the four *varna* systems would be as old as the *Rigveda*. On the other hand, Ambedkar observed that "the *Shatapatha Brahmana* mentions only the three *varnas* and *shudras* do not form a separate *varna*. Therefore, the *Purushasukta* is a later incorporation in the *Rigveda*,"[14] which signifies that Ambedkar indeed took into account the tradition of compilation of the text. At the same time, the references not only in a single text but also in the other texts are correlated and internalized to bring out a possible meaning in the historical formations of the society.

The observance of discrepancies in the *Rigveda* and the other texts clearly implies that a particular reference in the text has a definite meaning and furthermore to reconstruct the situation of a time, as per the tradition; the later texts should also have similar denotations. It can be considered as a general law for historical explanations. So, the meaning derived in a single text has an implicit meaning. Thus, instead of considering one single unit of the text, the other units of different texts also have bearing in their respective connotations. It is precisely by relating different units of one text with various meanings in different texts, Ambedkar made historical reconstruction of the ancient past. Even a single reference of Paijavan in the *Mahabharata* is treated as a crucial link to unfold the chains of events in different texts, which has been done keeping in mind the importance of ritual-based religious practices of societies holding their ritual-based values as instrumental objects to form a particular code of functioning along with the positional values among the different social groups. Ambedkar also observed that "social organization of the Vedic Aryans has yet to be studied"[15] and he further explained functioning of social groups and the clan system by using anthropological frame of reference. The other noteworthy question he raised was the question of slavery. He observed that "the Aryans knew slavery and permitted the Aryans to be made slaves".[16] Though the explanation is too short to critically examine this question but later many other writers, including Sharad Patil,[17] have probed it in detail.

The reference to untouchability in the entire book is only at one instance. The distinction is made on the basis of notion of *avarna* and *savarna*.[18] The *avarnas* would logically mean the ati-Shudras, the concept is enlarged in the next volume. The Shudras, according to Ambedkar, were the Kshatriyas, and they had conflict with the Brahmanism. He meticulously explained the power conflict in the ancient society and because of the denial of the Upanayana, the Shudras were degraded as the fourth Varna.[19] The sources he referred in order to arrive at this conclusion ranged from the Vedic literature to the Puranic literature and the *Smritis*.

It is true that earlier scholarship was concerned with the institutionalization of cultural practices in Indian society just to emphasize homogeneity in the tradition. In the process, large number of operating social codes and religious rituals caused considerable discomfiture because of sanctioning of such practices in the sacred texts. However, its opposition too was sought in the sacred texts itself in order to bring certain amount of credentials to the affected population. Nevertheless, the problem of a particular section of the society remained within the realm of the hegemonic cultural practices. Ambedkar was well aware of this attitude. Later, when other scholars wrote about the problem of the Shudras in ancient India, it is significant to note that their attitude towards his writing is in the realm of the articulated system of intellectual domination. While acknowledging that Ambedkar's book is the only monograph on the subject, R.S. Sharma further adds that "...published by a well-known Indian politician, who confined himself to the question of their origin. The author was entirely dependent for his source material on translations, and what is worst, he seems to have worked with the fixed purpose of proving a high origin for the Shudras – a tendency which has been very much in evidence among the educated section of the lower caste people in recent times"[20].

A single passage of the *Shantiparva*, which states that the Shudra Paijavan performed sacrifice, is sufficient to establish the thesis that Shudras were originally the Kshatriyas. The author did not bother himself about the complexity of various circumstances, which led to the formation of the labouring class known as the Shudras. The remark by Sharma shows his prejudice in not accepting Ambedkar's writings in Indian history as a serious writer grounded in research but as a politician with fixed ideas. It signifies his connection to the dominant forms of systematized hegemonic discourse. Sharma failed to understand the situational logic of Ambedkar's conditionality. In the preface of the book, Ambedkar categorically clarifies his position as a non-Brahmin scholar and a non-Sanskritist, therefore, reliance on the translation becomes a natural process, but, this does not mean that he ever sidelined the source material; nor had he violated the cannons of historical writings. Sharma failed to acknowledge the inductive logic in Ambedkar's writing, and his categorical position as a non-Brahmin scholar. Ambedkar in his analysis, as stated earlier, makes critique of western imperial discourses as well as Brahmanical discourses[21] and never showed a tendency to romanticize and idealize the Shudras as a community since ancient times. Sharma was concerned with the material aspects of the problem and viewed the Shudras as a servant class, situating them in the present-day profession, thus keeping outside the 'intentionality' of hegemonic cultural practices as described in the texts itself.

For Ambedkar, the analysis is from the non-Brahmin premises based on the logical explanation of the human problem. It is also significant to observe that Ambedkar stated that a denial of *upanayana* resulted in the downgrading of the Shudras, Sharma agreed to this observation and wrote: ".... it helped to bring about the social degradation of the Shudras".[22] Ambedkar stated that (a) *Dasas* and *Dasyus* are different social groups than the Shudras and that people of multi-coloured complexion lived in Rigvedic times, (b) Aryans are of two kinds: (1) Vedic Aryans, (2) non-Vedic Aryans, Shudras are Aryans.[23] Sharma also arrived at similar conclusion, and according to him, Shudras are old tribe, some *Dasyus* were converted to Aryans and some were denied the Aryan status; there was hostility among the Aryans themselves.[24] Ambedkar mentions that the *Dasas*' and *Dasyus*' disappearance from the later Vedic literature means that they have been completely absorbed by the Aryans as early Vedic literature is silent about the Shudras and later Vedic literature exclusively talks about them.[25] The contention is born out by considerable references in the text itself. Sharma also states that (a) the Shudras are found with slight changes in the later Vedic literature, the epics, the *Puranas* and the *Dharmashastras*; and (b) the earlier opposition between Aryans and *Dasas* and *Dasyus* is replaced by one between Aryans and Shudras.[26] Such are the broad generalizations of Ambedkar and R.S. Sharma's understanding. Irrespective of such generalizations, Sharma would not like to accept Ambedkar's historical explanation.

It is evident from R.S. Sharma's remarks that he did not care to read Ambedkar carefully. While citing the cause of denial of *upanayana* as an instrument to degrade the Shudras, Ambedkar states that the *upanayana* is an important instrument for right to property and right to knowledge; without *upanayana* a person was doomed to social degradation, to ignorance and to poverty.[27] The Kshatriyas could afford to have conflict with the Brahmins because they were equally powerful and some Vedic hymns were composed by Kshatriyas.[28] Ambedkar again emphasized the functioning of the system in a society: "what was done by one individual belonging to the tribe was deemed to be done by the whole tribe. In all ancient societies the unit was the tribe or the community and not the individual, with the result that the guilt of the individual was the guilt of the community, was the guilt of every individual belonging to it". [29] This statement would clearly signify that the reflection of a social action lies in the collectivity of the society, which is further rooted in the already existing distinct social and ritualistic functions that are the mainstay of society. The deprivation of any right to knowledge at collective and individual level is bound to result in the denial of general accessibility to knowledge itself. The process may not be quick one. It is a process, as Ambedkar signifies, a deep-rooted conspiracy.

Ambedkar has not stopped here. According to him, the Shudras of Indo-Aryan society were different from the Shudras of Hindu society. Ambedkar offered the following explanation: "in the Indo-Aryan society, the word 'Shudra' was proper name of one single people. It was the name of people who belonged to a particular race. The word 'Shudra' as used in the Hindu society is not a proper name at all. It is an epithet for low and uncultured class of people. It is a general cognomen of a miscellaneous and heterogeneous collection of tribes and groups, who have nothing in common except that they happened to be on a lower plane of culture. It is wrong to call them by the name Shudras".[30] Ambedkar further drew his conclusion from the

Dharmasutrakaras: "...The *Dharmasutrakaras* make distinction between the *Sacchudras* and the *Asacchudra* and between the *Nirvasit Shudras* and *Anirvasita Shudras*. *Sacchudras* means a cultured *Shudra* and *Asacchudra* means an uncultured *Shudra*. *Nirvasit Shudra* means a *Shudra* living in village community. *Anirvasita Shudra* means a *Shudra* living outside the village community. The *Asacchudra* and the *Anirvasit Shudras* are the one who began to become the part of Hindu society."[31] This broad generalization also became the basis for his thesis on 'Untouchables'. However, it may be noted that Ambedkar also mentions Shudras as a separate race, a concept, which is in conflict with his own interpretations. Can there be a more glaring example than this, which would suggest that Ambedkar worked with fixed ideas? Ambedkar clearly mentions the Shudras as a distinct social group or a separate tribe. The statement in the *Mahabharata* can support this contention that the Abhiras and Shudras were settled near the Saraswati river.[32]

R.S. Sharma also criticizes Ambedkar for relying on a single reference about Paijavan, who is described as Shudra in the *Mahabharata's Shantiparvan* as no other text records this tradition.[33] However, Ambedkar states that "it is a well known principle of the law of evidence that witness must be weighed and not numbered".[34] He did not stop with this conclusion as he also states that "the Shudras were Aryans, ministers and rich people and kings".[35] However, he emphasized on the Paijavan episode and its possible historicity through other textual sources. Sharma's understanding is narrow-minded because Ambedkar being non-Brahmin and non-Sanskritist, ventured into the area, which is the domain of Brahmanical scholarship. It may be noted that a single piece of evidence such as artisans had a 5 per cent share in the donations of the cave at Junnar suffices to understand the nature of the earning pattern of the artisans in the early historic period,[36] similarly, the reference to the *Sutradhar* in Ajanta painting would prove the nature of execution of the painting,[37] and reference to the polisher, stone-cutter would mean the categories of artisans in different fields.[38] There are numerous such single references, which give the idea of the pattern of living in the past. Therefore, a single reference in a particular text also has historical validity. What Ambedkar did was that he shifted the western imperial theory of race and Brahmanical explanation of sacredness as a historical process to a instrumental form of reasoning. It is not intended that any other explanation is not accepted in the subject, but for Sharma, the subject and subjective attributes are within the systems of power, and within that domination of knowledge, rationality is addressable within and for particulars only.

Sharad Patil also made a significant contribution in understanding the evolution of the *varna* and *jati* systems from ancient times. He acknowledged that "the analysis is based on the Marxist-Phule-Ambedkar's methodology which helped to remove the limitation imposed by traditional historical materialism on studying various human societies – past and present – exclusively by class methodology".[39] Though, Patil accepted methodology adopted by Ambedkar, but he did not agree with Ambedkar's conclusion. Patil's analysis functions mainly at two levels: (1) how the moieties of the Indian gynocratic tribal society came to be called *varnas*, and (2) the nature of society from the point of view of Aryan and pre-Aryan groups; and *Dasa* slavery as a manifestation of pre-Aryan society whereas Shudra slavery was Aryan manifestation of the social system. According to Patil, the *varna* system evolved from the clan or tribe itself. But, there is one difference between standpoints of Ambedkar and Patil. Ambedkar ruled out the Aryan invasion theory whereas Patil accepted it.

Patil equated *Dasas* with Shudras, but, according to Ambedkar, *Dasas* were different class of people. Patil traces the origin of Brahmin *varna* not only from the priestly function of the Aryan tribe but also from the non-Aryan tribe.[40] He observed that the two *varna*-system of the classless matriarchal society was transformed into the three-*varna* system of the matrilineal class society.[41] It may also be observed that Patil has probed the problem of *varna* system from the Aryan and non-Aryan perspectives in which, he regarded the Aryan tribes as destroyer of the Indus cities.[42] On the other hand, Ambedkar did not accept the invasion theory. Ambedkar indeed worked with the idea of existence of three *varnas* in the ancient Indian society, and therefore, focused mainly on the origin of the Shudra varna, which Patil regarded as an origin of the Aryan society. Patil preferred to equate the *Dasas* and Shudras as one category of a class/*varna* system.[43] Ambedkar observed that Dasas and Dasyus were different communities and on the basis of references in the *Rg Veda* (VI 33.3, VII 83.1, VII 51.9, X

102.3), he concluded that the Dasas and Aryans have stood as one united people against a common enemy.[44] Ambedkar further adds that "it was a conflict which had arisen on account of differences of religions".[45]

III

The sequel to the earlier treatise *Untouchables* was written in 1948.[46] This work is considerably different from the previous one. It deals with the historical period. The social and economic history remained relatively less explored areas. Many of the researchers were confined to the histories of the political dynasties. Dr. Ambedkar mentioned in the preface that "... in the course of my investigations into the origin of untouchability and other interconnected problems, I have been confronted with many missing links. It is true that I am not the only one who has been confronted with them. All students of ancient Indian history have to face them".[47] This would indicate his acquaintance with the kinds of research that were being conducted during that time. To solve the problem, which was due to non-availability of the possible evidence and sources, Ambedkar believed in writing with his own imagination and intuition to bridge the gaps left in the chain of facts by links not yet discovered, thus, he propounded a working hypothesis suggesting how facts which can not be connected by known facts might have been interconnected.[48]

Ambedkar was well aware of the fact that critics might not accept his propositions and his unfolding of the events by applying his imagination (which may have historical validity) as it violates the very canons of history.[49] He wrote that "if there is a law which governs the evaluations of the results of historical results, then refusal to accept a thesis on the ground that it is based on direct evidence is bad law".[50]

Ambedkar took into account the then demographic structure of Indian towns and villages. The whole situation and its condition is corroborated with quotations from the *Manusmriti*. According to him, "the distinction between the Hindus and untouchables in its original forms, before the advent of untouchability, was the distinction between tribesmen and broken men from alien tribes. It is the broken men who subsequently became to be treated as untouchables".[51] The other two reasons he cites are hatred towards the Buddhists by Brahmins and continuation of beef eating.

The beef eating pertains to the idea of cow as a sacred animal, and therefore, Brahmins propagated against the eating of beef. Ambedkar cited the Brahmanical texts to support his contention. The idea appears to have emerged from the existing tradition of beef eating prevalent among untouchables and other backward communities. Thus, Ambedkar could reconstruct the past, which was seen in the present context. He quoted *Manusmriti* which sanctions only the four *varnas*.[52] Thus, the above statement in the *Manusmriti*, according to Ambedkar, implied the existence of the other class and subsequently he quoted the *Narad Smriti*, which states the existence of fifth class as slaves. Manu does not mention the fifth class as part of the *varna* system.[53] Ambedkar, then, considered the word *asprishya* in the *Dharmasutra*, which does not have the connotation of untouchability.[54]

As far as the sacredness of the cow is concerned, Ambedkar tried to construct his interpretation by using the textual and epigraphical evidences. He observed that the *Gayatri Purana* was a propaganda for cow worship and the idea of deification of cow was a manifestation of the *Advaita* philosophy, consequently, he also rejected the idea of Brahmins becoming vegetarian due to the doctrine of transmigration of soul.[55] He questioned the very notion by saying that "if the doctrine of transmigration of soul was so important, then, vegetarianism should have been propagated to the non-Brahmin population also".[56] Ambedkar mentions that the *Manusmriti* does not regard the killing of a cow as the sin.[57] The reason, therefore, he arrived at, is very significant. He attributed the possible reason to the onslaught of Brahmanism on the Buddhism that challenged the religion of the Vedic sacrifice.[58] He has also quoted the inscriptional evidence from the Ashokan rock-edict to state that the cow killing was not banned by the king as such, and on the contrary, it was from the time of the Gupta kings that the cow killing became a capital punishment.[59] This, according to him, may be the origin of untouchability. This also implies that Ambedkar disagreed with the nationalist discourse of a 'Golden Age'.

Ambedkar further went into the question of the dating of the *Manusmriti*. For him, the statement of *Manusmriti* is highly important as it does not recognize the fifth *varna*. This, according to him, implies that the fifth class must be the class of the slaves. Though the Aryan society had a tradition of slavery, Manu does not consider them as part of the separate *varna* of the Aryan society.[60] It is significant to note that he does not go into the historical analysis of the slavery. Thus, he quotes Buhler and Daphatari for the dating of the *Manusmriti*. The former dated it to second century AD whereas the latter dated it after 185 BC.[61] Daphatari observed a link between the killing of the Buddhist Mauryan king by his Brahmin commander, Pushyamitra Sunga, but does not provide any strong evidence. Ambedkar, on the other hand, considered this event as a revolutionary event and explains that "the *Manusmriti* justifies/sanctioned the killing of the king by the Brahmin to strengthen the revolutionary deeds of Sungas because the Brahmins lost ground to the Buddhist on every account, and therefore, the strife between Buddhism and Brahmanism is a crucial fact in Indian history. Without the realization of this fact it is impossible to explain some of the features of Hinduism. Unfortunately, students of Indian history have entirely missed the importance of this strife".[62] This crucial statement is further explained as a historical explanation in his *Revolution and Counter-Revolution in Ancient India*.

The conclusion that the untouchables were Buddhists is drawn from the evidence that Buddhist monks were permitted to eat beef and Ambedkar cited Nilakant who in his *Prayaschit Mayukha* quoted a verse from *Manu*, which says that if a person touches the Buddhist or (offer) flowers to *Pachupata, Lokayata, Nastika* and *Mahapatki*, he shall purify himself by a bath.[63] Ambedkar's conclusion that the untouchables were Buddhist was based on the study of V.R. Shinde in *Bharteeya Asprishyacha Prashna* in 1933, who also referred to earlier works of Babu Nagendranath Basu, Col. Olcott and M.S. Iyenger and V. Sheshagirirao.[64] Thus, Ambedkar tried to establish a missing link by explaining the nature of beef eating and the subsistence pattern of population for not only affording cow as a commodity but also the killing of a cow along with dependency over the settled population by the non-settled population.[65] This has not received any attention in later historical studies. For Ambedkar, the chain of events is unfolded through the chronological position of the texts and the perception of the community by the authors of the texts. Perhaps he was the first one to study the religion and society by acquainting himself with Durkhiem's idea of sacred and profane as well as the nature of social formation in the tribal societies based on anthropological reconstruction. [66]

IV

The Revolution and Counter-Revolution in Ancient India[67] became available in its incomplete form to the readers in 1987 and subsequently *Riddles in Hinduism*[68] was published. Both the works deal with the history of religion and society. The former was being written in 1956, according to one available evidence.[69] The significance of Ambedkar's writing in *Revolution and Counter-Revolution in Ancient India* lies in the fact that in his earlier writing on *Untouchables*, he tried to establish a possible link between the two events of Indian history: (i) the killing of the Mauryan king by Pushyamitra Sunga, and (ii) the writing of *Manusmriti*. Ambedkar observed that Brahmanism was on the defensive from Buddhist and therefore lost prestige and power at the Royal Court and among the people.[70] This made Ambedkar to believe that the nature of ancient past of India needs to be understood through the underlying principle of 'power conflict' in the Indian society. It also convinced him that since the Buddhists were scientific in their approach to philosophy, and completely moved away from the concept of divinity, Brahmanism had to defend itself in such an emerging situation. Far from emphasizing divinity, the kings of the Mauryan empire were patron of the heterodox sects which denied the existence of any god and ignored the notion of divinity.[71] Therefore, the act of killing the king by a Brahmin became a significant factor in the revival of Brahmanical *karmakand* theories along with its philosophical justification. His conclusions are based on a detailed study of the textual sources. As noted earlier, in his previous works, he strongly refuted the theory of Aryan race, which was very dominant, when he was writing in 1956.

At the academic level, the insistence on ascribing Indo-European roots to all aspects of Vedic culture has acted as a restrain on the analysis of mythology, religion and cultural symbols from the historical point of view.[72] Ambedkar observed this problem of studying Indian history much earlier and writes that "it has been made mythology to amuse women and children".[73] For the development of this attribute in the writing of Indian history Ambedkar reasoned that "it has been commonly supposed that the culture of India has been one and the same all throughout history; that Brahmanism, Buddhism, Jainism are simply different phases and that there has never been any fundamental antagonism between them. Secondly, it has been assumed that whatever conflicts have taken place in Indian politics were purely political and dynastic and that they had no social and spiritual significance. It is because of these wrong notions that Indian history has become a purely mechanical thing, a record of one dynasty succeeding another and one ruler succeeding another ruler".[74]

What Ambedkar remarked during that time undoubtedly implied a fresh look into the past. It is because of the historical explanations offered by the two hegemonic discourses: one, the dominant imperial theory and another, the native Brahmanical theories, where the perception of the past is coloured in terms of the social power which lies in their own hand, they never tried to locate the other section of Indian society in their historical writings. The framework for many of the writers was that of a 'Brahmanical attitude' whereas for Ambedkar it was 'non-Brahmanical'. To qualify his reasoning, it may be added that much of the social and political writing of ancient history received a different dimension after D.D. Kosambi.[75] Coming back to the notion of common cultural Vedic past, the explanation of destruction of the cultural past was attributed to the invasion of Muslims. This has always been the mainstay in historical interpretations during the British Raj. Moreover, the invasion of Muslims was regarded as the beginning of the medieval period.[76] Today, historians do not agree with these assumptions of periodization, some even dubbed them as 'communal'. But, even those so-called secular historians fail to understand the very logic of Indian society, which has always centred on Vedic and non-Vedic theories. This is where Ambedkar's writings assume significance. Though he is very empirical in his analysis but nevertheless the reconstruction of past in his writing has a purpose of highlighting the conflict between different philosophies with wider social implications, which was indeed part of historical past.

Ambedkar did not go by the normative interpretation of the Muslim invasion theory as the sole reason for destruction of Buddhism in India. His principle objection to the Muslim invasion theory was that the nature of Indian society was unchanged as Brahmanism remained a powerful social system even during the Muslim rule. He emphasized the need to make use of Buddhist literature to study the nature of society and also illustrated examples by making comparative analysis of society in the Buddhist and Brahmanical texts. According to him, the emergence of Buddhism in ancient India was a revolution whereas the triumph of the Brahmanism was a process of counter-revolution. The analysis is from the point of view of a Vedic and non-Vedic conflict. While describing the functioning of Aryan society, Ambedkar extensively quoted the *Brahmajal Sutta* and *Ambattha Sutta* of *Digha Nikaya*.[77]

The most important chapter in this essay is the 'Triumph of Brahmanism'. Ambedkar reasserted what he had said at the end of his earlier book, *Untouchables* that the accession of Pushyamitra Sunga to political power in second century BC was not an event merely confined to political conflict; it also had other dimensions. He relied on secondary sources for citing the causal factors. According to him, if the event was so much political, then, the Pushyamitra Sunga had no reasons to have an antagonist attitude towards Buddhism. The second event, he cites, is the writing of the *Manusmriti*. However, he did not stop at *Manusmriti* alone and further tried to understand the whole literature of Brahmanism as a body of key evidence to displace meaning from its centrality. Therefore, for him, the assertion of chronological position of Brahmanical texts and its analysis in propagation of certain principles that were central to the Vedic philosophy became important.[78]

What Ambedkar argues is that a single event not as a causal factor but series of events that are related to the earlier single event have considerable implications on polity and functioning of the state. Thus, he observed that the pre-Muslim invasion period in the Indian history as a period of mortal conflict between Brahmanism and Buddhism,[79] which prompted him to use a periodization of Brahmanic India, Buddhist India and Hindu India.[80] This periodization needs to be understood as an intellectual opposition to the Brahmanical concept of the homogeneity of Indian tradition and society. Today, the historians do not agree with this periodization, but what Ambedkar emphasized was that the historical events that are under study have to be questioned and without such questioning no true meaning or viability of an event can be reconstructed. Thus, the emphasis was more on the deeper meaning analysis, which has larger implications. He was well aware of the fact that differences in certain philosophical discourses were not mere differences at a theoretical level alone but has wider sociological implications, which he understood by comparing description of society in the Buddhist and Brahmanical texts. It is precisely because of this reason that he quoted extensively the *Brahmajal* and *Ambatta Suttas*. It may be noted that Swami Dharma Theertha called Buddhism a national identity.[81] The re-emergence of Brahmanism in India is termed as the invasion of Buddhist India by the Brahmanism and thus:[82]

(1) established the right of the Brahmins to rule and commit regicide;
(2) made the Brahmins a class of privileged person;
(3) converted the *varna* into a caste;
(4) brought about a conflict and anti-social feeling between the different castes.
(5) degraded the Shudras and woman;
(6) forayed the system of graded inequality; and
(7) made legal and rigid social systems.

The next task for Ambedkar was to go into the nature of the Brahmanical textual sources in their chronological order, and by the studies conducted by different scholars, he proved that how certain portions of the texts were composed from early historic period. The most notable are the examples of the *Vedanta Sutras*, *Geeta* and the *Puranas*. The *Vedanta Sutras* have been composed after the rise of Buddhism as they explain the *karamkand* theories, whereas *Geeta* and *Puranas* are composed after the *Manusmriti*.[83] Much emphasis is laid on the analysis of the *Bhagvat Geeta*. His approach to the analysis of the fact is that of decoding the intentional human action and mind, which has intrinsic hidden meanings. He did not regard the text as something sacred. He observed that *Geeta* defends the dogma of counter-revolution of Jaimini's *Purvamimansa*.[84] He explained by citing these examples: *karma yoga* or action *Geeta* means the dogmas contained in Jaimini's *karmakand* and by *jnana yoga* or knowledge it means the dogmas contained in Badaryana's *Brahma Sutras*.[85] It gives philosophical support to the *karmakand* theory. Krishna defends *chaturavarna* on the basis of *guna* theory of *Sankhya*; however, *chaturvarnas* are four whereas *gunas* are three.[86] After considering all the interpretations of western as well as Indian scholars, Ambedkar arrived at his own assessment and, according to him, the text has four parts (which shows its compilation):[87]

(1) Original must have been heroic story.
(2) Krishna as *Ishwar*, god of *Bhagvat* religion (which Ambedkar considered that it must have been added later than Megasthenes because if the Krishna cult existed during Megasthenes, then it must be in tribal worship and not as *Ishwar*. This conclusion is contrary to what Bhandarkar has observed).[88]
(3) The stage where *Sankhya* and *Vedanta* philosophy is added as a defence to *Purvamimansa*, which must have been added between 200 and 450 AD.
(4) Krishna elevated from *Ishwar* to *Parameshwar* between 400 and 464 AD.

Thus, Ambedkar's conclusions are based on the nature of the philosophical doctrines that are observed in the different texts as well as the social meanings, which lie outside the text. This shows how the philosophical doctrines were being shaped in ancient India by rivalry between the Vedic and non-Vedic philosophical schools and their possible social manifestations. Later, Sharad Patil has extensively described this philosophical conflict right from the early historical times till the establishment of Islam.[89]

While dealing with the conversion of *varna* into caste, Ambedkar does not mention his previous books, namely, *Who Were the Shudras* and *Untouchables*; instead, he has marked three important stages for the change of varna into the caste. The whole analysis is based on the studies made by Daphatary and Yati, which Ambedkar not only considered as an important understanding of the problem but also emphasized for the further investigation.[90] In the first stage, the duration of *varna* is for the prescribed period of time, and then, there is a shuffling of the *varna* of person. The second stage marks the *gurukul* system where after a period of education a *varna* is conferred by *upanayana*, thus, *varna* became for life, but was not hereditary in this stage. Ambedkar observed that Brahmanism was dissatisfied with this system due to danger of a Brahmin child becoming a *shudra* for life. Thus, in the third stage, the *upanayana* of the child was permitted to be performed by the father of the child at home and not by a guru. The evidence in this case is cited from the *Manusmriti*. The third stage is marked by the prohibition of the intermarriage and interdining among the different *varnas* together with the sanction of the degradation of woman along with child marriage and *sati*. Here, Ambedkar again quoted his earlier essay 'Castes in India' extensively and criticizes A.K. Coomaraswamy for providing a philosophical defence for the tradition of *sati*.[91] It may be added that Coomaraswamy became a strong supporter of the philosophical justification of Indian cultural traditions as spiritual, therefore, according to him, *sati* was a union of *Shiva* and *Shakti*. For Coomaraswamy, the construction of the nationalist discourse along with its political context was addressed to certain intellectuals of a social class, which is confined to the glorification of past.[92] It also affected later scholarship in various cultural studies.

Ambedkar himself observed that the proposed stages might not be as accurate as one wishes to be. The statement is born out of the fact that the nature of society as described in the Brahmanical text represents its own point of view, and therefore, the task is difficult. But, the drawback in the analysis is the proposition of the likely chronology of events. But, in this case, by quoting Manu, Ambedkar indeed makes an explicit statement that the rigidity in the *varna* system is systematized in the social structure as a means to counter Buddhism.

As stated earlier, there was widespread debate in the newspapers when *Revolution and Counter-Revolution in Ancient India* was published during the 'Riddles' issue. The main contention was that whether or not the Sunga power really made an assault on Buddhism and the evidences are drawn from the early historical monuments of Barhut, Sanchi, Krishna valley and western Deccan to contest the argument. According to some, there was an increase in the Buddhist activities at that time. However, it may be observed that many of the sites such as

Sanchi and Amaravati show activities from the Mauryan times. So far as the emergence of many new cave sites in western Deccan is concerned, it may be observed that the patronage received by the Buddhist Sangha was from the masses, including the merchants and traders. If a comparison is made between the trader's and merchant's patronage, the local population and the masses were the patrons of the Buddhist Sangha activity. There appears a collective form of donations and the occupations of the donors are mentioned without caste and *varna*[93] because Buddhism was against the *varna-jati* concept. It may be added that royal patronage to Buddhism was minimal and patronage was extended by royalty mainly due to political compulsions.[94] For example, Gautamiputra Satkarni was upholder of the *chaturvarna* whereas the Vakatakas were Vaishnavites and never patronized Buddhism.

As has been observed earlier that Ambedkar's assessment is based on the internal textual evidences within the Brahmanical texts and their philosophical standpoints; it is the meaning in the texts, which Ambedkar was mainly concerned with. The earlier studies have considered various logical systems such as Buddhist, Jain, *Lokayat*, *Charvahaka* as mere branches of the Vedic system. But, Ambedkar rejected this suggestion because the theoretical proposition, as propounded by the Brahmanical and Buddhist texts, forms binary sets of oppositions, different from each other in their meanings, and therefore, the interpretations of the non-Vedic philosophies need to be studied from the non-Vedic point of view. It is also for this reason that Ambedkar is dissatisfied with the writings on Buddhism, which he explained in a preface to P.L. Narasue's book *Essence of Buddhism*.[95] Later, he wrote, *The Buddha and His Dhamma*, which is a very significant contribution. He mainly quoted the *Nikayas* to decode Buddha's views with their scientific principles, but this would require a different discussion.

Coming back to the interpretations of ancient history, Ambedkar emphasized on the unfolding of the events that are socially relevant to the society. *Revolution and Counter-Revolution* is though not in its complete form, but, nevertheless, his contention that the Brahmanism in India propagated the doctrine of graded inequality and the notion of divinity, may not be as clear as Ambedkar summarized it. However, one example will suffice to make his contention explicit: in the post-independent India the *Ramjanambhoomi* movement is an example of counter-revolutionary propaganda. In the ancient Indian philosophic tradition, the distinction between the two traditions of Vedism and Buddhism would indicate two different natures of a society, which had a historical existence and unless and until the historical reconstruction is done on these lines, the social structure cannot be understood as it also reflects the continuous power struggle in the society. To illustrate this point, the emergence of Vaishnava and Shaivite monasticism in western Deccan is a good example. If one goes into the chronology of the entire Ellora caves, one reaches to the conclusion that the conflict to overpower a site between the Buddhist and Brahmanical faiths was strong and clear.[96] The other good example is the Elephanta caves, where the earlier Buddhist caves are overpowered by the Brahmanical caves. The monastic establishment of Brahmanism emerged after the emergence of the Buddhist Sangha as an organized activity. Perhaps, because of these reasons, Ambedkar called the Buddhist monks as an intellectual class who were open to ideas and the Brahmins as merely an educated class with self-interest.[97]

Ambedkar deals with the text. The reading of different texts made it possible for Ambedkar to read the meaning as what is said and what they want to say and their conceptualization of the world is understood by the present point of view. The meaning unfolded through the textual data consisted of two components: (1) the world in its formation, and (2) the intentional aspect of the reconstruction of the text itself, which are different ways of representing historical realities. It is these sets of conditions and its political strategy, which forms the basis for Ambedkar's historical writings. Ambedkar pointed out the problems in accepting the views of westerners as well as those of Brahmanical scholarship. The former adheres to the imperial discourse whereas the latter adheres to native hegemonic discourses. Situating the non-Brahmanical population in the larger realm of historical writing was also important for Ambedkar, which is done by a historical subject and through subjectivity, but by this count it definitely does not become unreliable.

Notes

1. For detailed discussion, see Mitter Partha, *Much Maligned Monster*, Oxford University Press, 1999.
2. The assumption is based on nature of origination to the problem, which in Buddhism is the law of dependent origination, for further discussion on the concept, see Kausalyayan Bhadanta Anand, *An Intelligent Man's Guide to Buddhism,* Buddha Bhoomi Prakashan, Nagpur, 1992, pp. 39-49.
3. *In Indian Antiquary*, Vol. XLVI, 1917, pp. 81-95, and now published in *Dr. Babasaheb Ambedkar: Writings and Speeches*, Vol. I, complied by Vasant Moon, Education Department, Government of Maharashtra.
4. Eleanor Zelliot writes: "Ambedkar's understanding of the reformer as politician was based on bitter experience, but it also reflects his grasp of comparative history" in chapter 'The American Experience of Dr. B.R. Ambedkar', *From Untouchable to Dalit: Essays on the Ambedkar Movement,* pp. 79-89, Manohar, Delhi, 1996.
5. The view is of M.S. Gore, in *The Social Context of an Ideology*, Sage Publications, 1993, p. 270.
6. *History of Hindu Imperialism*, Dalit Educational Literature Centre Madras 1992 (reprint), earlier published as *The Menace of Imperialism* in 1941, see the back cover for Dr. Ambedkar's remarks.
7. First published in 1946 by Thacker and Co. and now published as *Dr. Babasaheb Ambedkar: Writings and Speeches* Vol. 7, compiled by Vasant Moon, Department of Education, Government of Maharashtra, 1990, henceforth *Writing and Speeches.*
8. *Writings and Speeches*, Vol. 7, op cit. See preface and p. 41.
9. Ibid., p. 18.
10. Ibid., p. 14.
11. Ibid., pp. 105-106.
12. Ibid., pp. 132-138.
13. Ibid.
14. Ibid., pp. 112-113.
15. Ibid., p. 130.
16. Ibid., pp. 112-113.
17. Sharad Patil, *Dasa Slavery*, part I, Allied Publishers, 1982, and part II is published by Sugava Prakashan, Pune, 1991.

18. *Writings and Speeches*, Vol. 7, p. 36.
19. Ibid., pp. 156-175.
20. R.S. Sharma *Sudras in Ancient India*, Montilal Banarasidas, Delhi, 1958, reprinted 1980, p. 5.
21. See the critic of western theory of race and Brahmanical theory of the caste in *Writings and Speeches,* Vol. 7 For the further discussion on the 'imperialism' see Edward Said, *Culture and Imperialism*, Vintage, 1994. Said quoted the subaltern studies but there is hardly any representation of the lower people as such as the discourse remained in the hands of the native oppressors.
22. R.S. Sharma, op. cit.
23. *Writings and Speeches,* Vol. 7, p. 77 and 107-108:111.
24. R.S. Sharma, op. cit., pp. 15:21-22:17.
25. *Writings and Speeches,* Vol. 7, p. 106.
26. R.S. Sharma, op. cit., pp. 32, 35.
27. *Writings and Speeches,* Vol. 7, pp. 171-172.
28. Ibid., p. 189.
29. Ibid., pp. 187-189
30. Ibid., pp. 200-201.
31. Ibid., p. 201.
32. As quoted by R. S. Sharma op. cit., p. 38.
33. R.S. Sharma op. cit., pp. 40-41.
34. *Writings and Speeches,* Vol. 7, p. 205.
35. Ibid., pp. 111-112.
36. Shobhana Gokhale 1984, 'Fresh Light on an Inscription of Junnar', in *Journal of the Asiatic Society*, Bombay, Vol. 56-59, pp. 169-174, 1981-84.
37. For detailed discussion, see Andhare Sridhar, 1991, '*Sutradhar* in Ajanta Paintings' in Ratan Parimoo (ed.), *Art of Ajanta*, Vol. 2, Books and Books, New Delhi.
38. For inscriptional evidences, see H. Luder, *Appendix to Epigraphia Indica*, Vol. X, No. 987.
39. Patil Sharad, *Dasa Shudra Slavery*, part II, Sugava Prakashan, Pune, 1991. p. 6.

40. Patil Sharad, *Dasa Shudra Slavery*, part I, Allied Publishers, New Delhi, pp. 142-143.
41. Ibid., p. 253.
42. Ibid., p. 143 and see chapter 10 & 12.
43. Ibid., p. 279.
44. *Writing and Speeches*, Vol. 7, p. 75.
45. Ibid.
46. *Writings and Speeches,* Vol. 7.
47. Ibid., p. 243.
48. Ibid.
49. Ibid.
50. Ibid.
51. Ibid., p. 242.
52. Ibid., p. 371.
53. Ibid., pp. 371-372.
54. Ibid., pp. 359-367.
55. Ibid., pp. 344-345.
56. Ibid., p. 345.
57. Ibid., pp. 341-343.
58. Ibid., pp. 346-347.
59. Ibid., pp. 330-333 and pp. 348-49
60. Ibid., pp. 371-372.
61. Ibid., p. 373.
62. Ibid., p. 345.
63. Ibid., p. 315.
64. M.S. Gore, op cit., pp. 200-201.
65. *Writings and Speeches,* Vol. 7, pp. 350-355.
66. It is significant to note that Dr. Ambedkar quoted Durkhiem's idea of *sacred* and *profane* on religion, which shows his theoretical understanding of religion but does not reconstruct the past entirely on Durkhiem's sociological reconstruction of religion. For Durkhiem's quotation by Ambedkar, *Writings and Speeches*, Vol. 7, pp. 351-352.

For discussion on anthropological reconstruction of the society, Ibid., pp. 274-277. The observation that Dr. Ambedkar was likely to be the first person to study religion by quoting Durkhiem is based on the historiography writing by K. M. Shrimali, 'Religion Ideology and Society', in *Proceedings of the Indian History Congress*, Dharvad, 1988.

67. *Writings and Speeches,* Vol. 3, pp. 149-462.
68. *Writings and Speeches,* Vol. 4.
69. *Writings and Speeches,* Vol. 3, see the end pages.
70. Ibid., pp. 268-278, also see *Writing and Speeches*, Vol. 7, p. 246.
71. Thapar Romila, 1992, *Interpreting Early India*, Oxford University Press, Delhi. p. 17.
72. Ibid., p. 18.
73. *Writings and Speeches,* Vol. 3, p. 351.
74. Ibid., p. 275.
75. It may be observed that Ambedkar's writings are even not addressed in the historiographical writings by the historians, which signifies how he is treated as academic untouchable. For the contribution of D.D. Kosambi, see Romila Thapar 1992, op. cit. and K.M. Shrimali, op. cit.
76. See M.S. Mate 1996-97, 'Urban Culture of Medieval Deccan (1300-1680 AD)' in *The Bulletin of the Deccan College Post-graduate Research Institute*, Vol. 56-57, pp. 161-217.
77. *Writings and Speeches,* Vol. 3, pp. 176-222.
78. Ibid., p. 267.
79. Ibid., p. 275.
80. Ibid.
81. op. cit., pp. 61-87.
82. *Writings and Speeches,* Vol. 3, p. 275.
83. Ibid., pp. 246-249, 361-379, 253-257.
84. Ibid., p. 362.
85. Ibid., p. 363.
86. Ibid., p. 364.
87. Ibid., pp. 376-378.
88. *Vaisnavism Saivism and Minor Religious System,* 1993.

89. Sharad Patil 1996, *Jativyavasthapak Samanti Sevakatva*, Vol. 2, Sugava Prakashan, Pune (in *Marathi*).
90. *Writings and Speeches,* Vol. 3, p. 286.
91. 'Sati: Defence of the Eastern Women', *British Sociological Review,* Vol. VI, 1913.
92. See A.K. Coomaraswamy, *Transformation of Nature in Indian Art*, 1934 where he discussed in detail the metaphysics of Indian Aesthetics, which became dominant in the later studies on Indian Culture.
93. H. Luder, op cit. And also see Romila, Thapar *Cultural Transaction and Early India: Tradition and Patronage*, Oxford University Press, Delhi, 1987.
94. For example, at Nasik, the son-in-law of the Kshatrapa King Nahapana made donations to the Buddhist Sangha when the region was under the control of Nahapana because the Buddhist Sangha being a dominant social group, political authorities made some donations to exercise their political authority, on the hand, when the Satanahana regained the region they too extended the patronage to the Buddhist Sangha at Nasik and Karla. This was just to follow the earlier practice set forth by the Ushavadatta. Besides in cave 3, inscription of Satakarni, he is addressed as the person who stopped contamination of the *Caturvarna*, the example is sufficient enough to show the intentional political action of the counter-revolution strategies.

    For Nasik inscriptions see E. Senart, 1905-6 in *Epigraphia Indica,* Vol. VIII, pp. 59-96.
95. *Essence of Buddhism*, Thakare and Co., Bombay, 1948, 3rd edition, first published in 1997.
96. M.N. Deshpande, Ex-Director General, ASI, personal communication.
97. *Writings and Speeches*, Vol. 3, p. 322.

16 Cultural Roots of Un-Democratic Order

G. HARAGOPAL AND SUKUMAR

At the commencement of the twenty-first century Indian society is passing through an unprecedented transformation. The transformation is marked by a move towards democratic governance but we also see emergence of authoritarian forces, embedded in out society that negate the few accomplishments of post-independence India.

There are indications that Indian society is becoming increasingly creative. There are movements, which embrace a large number of issues engulfing a cross-section of society. There are articulate dalit movements, tribals carrying on uncompromising struggles, peasants and landless poor waging a struggle for an alternative politics, ethnic movements for autonomy and self-determination, working- class assertions against the very model of development, struggles of women for dignity and self-respect at one level and for equality and expansion of public space at another level, environmental movements, and civil liberties, democratic rights and right to information movements. These movements and consequent changing consciousness have thrown up men and women of integrity and conviction, symbolizing the dissenting democratic voices.

Ambedkar was one activist analyst who tried to locate sources of both democratic and authoritarian culture. If Jawaharlal Nehru tried to discover unity in diversity, Ambedkar discovered disunity in the apparent unity. While there were several attempts to study history from above or from below, he seriously attempted to look below from above and above from below. Above all he looked at history and its processes from the perspective of the oppressed.

Ambedkar, in his essay on the philosophy of Hinduism puts "Hinduism on its trial to assess its worth as a way of life" (Ambedkar, 1987: 5). He observes, "as for myself I think it is safe to proceed on the view that to know the philosophy of any movement or any institution one must study the revolutions which the movement or the institution has undergone". He traces the revolutions causing the religion at one level and the religion that passes through that revolution. He admits that many religions as a part of a historical process played a positive role in terms of providing a moral reference point. This is evident from his statement that "in my mind there is no doubt that they are real norms by which to judge the philosophy of religion. In the first place the norm must enable people to judge what is right and wrong in the conduct of men. In the second place the norm must be appropriate to current notion of what constitutes the moral good" (p. 22).

Ambedkar maintains, that religion is a social force, and approvingly cites Herbert Spencer, who described religion as "the weft which everywhere crosses the warp of history", and adds that Hindu social order not only crosses the warp but formed the warp and woof of Hindu mind (p. 23). He observes:

> The life of the Hindu is regulated by religion at every moment of his life. It orders him during life how he should conduct himself and how on death his body shall be disposed of. It tells him when he shall indulge in his sexual impulses. It tells him what ceremonies are to be performed – when a child is born – how he should be named, how he should cut the hair on its head, how he should perform its first feeding. It tells him what occupation he can take to, what woman he should marry. It tells him with whom should he dine and what food he should eat, what vegetables are lawful and what are forbidden. It tells him how he should spend his day, how many times he should eat, how many times he should pray. There is no act of Hindu, which is not covered or obtained by religion.

Given the space that Hindu social order occupies and the grip it has over the mind, its influence on the day-to-day life of the individual and society is tremendous. The important part of this influence in the form of un-democratic force emanates from inegalitarian roots on which it stands. Ambedkar applied the test of justice and utility to social order is Hinduism. He interprets the principle of justice as a "compendious one and includes the foundations of moral order" and adds that "justice has always evoked ideas of equality, liberty and fraternity". Based on this criterion the entire Hindu social order is unjust. The best example of this injustice is the caste system, "a system in which the different castes are placed in a vertical series one above the other". He adds, "this system of rank and gradation is, simply another way of enunciating the principle of inequality so that it may be truly said that Hinduism does not recognize equality" (p. 25). The worst part of this inequality "is a permanent social relationship among the classes to be observed – to be enforced – at all times in all places and for all purposes". "The hierarchical organization of the caste system", Ambedkar writes, is "responsible for producing a social psychology which in the first place produces a spirit of rivalry among the different castes for dignity and secondly it produces an ascending scale of hatred and descending scale of contempt" (p. 48). Manu, who theorized and legitimized this unjust and unequal social order, did not leave any part or space of life and social order for individual initiative or societal creativity.

The absence of fraternity in social order of Hinduism is equally striking. Ambedkar observes:

> The fundamental condition for the growth of the sentiment of fraternity is not preaching that we are children of God or the realization that one's life is dependent upon others. It is too rational to give rise to a sentiment. The condition for the growth of this sentiment of fraternity lies in sharing in the vital process of life. It is in sharing the joys and sorrows of birth and death, marriage and good (p. 65).

He further observes, "there is no sharing among Hindus of joys and sorrows involved in the vital facts of life ... everything is separate and exclusive all through his life and joys and sorrows of one caste are not the joys and sorrows of another." He asks, "Is there any wonder that the sentiment of fraternity is foreign to Hindus? ... With a complete refusal to share the joys and sorrows of life how can sentiment of fraternity take roots?" From the point of view of justice, the philosophy of Hindu social order is "inimical to equality, antagonistic to liberty and opposed to fraternity" (p. 66). Lord Acton, who held that "inequality has grown as a result of historical circumstances and it has never been accepted as a creed" did not take Hindu social order into account. In Hindu social order inequality is a religious doctrine adopted and conscientiously preached as a sacred dogma. It is an official creed and nobody is ashamed to profess it openly. Inequality for the Hindus is a divinely prescribed way of life as a religious doctrine and as a prescribed way of life, it has become incarnate in Hindu society and is shaped and moulded by it in its thoughts and its doing, indeed inequality is the soul of Hinduism.

Ambedkar thinks that in the normal pattern, religious ideals fall into two classes – one in which society is the centre and the other in which the individual is the centre (p. 67). For the former the appropriate test of what is good and what is right, i.e., the test of moral order is utility, while for the latter the test is justice.

The philosophy of Hinduism does not answer the test either of utility or of justice because the religious ideal of Hindu social order for divine governance of human society is an ideal, which falls into a separate class by itself. The centre of the ideal is neither the individual nor society. It is a class – the class of supermen called Brahmins. It holds that to be right and good the act must serve the interest of this class of supermen.

In this whole arrangement Ambedkar tends to suggest that Hindu social order is akin to the ideas of the German philosopher Nietzsche who pronounced, "realize the ideal and idealize the real".

Ambedkar asserts that Nietzsche drew his inspiration from Manu. This philosopher, while attacking Christ in his work *Anti-Christ,* observes, "when I read the law book of Manu, an incomparably intellectual and superior work, it would be a sin against the spirit even to mention in the same breath with the Bible." That *Manusmriti* was placed far above the Bible is a sufficient indication of Nietzsche's inclinations. However, Ambedkar maintains that while

Nietzsche was genuinely interested in creating a new race of men that will be a race of supermen as compared with the existing race of men; Manu was interested in maintaining the privileges of a class that had come to arrogate to itself the claims of being supermen. Nietzsche's supermen were supermen by reason of their worth. Manu's supermen were supermen by birth and this status was not to be lost even if they lost their virtue (p. 78).

With its overemphasis on supermen or this class, Hindu social order if it penetrates, does not vitrify the inmost life of ordinary humanity. In Hindu social order there is no nourishment for ordinary human souls, no comfort for ordinary human sorrow, and no help for ordinary human weakness. It leaves men in darkness, face to face with the unthinking energies of nature, which gives them birth to which after a few fruitless struggles they succumb. It is superman's heaven and the common man's damnation (p. 78).

The consequence of such a social philosophy and approach to life and society has been that millions of people are left far behind. If indeed Hindu social philosophy were a superior and old one, how could these millions have remained in the state of moral, material, social and spiritual degradation surrounded as they have been by Hindu social order? Ambedkar retorted, "how is it that Hinduism failed to elevate these people, bring them enlightenment and hope; how is it that it failed even to reclaim them; how is it that it stood with folded hands when millions and millions were taking to a life of shame?" The advocates of this religion remain silent to these questions, as it has no clues to answer these pressing questions. It has no impulse to serve (p. 92).

Hindu social order does not at any level recognize the principle of equality. That men are born equal is a doctrine repugnant to the Hindu social order. In the spiritual sense it treats the doctrine as false. It does not bother to examine whether the doctrine is founded on facts. It refuses to recognize that men, no matter how profoundly they differ as individuals in capacity and character, are equally entitled as human beings to consideration and respect and that the well-being of a society is likely to be increased if it so plans its organization that, whether their powers are great or small, all its members may be equally enabled to make the best of such powers as they possess. It will not allow equality of circumstances, and equal opportunities in mortal life. It is against egalitarian temper. It has therefore created a social order based on the principle of graded inequality. There is no sphere of life, which is not regulated by this principle of graded inequality. This principle replaces the principle "from each according to his ability to each according to his need, with the principle from each according to his ability to each according to his nobility".

There are classes even in a free society. What a free social order aims at is preventing isolation and exclusiveness, which makes the social relations non-social in their relation towards one another, whereas in the Hindu social order the isolation and exclusiveness are such that it makes members of the classes anti-social and inimical towards one another. "Isolation makes for rigidity of class consciousness, for institutionalizing social life and for the dominance of selfish ideals within the classes ... isolation makes life static, continues the separation into a privileged and under-privileged, masters.... What is striking about the Hindu social order is its ban on free interchange and intercourse between different classes." In the absence of social interaction, the social structure loses its mobility and vitality resulting in prolonged stagnation.

Such contexts and situations can be changed through rebellions, while this right to rebel has been given to the three higher classes, it was denied to the Shudras. The outbreak of a revolution "is conditioned by three factors: (1) the existence of a sense of wrong, (2) capacity to know that one is suffering from wrong, (3) availability of arms. When the social order denies the opportunity to rise, denies the right to education and denies the right to use arms, it is in a position to prevent rebellion against the social order." The Hindu social order fixes the social status of the lower orders for all generations and also fixes the economic status. There being no disparity between the two, there is no possibility of a grievance growing up.

The Hindu social order denied education to the lower orders, with the result that no one is conscious that his low condition is a ground for grievance. If there is any consciousness it is that no one is responsible for the low condition. It is a result of fate. Assuming there is grievance, assuming there is consciousness of grievance, there cannot be a rebellion by the lower order because the masses are denied the right to use arms. To deny freedom of opportunity, to deny freedom to acquire knowledge, to deny the right to use arms is the most cruel wrong. This approach was found as the most effective method of preserving the established order.

This is the only society where the social order – the relation of man to man – is consecrated by religion and made sacred, eternal and inviolate. A section of the Hindus argued that this social order had changed since the advent of the British, but in Ambedkar's view, "Hindu social order defies the ravages of time and onslaught of time". Those who argued that there had been changes "omit to take note of the fact that institutions which have died as creeds sometimes continue, nevertheless survive as habits. No one can deny that the Hindu social order has become the habit of the Hindus as such is in full force".

There is yet another aspect of Hindu social order, namely, counter-revolution. Historically there has been a tendency towards counter-revolution, if there is any revolution in social thought and practice. This capacity is nowhere more demonstrated than in the triumph of Brahmanism over Buddhism. Given the stagnation, the social order degenerates. The dehumanization in the Hindu social order reached a point where there were objective conditions for a revolution. This came in the form of Buddhism, which was an antithesis to Brahmanism. It was an enlightened and forward-looking world-view. In any historical process such a revolution should march forward. Buddhism did move forward, it spread to different parts of the globe but got smothered in the land where it was born. Ambedkar addresses these issues and developed as alternative approach to interpret evolution is the Indian context.

For Ambedkar "the history of India is nothing but a history of mortal conflict between Buddhism and Brahmanism". The conflict originated not only because Buddhism was a refreshing alternative but Brahmanism lost state patronage and they lost their occupations. By the time of Mauryan empire Brahmins lost their privileges. From such a situation they rose to the position of rulers and were able to produce a counter-ideology in the form of *Manusmriti,* which held sway over society for centuries. How Brahmanism succeeded in staging the counter-revolution is a question that received considerable attention from Ambedkar. The Brahmin rulers invaded the areas and kingdoms, which had come under the Buddhist influence. The Buddhist organizational structure lacked the strength to defend itself. "Brahmanism in its conflict with Buddhism made a clean sweep. It emptied the bath with the Buddhist baby in it and filled the bath with its own waters and placed in its own baby. Brahmanism acquired by its invasions political power to annihilate Buddhism and it did annihilate Buddhism."

Buddhism came as a liberating influence. The freedom that women and Shudras enjoyed under Buddhism was counterpoised to the severity of Manu's laws against them. The phenomenal rise of these classes during the Buddhist times not only offended the Brahmins but had also become intolerable to them. It was a complete reversal of their sacred social order from top to bottom, the first having become the last and the last the first. Manu's laws also explain the determined way in which the Brahmins proceeded to use their political power to degrade the Shudras and women to their old status. The triumphant Brahmanism began its onslaught on both the Shudras and the women in pursuit of the old ideal, namely, servility, and Brahmanism did succeed in making Shudras and women the servile classes, and the Shudras serfs to the three higher classes. The colossal character this deed of degradation perpetrated by Brahmanism is unfortunately not fully realized. It is this huge mass of people that has been doomed by Brahmanism to degradation. It is because of the colossal scale of degradation whereby 75 per cent of her people were deprived of their basic right.

The long-range implications and consequences of the grip of Brahmanism have not been fully comprehended. Ambedkar complains that students of social organizations have been content with noting the difference between equality and inequality and it is hardly recognized that there is graded inequality.

Inequality carries within itself the seeds of its own destruction. For it creates general discontent that forms the seed of revolution and it makes the sufferers combine against a common grievance. In contrast, the nature and circumstances of the system of graded inequality leaves no room for either of these two things to happen.

For, the system of graded inequality prevents the rise of general discontent against inequality. Then, it cannot become epicentre of revolution.

The people who suffer under inequality become unequal both in terms of benefit and the burden. There is no possibility of a general combination of all classes to overthrow the inequality. One of the reasons why there has been no revolution against Brahmanism and its inequalities is due entirely to the principle of graded inequality. It is nothing else but inviting the people to share in inequality in order that they may all be supporters of inequality. This counter-revolutionary strategy not only worked at that point of time in history but also continues to influence Indian society till today.

Ambedkar's historical analysis and his world-view reinforce each other. His reading of history is full of insights and his analysis reveals that Hindu social order in the form of institution of caste system and untouchability has all the conditions that contribute to the rise of undemocratic society and polity. This un-democratic order, supported and sustained by graded inequalities, can last longer than most of the authoritarian regimes in history. The Indian social order did undergo some changes because of its encounter with other egalitarian religions and also due the two hundred years of colonial exploitation. The freedom movement or the anti-colonial struggle had its own positive impact on society. In fact, Ambedkar and his world-view is a product of those historical forces. The developments of post-independence era did give rise to new democratic forces. These hold the key to the process of transformation. However, the emerging scenario indicates that the contradiction between the forces of revolution and counter-revolution is getting accentuated. At this juncture, Ambedkar's analysis would be extremely useful. How these challenges would be overcome should constitute the socio-political agenda of the emerging democratic forces.

Reference

Dr. Babasaheb Ambedkar: Writings and Speeches, Government of Maharashtra, Vol. 3, 1987.

17 Indian Counter Culture

KANCHA ILAIAH

Whether Ambedkar has constructed a cultural alternative is a pertinent question in the modern Indian discourse. Different schools have different approaches to this question. Many Marxists treated Ambedkar merely as a bearer cultural transformation. At one level Indian communists treated the question of caste as a cultural question and Marxism considered culture as superstructure. In the discourse of base-superstructural dependence theory, cultural transformation is the superstructural issue, which does not deserve serious attention.[1] Ambedkar considered caste as both an economic and a cultural question. According to him, abolition of caste was central to Indian democratic transformation.

Ambedkar never considered his struggle as a cultural struggle but basically a political and ideological one. Caste was a political and ideological issue, an entity that could be annihilated, just as Marx and Engel's saw class as an entity that could be abolished.[2] While critiquing Hinduism, Ambedkar focused his attention on the socio-cultural contradictions it institutionalized in India. But, the attempt of the post-Ambedkarist studies is to construct the entire edifice of an alternative based on the real life of Dalitbahujan masses.

Cultural Studies

Though there have been cultural studies in India, by and large, they constructed cultural texts on the Hindu mythological discourses. During the colonial and nationalist periods the discourse centred on the cultural modes of Hindu ritual and cultural practices. Hindu culture was sought to be projected as Indian national culture. This cultural mode highlighted war, sex and conspicuous consumption. Missing in Hindu cultural ethic was the essence of a human being's labour, unlike in other nations where the base or core of culture gets reflected in the labour process of the productive masses. The productive masses in ancient India were called Shudras and Chandalas. In Mahatma Jyotirao Phule's language they were Shudras and Ati-Shudras and in Ambedkar's language they were 'depressed classes'. Indian culture in fact was shaped by their labour.

Ambedkar and the Theory of Labour

Ambedkar did not propose a distinct theory of labour, but his writings reflect the process of hegemonizing the culture of labour. Caste, according to him, not only established division of labour but also divided the labourers. The depressed classes are a historical bloc. The axis that formed the bloc is their involvement in the labour process and their continuous engagement in productivity. As understood by Ambedkar, the cultural edifice of this country rests up on the labour and productivity of the depressed classes.

Culture is a mode of relationship between individuals or communities. Indian culture seems to have formed in continuous conflicts between different communities. Caste struggles occurred in India as a result of differentiated culture. Positive relations germinate among human beings in the labour process. Hinduism negated this process. As I have shown in *Why I am not a Hindu*, the Dalitbahujan bloc lives in 'labour as life' whereas the Hindu bloc lives in 'leisure as life'. Post-Ambedkarite discourse is aimed at the cultural alternative sought to be constructed from the life experience of Dalitbahujans.[3] But, methodologically, Ambedkar has offered a critical tool of analysis of the 'life experience' while examining the source of untouchability. He wrote:

> According to Mr. Rice, the origin of untouchability is to be found in the unclean and filthy occupations of the untouchables. The theory is very plausible one. But there are certain difficulties in the theory

> being accepted as a true explanation of the origin of untouchability. The filthy and unclean occupations, which the untouchables perform, are common to all human societies. In every human society there are people who perform these occupations. Why were such people not treated as untouchables in other parts of the world?[4]

Ambedkar, however, left another fundamental question unasked. What are the notions of filth and unclean? Who constructed them? What are the implications of such notions to human development?

Brahmanism had constructed the acts of tilling the land, removing a carcass from the village, skinning a carcass, and transforming hide into leather as filthy. In other words, the whole process of human intercourse with nature, land, plants and animals in productive and creative modes was constructed as unclean. The Hindu negation of science and technological development begins here. With a certain disagreement with Ambedkar if we presume that the Aryan social forces that invaded (but did not migrate) began to construct their hegemonic power relations by hegemonizing war, violence and sex, constructed in the process Aayudha Pooja (worshipping weapons) as an early mode of spiritualism.[5] The native Dravidian masses, it appears, worshipped *bhoomi* (land) and other natural elements, and more importantly, they worshipped the productive tools. Dussehra or Vijayadashami, before the Brahaminical nationalists constructed it as a festival of all Indians, was not a festival of Shudra productive masses: it was a festival of rulers and priests.[6] Wherever Shudras like the Mysore rajas became powerful, they too resorted to Aayudha Pooja conspicuously. Makara Sankranti (the festival of crops), on the other hand, was the main Shudra festival. The Shudra masses worshipped instruments of production – the sickle and the hammer – but not weapons of war, the trishul, which the Hindutva forces extol.[7]

With some modifications, even the Indian sociologists took up constructed notions of filth and unclean into "purity and pollution" discourse.[8] In non-Indian (non-Brahmanic) societies class division was essential by a civil societal aspect. But religious society never officially recognized the civil societal categorization and hence civil society was not hierarchized in religious society. Brahmanism constructed a particular mode of civil societal relations and carried them into religious society also. For example, neither Buddhism nor Christianity nor Islam defined the process of human intercourse with nature as filthy and unclean. Handling soil, mud, carcasses and hide in themselves do not become filthy acts. It is an inevitable part of the productive process. By categorizing this process as filthy, Hinduism negated a natural process of human living. Even contemporary Hinduism does not assign a historically significant place to labour. Other societies recognized labour as positive, constructive and even divine. Socialist and Marxist thought gave the labour process the highest place in historiography. In Rossiter's view, "In Marx's deepest and most imposing thoughts labour is the essence of the life". Engel's wrote with precision: "Labour is the source of wealth. ... It is the prime basic condition for all human existence, and this is to such an extent that, in a sense, we have to say that labour is man himself."[9] Buddhism and all western religions thought along similar lines.

The untouchable homes are the centres of human labour process even today. Tilling, seeding, cutting, crushing of grain and so on involve soiling of hands. The human language, songs, proverbs and festivals are rooted in this agrarian labour process. By defining this process as unclean, Hinduism took the first negative cultural step.

The collective life of humans is an essential condition of village formation. But, a village is not merely a collectivity of humans. It is a combination of several species – cows, bulls, buffaloes, dogs, pigs, donkeys, horses and birds. Their birth and death are also an inevitable process of that collectivity. The whole construction of spiritual thinking is done around birth and death. In fact, the essence of human philosophy developed around death. All born creatures have to be touched and nursed and the dead have to be touched and need to be removed. Even divine bodies are subject to these processes. How do human acts like midwifery, child rearing and removal of carcasses become an avoidable process of life within the village. This is where two schools of thought got bifurcated within the Indian village system. One school was known as Shudratwam (philosophy of Shudras) and the other as Brahmanatwam separated in their fundamentals.[10]

For Shudra labour is an integral part of life. For Shudras labour is neither filth nor polluting. It is a process of creation and recreation. Their ideas, communicative processes, human relations, language and every dimension of life are related to their labour process. Hinduism, by negating this whole process in its philosophical discourses, destroyed the very scope of development of a positive thought in India.

By describing the labour process as filth or polluting, Hinduism constructed its own self in relation to pooja. No other religion has constructed pooja as full-time activity; they combined science and myth. Hinduism, on the other hand, made myth alone the totality. A Brahmin priest is essentially a mythmaker. In the process of myth making he not only negated the Shudras and Chandalas as human beings but also their productivity and creativity. It was here that human cultures fundamentally got dehumanized. The roots of Hindu dehumanization lie in negating labour, in constructing science as pollution, in treating humans who convert nature into commodities that could be used for survival of society as sub-human. Hinduism attempted to cut the branch on which it was sitting. This was the reason why it could not spread as a religion beyond the Brahmanical boundaries. Of course, geographically, it did not go beyond the boundaries of India.

The Food Culture

Hinduism again is the only religion that constructed the notions of 'we' and the 'other' based on the food cultures of Indians. Even today, not all Indians, who are non-Muslims, non-Christians, non-Buddhists, non-Parsis and non-Sikhs, are considered to be Hindus. While the Brahmins, particularly the priests, the sadhus and sanyasis treat themselves and others as non-intractable groups, the Dalitbahujans consider themselves in terms of their own spirituality. The bifurcation of Dalitbahujans and Brahmanical forces is also done on the basis of their food habits.

A people's culture is also reflected in their food habits. Spiritual modes also relate to the food habits of different castes. The food that we eat, and the tastes that we relish, have a close connection with our caste background. Hindu and non-Hindu society got divided on this basis.[11] A fundamental issue in this division is between eating beef and meat and vegetarianism. Ambedkar examines the food-related cultural process and critiques Brahmanism as to how unscientific ideological formations were worked out to keep a section untouchable and another section touchable subordinates and how they constructed their food habits like vegetarianism to practice hegemony. Ambedkar writes:

> For ordinary purposes the division of Hindus into two classes Mamsahari and Shakahari may be enough ... for exhaustive classification, the class of Hindus called Mamsahari shall have to be further divided into two sub-classes: (1) those who eat flesh but do not eat cow's flesh; and (2) those who eat flesh including cow's flesh.[12]

Ambedkar's presumption that they all can be treated as Hindus was misplaced and he himself got divorced from that idea later. He, however, says, "it is difficult to understand why a person who is a flesh eater should object to one kind of flesh, namely, cow's flesh".[13] Ambedkar considered the Brahminac negation of eating meat and especially beef as double revolution. He writes:

> The non-Brahmins have evidently undergone a revolution. From being beef-eaters to have become non-beef-eaters was indeed a revolution. But if the non-Brahmins underwent one revolution, the Brahmins had undergone two. They gave up meat-eating altogether and became vegetarians, which was another revolution.[14]

This definition of revolution is, however, negative.[15] What the Brahmins actually did was to negate a universal mode of cultural construction of food habits and carry that negation into the discourse and practice of religion. After organized religions emerged, all organized religions except Hinduism gave up offering food to divine spirits or deities. Before the eyes of Hinduism itself Buddhism separated the connection between food habits, offerings and religious performances. Ambedkar himself proved with evidence that Hindu

Brahmin priests once used to offer beef and meat. When they turned to vegetarianism, they made vegetarianism compulsory both for personal and familial consumption and also for religious offerings. Hinduism also gave vegetarianism religious status and the offering of vegetarian foods was regarded as superior. Here again, Hinduism did not care for the implications of the imposition of such subjectively constructed food cultures on the entire civil society. They had never shown an interest in examining the relationship between beef-meat-vegetarian foods and generation of energy in relation to production of goods and commodities in the agrarian, artisan and industrial (though operating with primitive capital) economy. Nor they showed an interest in understanding the relationship between human food availability in terms of beef-meat-vegetables and the socio-cultural relations that get established in the civil societal system, including the nurturing of animals and birds around the human habitats, and using their flesh for acquiring the required calories of food that sustains them and their hard work day after day. In the face of condemnation of their work, their cultural life, and their food habits by those who considered themselves knowledgeable, the Shudras constructed their own philosophical discourses to live a 'life of labour'. But, what are the requirements of the life of labour? How do the divine and spiritual relations operate within the social forces, which live a life of labour?[16]

By negating the Dalitbahujan food culture and by considering the social forces that produce for the well-being of the whole society as spiritless, Brahmanism slipped into degeneration.

People's food cultures are essentially secular. They are geo-political-cultural but Hinduism made them religious. The Dalitbahujans' universal food culture is non-spiritual, and thereby non-Hindu. This mode of rigidification of food cultures of Hinduism constructed a deep counter-revolutionary process into Hinduism itself.

Ambedkar subsequently locates the reasons for constructing such a counter-revolutionary psyche leading to schisms that operated between Buddhism and Hinduism. Both Manu's legality and Kautilya's statecraft gave us clues about the modes of food exploitation. Kautilya lists Mahisha (buffalo) flesh as a main food item of ancient human beings. Eating beef by all communities is a known aspect of ancient history. Why did the Brahmins give up eating of beef and meat? Ambedkar draws the correct conclusion about the politico-ideological reasons for giving up beef and meat eating by Brahmins. He says, "to my mind, it was a strategy which made the Brahmins give up beef-eating and start worshipping the cow. The clue to the worship of the cow is to be found in the struggle between Buddhism and Brahmanism and the means adopted by Brahmanism to establish its supremacy over Buddhism".[17] This ideological strategy of Brahmanism and the campaign let loose against Buddhism established Brahmanical supremacy.

Vast food resources went unused as Brahmanism built superstitious values around such food resources. All our food resources come from animal and plant kingdoms. Brahmanism negated the animal food resource and as a result very strong barriers were built to checkmate human advancement. The growth of human resource, both in terms of mental and physical abilities, through proteineous food resource, was always the key link. By negating economically available food, it destroyed the historical potential for community development and when some communities disobeyed the Brahmanical dictum, they suffered the attacks of Brahmanism, such as constructing them as untouchables and marginalizing them, attacking them as Shudras, Chandalas, Mlechas and so on. Based on food habits and modes of cooking, Brahmins divided civil societal communities as higher and lower. While constructing the lower-higher gradations, the most productive and creative communities were constructed as lower and the most leisure-bound communities as higher.

Ambedkar and Cultural Nationalism

The struggle between Buddhism and Brahmanism led to several revolutions and counter-revolutions. The Brahmanical priesthood, according to Ambedkar, was a 'sunken priesthood'.[18] He said:

> The Brahmins monopolized the priestly profession in the ancient Aryan society. None except a Brahmin could become a priest. As custodians of religion, the Brahmins were the guides of the people in

> moral and spiritual matters. They were to set the standard for people to follow. Did the Brahmins act up to the standard? Unfortunately, all the evidence we have shows that the Brahmins had fallen to the utmost depth of moral degradation.

The *Yagya* culture was the most superstitious culture. Ambedkar writes: "The animals most commonly offered for sacrifice were, the cattle which were used by the people for their agricultural purposes. They were mostly cows and bullocks."[19] The Buddhist revolution mainly starts at this juncture. Buddha and his Sanghas resisted the killing of thousands of agrarian cattle in the yagyas, the flesh of which was feasted on by Brahmin priests themselves. At a time when animal power was being deployed in agrarian production, the process of animal sacrifice destroyed the basis of the new economy.[20] Ambedkar's utmost concern was the indulgence of Brahmanical forces in eating, drinking and gambling. Ambedkar writes:

> The *Yadnas*, besides involving a terrible carnage, was really a kind of carnival. Besides roast meat there was drink. The Brahmins had Soma as well as Sura ... almost every Yadna was followed by gambling.

The Brahmanic culture of worshipping the violent killers was the most negative basis of Hindu spiritualism. Ambedkar critiques the so-called great Rigvedic culture as nothing but the worship of violence. He asked:

> Do they [the Brahmins] ask the gods to be kept [themselves] away from temptation? Do they ask for deliverance from evil? Do they ask for forgiveness of sins? Most of the hymns [of Rigveda] are in praise of Indira. They praise him for having brought destruction to the enemies of the Aryans. They praise him because he killed all the pregnant wives of Krishna and Asura. They praise him because he destroyed hundreds of villages of the Asuras. They praise him because he killed lakhs of Dasyus. The Aryans pray to Indira to carry

> on greater destruction among the Anaryans in the hope that they may secure to themselves the food supplies of the Anaryans and the wealth of the Anaryans.[21]

The construction of such texts itself shows that the Brahmanical social order reached very decadent levels. Worshipping violence became the essence of Brahmanical life. All the Aryan war heroes, who killed thousands of Shudras and Chandalas, were the backbone of production. Ambedkar examines this historical fact and draws serious lessons reconstructing why the nationalists were projecting the Rigveda as the most sacred nationalist text. By deconstructing that text to show the anti-Dalitbahujan ideology that got constructed into Rigveda and by showing the main reason for degeneration of the Indian system, Ambedkar squarely faced all the nationalists by writing texts that show up the nationalist myth.

Ambedkar focuses on documenting the Hindu-Aryan cultural decadence they had undergone over a period of time. Several Hindu nationalists perceived this attempt as unwarranted and untimely, because Hindu nationalism was being constructed to negate the Christian colonial hegemony. Ambedkar making a scathing attack on Hindu Brahmanism at this time was considered anti-national. Ambedkar saw the nation differently. What Brahmin-Bania leaders were constructing as Hindu nation was going to re-establish Brahmin supremacy. For him, the Shudras or Asuras constituted a separate nation within the boundaries of the Indian subcontinent.

For Ambedkar the notion of nation was entirely different. The depressed classes on their own constitute a nation. The culture of the depressed classes was entirely different from the culture of the Hindu classes. He located the cultural roots of the depressed classes in the Buddhist tradition. He said: "Religion is necessary for a free society. ... Religion must relate to facts of life and not to theories and speculations about God, or soul or Heaven or earth."[22] He seems to have felt that Buddhism was nearer to the facts of life of Dalitbahujans.

The Buddha's vision and understanding, Ambedkar thought, was in close proximity to his belief and thinking. He says, "it is not enough for morality to be the ideal of life. Since there is no God it must become the law of life."[23] He sees scope within even a religious society to abolish inequalities of property. Unlike in Hinduism 'everyone should have a right to learn' Ambedkar thought that Buddhism aimed at providing scope for all human beings to be equal.

Ambedkar, therefore, tries to compare the Buddha and Marx to evolve his own understanding of social change and of construction of new society. He borrows four essential principles from Marx as necessary to reconstruct India. The function of philosophy is to reconstruct the world and not to waste its time in explaining the origin of the world. There is conflict of interest between class and class. Private ownership of property brings power to one class and sorrow to another through exploitation. It is necessary for the good of society that the sorrow be removed by the abolition of private property.[24] Ambedkar tries to synthesize the Buddha and Marx on many fundamental questions.

Conclusion

The Buddhist alternative that Ambedkar offered has manifest limitations, which have become clear in the post-Ambedkarite experience and praxis. The Dalit democratic revolution that he visualized showed more vibrant expressions than conversion to Buddhism as an alternative. The Dalit movement in the country has started constructing very powerful identity movements by hegemonizing non-spiritual productive and creative historical contribution they made to the development of the socio-economic and cultural process of this country. The post-independence capitalist development has also created new conditions for reconstructing social relations based on the dignity of labour. Ambedkarism can now play its role in more vibrant ways than it did earlier.

In the realm of culture, more than the Buddhist sanghas, the dalit wadas and the cultural life that dalits live has a powerful potential to become universal. As of today, the dalit wadas have universal food habits; their body and mind are trained to learn anything that can split like atom to spread energy not for destructive purpose but for the development of society. Dalit energy gets released only when they seize political power. Dalit music and song will acquire a place of its own by overthrowing all the Brahmanical cultural forms.

Notes

1. In all democratic revolutions culture played a key role. In India culture plays a much more central role because Brahmanism established its hegemony specifically though cultural means. Though Brahmins were the first Granada landlords, more than their grip on land their manipulative skills in the field of culture put them in a hegemonic place for several centuries. The Indian communist intellectuals, since the majority of them came form the Brahmin background, to some extent, consciously underplayed the role of culture in India. Education, for example, was treated as a cultural asset, which played a more hegemonic role than landed property. Brahmins had total monopoly on such educational property. Indian communists, though they knew the powerful role of education, deliberately undermined it to their cadre at the same time their own children were given the best education available in the country. The base and superstructure debate in India must be understood in this background.
2. See B.R. Ambedkar, 'Annihilation of Caste', *Writings and Speeches*, vol.1, Government of Maharashtra, Bombay, 1979.
3. Kancha Ilaiah, *Why I am not a Hindu*? A Shudra Critique of Hindutva Philosophy, Culture and Political Economy, Samya, Calcutta, 1996, pp. 114-132.
4. Ambedkar, *Writing and Speeches*, vol. 7, Government of Maharashtra, Bombay, 1990, p. 305.
5. Ambedkar did not agree with the theory that Aryans were non-Indian invaders. He was of the opinion that Aryans were always Indians. Thus, he treats India as a multi-racial country. See *Who were the Shudras*, *Writing and Speeches*, vol. 7.
6. In south India, till recent times, Dasara was not a mass festival. It was basically considered to be the Kshatriya festival but Brahmins were also central to the process of worshipping weapons. There are a number of story narratives in the rural Telugu country, which indicate the non-Shudra character of Dasara. When the Brahmanical nationalists expanded this festival the Shudras in the villages converted that festival into a festival of meat eating and drinking of intoxicants. Thus used their

cultural modes to debrahminize Dasara. In many Telangana villages Dasara has now become a festival of invoking the spirits of villages at Bodrai (stone deity erected in the centre of the village).

7. Consider the symbols of contemporary Hindutva organizations. The Shiva Sena and the Bajrang Dal openly worship war weapons. The RSS propagates about the godhood images where war weapons become visible. Except the BJP's election symbol-Lotus-all other symbols that the Hindutva forces use are related to war and destruction. Since the Dalitbahujan castes had an opposite tendency of worshipping productive tools, in spite of their contribution to production, their share in the national wealth is meagre. The cultural divide of production and destruction between the Dalibahujans and Brahmanical forces s clear in many fields even today. The Brahmanical euphoria of celebrating even at the societal level after the Babri Masjid demolition and also the tremendous euphoria of the Indian Brahmanical forces in the context of Pokhran II unclear tests must also be seen in this light.
8. See M.N. Srinivas (ed.), *Caste and its Twentieth Century Avatar,* Viking, *Delhi, 1996.* For this volume several upper-caste sociologists contributed articles and all of them upheld the notions of purity and pollution as natural. Even an attempt to problematize the notions of purity and pollution is not made. Constructing such sociological texts is necessary for the maintenance of Brahmanical hegemony.
9. Karl Marx and Frederic Engel, *Selected Works*, Progress Publishers, Moscow, 1973, p. 66.
10. I have observed during my fieldwork in Telugu villages that the villagers treat Shudratwam as a full-fledged philosophical concept. In their view *Shudratwam* and *Brtahmanatwam* (they call it *Bapanatwam*) are two opposite philosophical positions. By and large, Dalitbahujan masses view *Bapanatwam* as negative philosophy, as an ideology of laziness and of gluttony.
11. See Kancha Ilaiah, *Why I am not a Hindu,* Ch. I & II.
12. Ambedkar, *Writing and Speeches*, vol. 7, p. 329.
13. Ibid., p. 330.
14. Ibid., p. 329.
15. What Brahmins did by becoming vegetarians was that they became counter-revolutionaries even in terms of food cultures. Brahmins did not contribute for the production of vegetables. If killing of any living organism even for the sake of human consumption was treated as

non-violence at least an alternative should have been worked out in the realm of labour, because agriculture basically centred around the labour process. While constructing a discourse on vegetarianism and putting it in a hegemonic position Brahmanism continued to condemn the labour process as Shudra-Chandala process. This contradictory process destroyed labour potential in the country.

16. Kancha Ilaiah, *Why I am not a Hindu*, see the last chapter, 'Dalitization but not Hinduization'.
17. Ambedkar, *Writings and Speeches*, vol. 7, p.354.
18. Ibid., vol. III, p.158.
19. Ibid., p. 174.
20. R.S. Sharma and Romila Thapar have shown enough evidence about the killing of thousands of cows and bulls in Yagyas and Yagas.
21. Ambedkar, *Writing and Speeches*, Vol. 7.
22. Ibid., p. 442.
23. Ibid., p. 444.
24. Ibid.

Part Six

On the Question of Women

18 Empowerment of Women

ELEANOR ZELLIOT

My premises for this essay are that Ambedkar's thought and action made important differences in the lives of Indian women in four ways. First, his organizations encouraged many Dalit women to become educated, to be active in public life, and especially to gain that all-important quality of self-respect. Second, this self-respect, education and activity resulted even years after his death in a creative spirit which produced poetry, fiction and autobiography of extraordinary quality and quantity, and in addition encouraged women to form or to participate in organizations for Dalit women at the state and national levels. Third, his concern for the status of all women is reflected in the Hindu Code Bill, which he promulgated as the Law Minister in Nehru's first cabinet and which eventually resulted in a more equal status for women in marriage, divorce, adoption practices, inheritance and property ownership.

The fourth category is more difficult to explain. As a historian, I am concerned that we recognize the essential quality of historical legitimization for change and that we recognize that change requires a philosophy that may be broader than the issue directly concerned. As an example of this philosophical legitimacy, let me refer to the final paragraph of a two-page flier published in 1986 by the Bharatiya Mahila Jagriti Parishad (Indian Women's Conference for Awakening). The two-page litany of protest, entitled "Dalit Women are Slaves of the Slaves" ends:

> Dr. Babasaheb Ambedkar urged us to develop strength and struggle and to give up superstitious customs. He said, "the appearance of Tulsi leaves around your neck will not relieve you from the clutches of the moneylender. Because you sing songs of Rama you will not get concession of rent from landlords. You will not get wages at the end of the month because you make pilgrimages every year to Pandharpur. ... Do not believe in fate; believe in your own strength."

The organization, which published this, is not anti-Hindu. The message here is that you can take your life in your own hands, that fate is not all-powerful; itself a powerful message for women, and those Hindu beliefs should not hinder women's freedom. The other philosophical problem, which must be examined, is the link between patriarchy and caste, between the social system as a totality and the role of women. Ambedkar began to explore this currently much debated issue. I shall take up this problem in the final section of this essay.

Women Activists in the Ambedkar Movement

Women's action began quite early. Meenakshi Moon and Urmila Pawar have investigated "Women in the Early Untouchable Liberation Movement" and found pre-Ambedkar action to bring women out of devadasi profession and find husbands for them as early as 1908.[1]

At the Mahad satyagraha of 1927, an historic effort to get water from a public pond after the Bombay Legislative Council had declared all public places open to untouchables, women not only participated in the procession from the conference site to the pond (where they were met with violence), they also "participated in the deliberations of the subject committee meetings in passing resolutions about the claim for equal human rights".[2] Women by the hundreds also participated in the five-year-long Nasik satyagraha to enter the Kalaram temple (1930-1935), a massive effort that went on until Ambedkar declared at Yeola near Nasik that he would "not die a Hindu" and all such efforts to enter the Hindu citadels ceased.

Women's conferences were held simultaneously with those of all the 'depressed classes' in the early days, and then women met on their own. In May 1936, women held an independent conference to support

Ambedkar's declaration to convert. Pawar and Moon report that the women expressed confidence that Ambedkar would not choose a religion that would make them live in purdah![3] One wonders if the place of women as well as the religions' commitment to social equality was a factor in the decision that led Ambedkar past Islam, and also past Christianity, Sikhism and various reform sects of Hinduism into Buddhism.[4]

Pawar and Moon report that resolutions of various conferences reveal that what women wanted was free and compulsory education for girls (still not a fact in contemporary India); representation in legislative assemblies; self-protection such as karate (interestingly enough, the Girls' Hostel run by the Trilok Bauddh Mahasangha Sahayaka Gana, TBMSG, in Pune, teaches karate); a women's branch of the Samata Sainik Dal (equality volunteer corps); and the prohibition of child marriages.[5] When other castes were 'sanskritizing' and adopting such older Brahmanical practices as child marriage and prohibition of widow remarriage, Ambedkar's followers opposed these practices. Ambedkar himself had been married at 13, so it is clear that such progressive reforms were part of a new movement, not the old Mahar pattern.

The Women's Conference, during the Scheduled Caste Federation meeting of 1942, was a very important event. Ambedkar told the women, "their dress, their cleanliness and the confidence with which they behaved in the conference brought delight to my heart".[6] Note that word confidence. Keer reports that Ambedkar's advice to the women on that 1942 occasion included injunctions to educate their children and remove from them any inferiority complex; not to have too many children; and to let every girl who married "claim to be her husband's friend and equal and to refuse to be his slave".[7] Sulochanabai Dongree of Amraoti, a very active centre of reform, was the president of this conference and both Keer and the Pawar/Moon sources indicate quite a number of women leaders in the movement at this time.

Not enough research has been done on women and education in the Ambedkar movement to allow any sort of analysis, but Moon and Pawar report a girls' school in the Central Provinces in the 1920s and a girls' school begun by a woman, Jaibai Chaudhuri, in Nagpur in 1924.[8]

More recently, Shantabai Dani has done a great deal of educational work for women in Nasik. There are no separate figures for Buddhists in the census so we do not know how women in the Ambedkar movement today rank in literacy with other groups although we do know that Scheduled Caste (SC) women in general are much less literate than their caste Hindu sisters or their male caste fellows.

Women have continued to be part of demonstrations and the various campaigns of the Ambedkar movement. A moving illustration of this is in a poem by a Dalit woman. Jyoti Lanjewar, who participated in the long campaign to rename Marathwada University, now Dr. Babasaheb Ambedkar Marathwada University, paints a picture of a poor, probably illiterate, but passionately active woman in her poem Ai (Mother). Her heroine, who is Every Buddhist Woman, is seen in the Namanter (change the name) campaign, this way:

> I have seen you
> at the front of the Long March
> the end of your sari tucked tightly at the waist
> shouting "Change the name",
> taking the blow of the police stick on your upraised hands
> going to jail with head held high ...

Toward the end of her moving poem is this passage on the *diksha bhumi*, the place of the Buddhist conversion, using 'Baba' and 'Bhim' as affectionate terms for Ambedkar:

> I have seen you on your deathbed
> giving that money you earned
> rag-picking to the *diksha bhumi*
> saying with your dying breath
> "Live in unity...fight for Baba...don't forget him..."
> and with your very last breath
> "Jai Bhim" (Victory to Ambedkar)[9].

Women in the Ambedkar movement have also been active in other ways. An example of this is Meenakshi Moon's *Maitrani,* which means "woman friend" in village Marathi and offers women (and sympathetic men) a chance to comment on religion and their social and political interests. Moon has also been involved in conferences that bring to public attention women's concerns, give women a chance to meet other socially concerned women, and bring as speakers both Dalit and non-Dalit women who are involved in women's activities.

Women who are part of the Ambedkar movement also participate in three women's organizations: the National Federation of Dalit Women, founded by Ruth Manorama in Bangalore and now about to open a north India branch; the Maharashtra Dalit Mahila Sangathna which has held meetings in Dhule and Nagpur and is open only to Dalit women; and the All-India Dalit Women's Forum, established by a Buddhist woman from Pune, which is open to all women. These conferences offer fellowship and stimulation and also a chance to present women's demands. The National Federation of Dalit Women was represented at the International Women's Conference held in Beijing.

Vimal Thorat reports that Maharashtrian Dalit women's groups, as a coda to the Mahad Conference of 1927, which are seen as the real beginning of the Ambedkar movement, has called for Dalits to gather at Mahad again on 25 December 1998. Just as the Mahad Conference of 25 December 1927 burned those portions of the *Manusmriti*, which limited the rights of untouchables and legalized extreme punishments for any supposed transgression, the Mahad Conference of 25 December 1998 will find women in the thousands burning the *Manusmriti* for its denial of human rights to women.[10]

An area that has not been explored involves all the Mahila Mandals (women's organizations) that dot the localities of Buddhists across the urban face of Maharashtra. Some of these groups concentrate on Buddhism, some organize classes for literacy or some skill such as typing. They are purely local and locally organized, and their strength depends upon the individual commitment of women. Gopal Guru reports that Mahila Mandals have proliferated even in the villages of Akola district. In the post-Ambedkar period women have been creating songs, which reflect their feeling about Ambedkar, about politics, about Brahmins, and this creative urge has led to cultural programmes with Buddhist motifs. He also notes that Mahila Mandals, besides staging cultural programmes at the *diksha bhumi* (place of convention) in Nagpur and the *chaitya bhumi* in Mumbai (Ambedkar's final resting place), have resulted in some Dalit women being invited to perform their cultural programme on Mumbai TV.

After recounting all this activity, one note of failure must be injected into the story. We must note that women do not play an important role in political leadership in Maharashtra. Aside from Shantabai Dani, one cannot point to a truly important female figure. Perhaps it might be noted, that a radical Brahman woman, Neelham Gorhe, was associated with Prakash Ambedkar's branch of the Republican Party for a brief period. I shall not analyze this lack of women's political power except to say that women in Maharashtra have achieved a political place only in Socialist and Communist parties, and that too rarely. But I might point out that Mayawati, a Chamar school teacher, has achieved extraordinary political power from time to time in Uttar Pradesh through the Bahujan Samaj Party (BSP). As an essential part of her programme, she promoted the creation of Ambedkar statues and parks in every possible area of that state, and designated 'Ambedkar village', which had large Dalit population, to receive special help.

Dalit Women in the Field of Culture

The poem fragments by Jyoti Lanjewar and the notes on song above lead us into a post-Ambedkar development in which women have made extraordinary progress. I think the most important new element in the twenty-five year history of Dalit Sahitya (literature) is the entrance of a number of women as fiction writers and poets. Urmilla Pawar has been very successful as a short story writer, and has represented Marathi literary ideas at international conferences. Jyoti Lanjewar, Hira Bansode, Surekha Bhagat and Mina Gajbhiye are published poets. Two minimally educated Dalit women, Baby Kamble and Shantabai Kamble, have published their autobiographies. Baby's is excerpted as an example of Marathi literature in *Women Writing in India*, the major collection of women's writing. Shantabai Dani, educator and political and social activist based in Nasik, has also written the story of her life as has Savita Ambedkar, Ambedkar's second wife, known as *Mai*. As an example of the contribution women have made and as their tribute to the power of Ambedkar's life and thought in their lives, here is Hira Bansode's poem about Ambedkar. Its thrust is to ridicule those who pay tribute to him now but opposed him during his lifetime. Note that Bansode writes as a follower of Ambedkar with no particular feminine interest, except perhaps that sarcastic last line of each verse sounds like a woman's scorn for hypocrisy:

O Great Man (Mahapurush)

O Great Man –

those who strewed thorns in your path
today offer you flowers
and sing your praises
– now this is really too much –
During the dark procession of time
you lit the flowers of light
but these impostors, these villains
crushed, extinguished those flowers.
today those flowers of light have turned into a wildfire
and those villains are fanning that wildfire
– O now, this is too much –
Like an elephant ramming a gate
you pounded on the temple door,
the stones of the temple shook.
Under the holy name of religion
they long ago enslaved the gods.
your honest painful claim
of the right to see the gods
was demolished, thrown out of the village.
Now they decorate the great tree
that sprouted on that spot
– now this is really too much –

It is clear that nature belongs to all
but these people bought that too.
Every drop of water in Chowdar Tank
was stamped with their name;
the alert watchman of this culture
guarded the imprisoned water.
They feared that your touch would poison the water and
they anointed you with your own blood
when you were dying of thirst.
And now they pour water
into the mouth of your stone effigy
– oh now this is too much –[11]

—Translated by Jayant Karve and Eleanor Zelliot

Chowdar Tank is the body of water in Mahad from which Ambedkar and the Mahad conference participants of 1927 attempted to drink. Driven away violently, they returned in December 1927 to burn the *Manusmriti*. Bansode's poem illustrates the centrality of Mahad in the Ambedkar movement and sheds light on the intent of the new women's movement to return to that place in protest of Manu's tradition. There are many other poems, often offering up new ideas and images, rigorous criticism of the community itself, perhaps some subtle anti-patriarchal ideas. And, there is one creative act, which goes beyond publishing and singing. Dr. Padmavathi of Andhra Pradesh took seven years of her life, leaving her clinic and her son in the care of her husband, and created a full-length feature film on the life of Ambedkar. Its language is Telugu, so it has won honours only in that language area, but it exists in video form with English sub-titles as a remarkable tribute to Ambedkar and to the creative ability of Dalit women.

The Hindu Code Bill

Even before the Hindu Code Bill was on the mind of anyone, Ambedkar supported legal measures to aid women. In 1928, as a member of the Legislative Council of Bombay, he supported 'vehemently'[12] the bill for maternity leave for working women and felt the financial responsibility should be on both the employer and the government. He also supported equal wages for women.

Volume 14 of *Dr. Babasaheb Ambedkar: Writings and Speeches* carries as its foreword a statement by Ambedkar on the significance of the Hindu Code Bill:

> No law passed by the Indian Legislature in the past or likely to be passed in the future can be compared to it [Hindu Code] in point of its significance. To leave inequality between class and class, between sex and sex, which is the soul of Hindu society, untouched and to go on passing legislation relating to economic problems is to make a farce of our Constitution and to build a palace on a dung heap. This is the significance I attached to the Hindu Code.[13]

These are strong words, and they underwrite my point that gender inequality, if related to other forms of inequality, a matter to be pursued in the final section of this paper, as well as illustrating the commitment Ambedkar brought to the consideration of the Hindu Code Bill in the Indian Parliament.

Ambedkar himself gives the history of the bill. It had its origin in the 1937 and from then has been "bandied from committee to committee" till 1941. In 1941 the Rau Committee report on Women's Rights to Property Act of 1937 was submitted. In 1942 two draft bills, one on succession and another on marriage, were presented. A Hindu Succession Bill was introduced in the Assembly in 1943 but was referred to Joint Committee. It should be noted that for the purposes of this Code, people who are not Muslims, Parsis or Christians, were included in the category of Hindu.[14]

The parliament of independent India settled down to consider the Hindu Code Bill in 1950. The failure of the bodies above to finalize the bill was to be repeated in the lengthy discussions of 1950 and 1951. As Law Minister, Ambedkar was in charge of presenting the facets of the bill, explaining the rationale of various sections, answering questions, and especially defending the very idea of equality for women in marriage, divorce, adoption and property rights. He and his many supporters, including all the women in the legislative body, were faced with a barrage of criticism. Among the objections to the bill, which were raised, were such statements that "ladies will be reduced from being an Alexander in the home to being a mere partner",[15] and a host of other ideas: the Code should apply to Muslims also; it is worded dictatorially; it should be submitted to all Indian in referendum; Sikhs find it regressive; Ambedkar does not have a mandate; "we do not want Ambedkarian religion"[16]; custom should dominate over law; there will be nothing but litigation; "Ambedkar has been egged on by aggressive ladies"[17]. Ambedkar himself noted that the Hindu Code Bill was introduced in parliament on 11 April 1947 and after a life of four years, it was "killed and died unwept and unsung, after four clauses of it were passed".[18] Ambedkar himself resigned in 1951, the failure of the Prime Minister to support the final passage of the Hindu Code Bill being one of his major reasons.

In the end, the Hindu Code Bill was for the most part passed bit by bit in 1955 and 1956, but was Acts, not the total Bill. Among its provisions are guarantees of property from the paternal home to daughters; abolition of caste in the matter of marriage and adoption; the principle of monogamy; and the principle of divorce. What I want to stress here, however, is Ambedkar's commitment to female equality and to legal measures to help women. Often he spoke about a particular measure by using examples of women's worth or international practice. For instance, during the fierce battle over women's property, in which one argument was that the joint family would be destroyed and another that women were incapable of good judgement in this matter, he said:

> I know a great deal of the argument that is always urged against women getting absolute property. It is said that women are imbecile; it is said that they are always subject to the influence of all sorts of people... My submission to the House is this. If the woman can be trusted to dispose of her *stridhanam* property (marriage gifts) in the best ways she likes... if in certain cases women were competent and intelligent to sell and dispose of their property, they must be held to be competent in respect of the disposal of the other property also.[19]

Also, in the matter of women's property, he noted that various systems of inheritance had been examined and "there is no system anywhere in the world where a daughter has been included".[20]

There were a few fairly humorous moments in the discussion. Pandit Lakshmi Kanta Maitra explained why he could not support the Code: "I am a married man. I have a humble wife – married according to Hindu shastric rites, a simple unsophisticated lady, bred up and nurtured in the ideals of our Hindu homes." When Ambedkar interjected, "What a pity!" he was besieged with opinions that 99.9 per cent of Hindu homes had that kind of wife and were happy.[21] N.V. Gadgil suggested that Ambedkar himself was of the race of Manu and Yagnavalkya, great rishis of the past, and Syamnandan Sahaya called Ambedkar the 'Kaliyugi Manu'.[22] During this time Ambedkar made one of the few jokes attributed to him: He wished he could find some fat Brahmin women to sit fasting in front of parliament until the Hindu Code Bill was passed!

As these notes show, the debate over the Hindu Code Bill was at times very personal. It is clear, however, that the basic objections were not directed against Ambedkar but against the idea of women's property rights, their right to divorce, the abolition of caste in the matter of marriage and adoption, and the prescription of monogamy. Reading the two thick volumes of debate gives one an impression of a very intelligent, well-informed and only occasionally impatient Ambedkar in battle with a vocal minority whose fear of change was emotional and often irrational. That there are new laws eventually prescribing women's rights is a tribute to Ambedkar, to the slow influx of new ideas, and to the women who spoke strongly for their sisters in parliament and outside it.

Ambedkar seems to have entered the debate with great optimism. Society has never accepted its own power and its own responsibility in moulding its social, economic and legal life. It is for the first time that we are persuading Hindu society to take this big step and I have not the slightest doubt in my mind that a society, which has bucked up courage enough to tolerate the large step that we are asking it to take by reason of this Bill, will not hesitate to march on the path that remains to be trodden and reach the goal that she [Mrs Hansa Mehta] has in mind.[23] This early optimism was not to last, but it demonstrates

Ambedkar's commitment to women's rights and the linkage of women's rights with social justice.

The Broader Context of Women's Empowerment

At the beginning of this essay I noted the relationship between broader social ideas and the empowerment of women in the flier, which advised women to reject faith in fate and take their lives in their own hands. The major arena, however, which must now be explored is that of patriarchy and caste. G. Dietrich has pointed out what she sees as Ambedkar's place in the date:

> Ambedkar, though aware of women's position in general, has not integrated his analysis of caste with an analysis of patriarchy. He confines himself to general observations like the following: "From time immemorial, man, as compared with women, has had the upper hand. He is a dominant figure in every group and of the two sexes has greater prestige. With this traditional superiority of man over woman, his wishes have always been consulted. Women, on the other hand, have been an easy prey to all kinds of iniquitous injunctions – religious, social or economic. But man, as a maker of injunction, is most often above them all."[24]

Dietrich continues with her analysis of Ambedkar's idea:

> While he sees a connection between social evils like *sati*, child marriage, ban on widow remarriage, caste and untouchability, his preoccupation is clearly with untouchability and caste. Yet, his writings are not only relevant to rethink drastically on racial theories of invasion, they also lend themselves for drawing further connections between caste and patriarchy and also for critical introspection, both among feminists and Dalits.

Dietrich, in conclusion, pleads for 'drastic rethinking' in the Delhi movement on patriarchy.[25]

Other sources for a discussion of the issue of caste and patriarchy include an article by M. Nalini, which traces Ambedkar's presentation of an 'innovative argument' on the relationship between the rise of the caste system and the decline of the status of women. Here, Ambedkar's argument is combined with that of Engles.[26] A pioneering article that links Dalit patriarchy and state-sponsored globalization as the rationale for separate organizations for Dalit women by Gopal Guru is titled very clearly: "Dalit Women Talk Differently".[27]

Ambedkar was ahead of his time in his thinking about women's empowerment, as a close reading of the debates surrounding the Hindu Code Bill will show, and it is perhaps enough that he pointed out the relationship between the caste system and the position of women. Hierarchy in a social system is reflected in hierarchy in the home. Rights and special privileges for one caste can be translated into rights and special privileges for one gender. The hegemony of caste translates into a hegemony of gender codes of pride, privilege and self-image. The necessity for a son in the continuance of the male line, which is related to caste, calls for the lessened importance of daughters. Ambedkar stood for annihilation of caste itself, and chose a religion which stresses rationality, equality and humanity for himself and any who felt it offered personal and social freedom. But these simple statements reveal just a bit of the "interface between caste, patriarchy and gender", to use Dietrich's words. It is up to those of us who think best theoretically to more thoroughly explore this issue. It is up to Dalit women themselves to explore ways to control the patriarchy they face both within and without the Dalit family. It is up to all who care about human rights to work for freedom, equality and justice for women.

Notes

1. Meenakshi Moon and Urmila Pawar, "We made History Too: Women in the Early Untouchable Liberation Movement", *South Asian Bulletin*, 9:2, 1989, pp. 68-71.
2. Ibid., p. 69.

3. Ibid.
4. In the Rise and Fall of the Hindu Woman, first published in *Mahabodhi* in 1950 and then as a separate pamphlet, Ambedkar lists all of the many women of early Buddhism, analyses why the order of nuns is subject to the order of bhikkhus, and affirms his belief that women were equal to men in the eyes of the Buddha.
5. Moon and Pawar, p. 69.
6. Ibid.
7. Dhananjay Keer, *Dr. Ambedkar Life and Mission* Bombay: Popular Prakashan, 1991, reprint, p. 352.
8. Moon and Pawar, op.cit.
9. The poem appears in full in "Stri Dalit Sahitya: the New Voice of Women Poets," in Anne Feldhaus (ed.), *Images of Women in Maharashtrian Religion and Society*, ed. Albany: State University of New York Press, 1996.
10. *Dalit Cultural Movement & Dialectics of Dalit Politics in Maharashtra*, Mumbai: Vikas Adhayn Kendra, 1997, pp. 25-29.
11. From Phiyadi. Pune: Samaj Prabodhan Sanstha Prakashan, 1984. First published in Bombay, *Sakal*, 16 April 1980.
12. R.R. Sonker, "Women's Liberation in India and Dr. B.R. Ambedkar" (typescript).
13. These volumes are edited by Vasant Moon and published by the Education Department, Government of Maharashtra.
14. Dr. *Babasaheb Ambedkar: Writing and Speeches*, vol. 14, parts One and Two: The Hindu Code Bill, Vasant Moon, ed. Education Department, Government of Maharashtra, 1995, pp. 37-40.
15. Ibid., p. 910.
16. Ibid., p. 1079.
17. Ibid., p. 891.
18. Ibid., p. 1324.
19. Ibid., p. 278.
20. Ibid., p. 282.
21. Ibid., p. 405.
22. Ibid., p. 1298.
23. Ibid., p. 41.

24. Garbriete Dietrich, "Dalit Movements and Women's Movements", in *Reflection on the Women's Movement in India*, New Delhi: Horizon India Books, 1992.
25. Ibid.
26. M. Malini, "Caste and Patriarchy: Ambedkar's Insight into the Status of Women", in K.S. Chalam (ed.), *Relevance of Ambedkarism in India*, Jaipur: Rawat, 1993, pp. 129-38.
27. Gopal Guru, 'Dalit Women Task Differently', *Economic and Political Weekly*, 14-21 October 1995, pp. 2548-50.

19 Problems of Hindu Women

P.G. JOGDAND

Ambedkar was the first leader of the Dalits who not only wrote on various issues but waged a series of protests against various evil social practices. He relentlessly struggled against social oppression and multiple deprivations. He is remembered for his many-sided contributions, as the architect of the Constitution, a thinker and writer, a great political organizer and as a true social revolutionary, and also as an emancipator of the weaker sections of India. But Ambedkar also needs to be acknowledged both for his analysis or explanation for degrading situation of Hindu women as well as effort to give the appropriate right and place to women, particularly by introducing Hindu Code Bill in the early 1950.

Improving women's position was one of the earliest tasks taken up by the social reformers in the nineteenth century. The problems attracting their attention were *sati*, the ill-treatment of widows, ban on widow marriage, child marriage, and the denial of property rights to women. Their main plank was to ensure women some dignity within the family and their basic message was that women must not be ill-treated and must be given some dignity and status because they are custodians of the family.[1] The reformers were hardly concerned with emancipating or liberating women from gender-imposed bonds. On the contrary, women's roles within the family as wife, daughter and mother were re-emphasized and extended, to be in tune with the requirements of the family in a changing situation,[2] which had more to do with the familial problems of the upper-caste women.

Non-Brahmin social reformers, on the other hand, made noteworthy efforts for the emancipation of women. Pandita Ramabai, V.R. Shinde and Jannka Shinde highlighted the problems, which touched women's lives, but they too failed to link up women's exploitation with that of the caste system. But reformers like Jotiba Phule, Ambedkar and Tarabai Shinde enunciated a revolutionary discourse for women's liberation.[3] In her book *Stri Purush Tulna,* Tarabai attacked male domination. Phule sought to demolish the slavery imposed by men on women. He attacked the patrilineal family, the caste system and Hindu culture as being responsible for the subordination of women.[4]

Phule's main project was to liberate women, Shudras and ati-Shudras from the slavery of Brahmanism. His whole project of education for women and Shudras was meant to give them a new vision.

Ambedkar and Women's Question

Ambedkar waged a series of protests with a view to establish a just society based on the principles of liberty, equality and fraternity. His effort for the upliftment of women in Indian society was a part of his major project of establishing a just society.

Ambedkar argued that the caste system itself was responsible for women's subordination and exploitation. He held that endogamy was a characteristic feature peculiar to caste: it was the essence of caste.[5] Numerical parity between the two sexes was maintained through *sati*, enforced widowhood and child marriage. These three customs were prescribed to maintain the caste system. Through exercising control on women's sexuality caste was preserved, women being considered the gateway to the caste system. During the Mahad satyagraha (1927), Ambedkar addressed the Dalit women, drawing linkages between caste exploitation and women's subordination and contested the claims of upper-caste women's progeny being pure and that of the lower caste being impure.

In Ambedkar's scheme of a just society, fraternity meant mutual respect, love and oneness, with equal sharing on the basis of equal status.[6] To put men and women on equal footing, Ambedkar included Articles 14, 15 and 16, which deals with the right to equality, in the Constitution. The official doctrine was to be equality as against the inequality doctrine of Hinduism. The Hindu Code Bill, which was intended to take the principle of equality further, was stalled from the beginning, its opponents believing that the interests of men and women were better served when women occupied a dependent position and men and women played different social roles. The bill was in fact, in accordance with the findings of a committee set up by the government in 1941, with B.N. Rau as its chairman and D.N. Mitter, J.R. Gharpure and V.V. Joshi as members. The committee advocated codification of Hindu law and recommended that the position of women in Hindu law be improved. The committee justified its recommendations on the basis of Hindu religious texts and on the basis of 'majority opinion' while responding to the questionnaire.[7] Ambedkar arranged the subject matter of the original bill in a more logical sequence. The bill would have done away with all customary laws in the areas of marriage (with a provision for judicial separation and conjugal rights), divorce (a two-year period of not resuming intercourse after a judicial separation), and inheritance and succession (the fixing of a daughter's share as equal to a son's share, and uniform law of succession for all Hindus).

Traditionalists vehemently opposed these recommendations with the plea that the sacred nature of Hindu marriage would be in jeopardy. Syama Prasad Mookerjee, founder of the Jan Sangh, said that the bill would "destroy the indissoluble nature of Hindu marriage, which is regarded as solemn and sacred by millions of people", and threatened that if it was passed "the whirlwind will come".[8] The law could be made voluntary for those who wanted to come under its provisions, he said. Ambedkar in his reply described the 'sacramental marriage' of traditional Brahmanic Hinduism as polygamy for the man and perpetual slavery for the women. Making the law voluntary would make a mockery of the law-making powers of parliament. Hindu society would not reform itself and would never give up its social structure that is responsible for the enslavement of the Shudras and of women. For this reason law had to come to their rescue.[9]

Finally, the bill was defeated. The Congress leadership did nothing to push it, even Rajendra Prasad said it would be 'undemocratic' to pass the bill since it had never been discussed in Congress conferences. Ambedkar resigned from his post and explaining his decision in parliament said:

> The Hindu Code was the greatest social reform measure ever undertaken by the legislature in this country. No law passed by the Indian Legislature in the past or likely to be passed in the future can be compared to it in point of its significance. To leave inequality between class and class, between sex and sex which is the soul of Hindu society untouched and to go on passing legislation relating to economic problems is to make a farce of our Constitution and to build a palace on a dung heap. This is the significance I attached to the Hindu Code.[10]

Ambedkar also tried to generate self-respect among the Dalit women. He said that he measured the progress of the Dalit community by the degree of progress which Dalit women had achieved.[11]

Ambedkar moved a resolution through P.J. Roham in the Bombay Legislative Assembly on 10 November 1938 regarding the measures for birth control. This resolution had a bearing on the health problems of women.[12] Ambedkar said that survival rate was more important than the birth rate.[13] Probably, Ambedkar was the only leader who had strongly advocated birth control, Gandhi being opposed to any artificial measures for birth control. Gandhi had faith only in the concept of self-control.

In a booklet entitled "The Rise and Fall of Hindu Women" Ambedkar pointed out how *Manusmriti* and Brahmin cultural ethos put restrictions on women. The Buddha's approach towards women was, on the other hand, progressive in terms of admitting women into 'sangha' and allowing them to receive education along with men (monks in this case).

Ambedkar organized several conferences of Dalits, ensuring that women's conferences were held simultaneously with those for men. By 1930 Dalit women started conducting their own meetings and conferences independently. They organized such conferences at Kanpur in 1944, at Bombay in 1945 and at Calcutta in 1946. Ambedkar's message inspired the Dalit women who, rather than being content to remain merely as the audience, shouldered the responsibility in Ambedkar's movement. Dalit women's participation in Ambedkar movement, documented by Moon and Pawar,[14] shows that Dalit women made great strides in achieving political consciousness. Their activism moved from a phase of organizing conferences and participating in *satyagrahas* to a more provocative one of criticizing Brahmanical customs and patriarchy.

Several associations of Dalit women exist today, which have been nurturing and asserting Dalit women's identity. Prominent among them are the Dalit Mahila Sangathana and the National Federation of Dalit Women. The emergence of autonomous Dalit women's organizations led to a major debate at least in Maharashtra. Feminist activists criticized the emergence of the organizations of Dalit women without realizing their gender specificities. Hitherto, the category of Indian women was treated as homogeneous and caste bondage and gender specificities did not figure in the debate. As the Dalit women become politically conscious, they started speaking differently in terms of their double deprivation and their exclusion in the feminist discourse.[15] They also criticized the post-Ambedkar Dalit leadership for its cavalier approach towards their problems.[16] Thus, the Dalit feminists recognize the need to reformulate the feminist discourse.

Conclusion

Deeply concerned about the subordination of women, Ambedkar wanted to change the old Indian social order, which was based on discrimination and inequality. His main project was to create a just society and his quest for social justice continued throughout his life. He vehemently criticized the idea of upholding purity of caste at the cost of women. He was against the bonds imposed on women in the name of religion. He drew linkages between women's subordination and caste exploitation and therefore he proposed to annihilate caste. It was the caste panchayat and family laws based on caste, which forced women to be dependent on men, he said. In Ambedkar's analysis of caste the analysis of women's subordination is subsumed. The bills he introduced from time to time reveal that he wanted to resolve the gender issue through laws. Hindu society could not reform itself, and hence law had to come to women's rescue. The issues that he raised in the Dalit women's conferences amply proved that he generated a sense of struggle among them.

Today, why are Dalit women subjected to double exploitation – of being Dalits and being women? Why are atrocities being perpetrated on a large scale on Dalit women? Why was the interconnection between caste and gender not brought to the fore and the category of 'Dalit women' figured neither in women's studies nor in caste studies? Why is the agency of upper caste women invoked in widely reported cases of violence against Dalit men? (Chundur in A.P. Gothala and Pimpri Deshmukh in Maharashtra are the cases in point). To address the complexities of caste and gender, Ambedkar's views are still relevant. If Ambedkar's emancipatory agenda is supplemented to the feminist discourse, it will go a long way in leading to the emancipation of all women in our society.

Notes

1. Veena Mazumdar, "The Social Reform Movement in India from Ranade to Nehru" in B.R. Nanda (ed.), *Indian Women: From Purdah to Modernity*, Vikas Publishing House, New Delhi, 1976, p. 64.
2. Ibid.
3. Pratima Pardeshi, *Dr. Ambedkar Ani Strimukti* (in Marathi), Savitribai Phule Prakashan, Pune 1996, p. 18.
4. Gail Omvedt, *Jotiba Phule Ani Stri Mukticha Vichar* (in Marathi), Lokvangmaya Griha, Mumbai, 1989; see also Saroj Kamble, *Strimukti Brahamani va Abrahmani*, Pardeshi, Pune, 1996.
5. Ibid.

6. Ambedkar addressed Dalit women at Mahad, the place where he waged a protest (satyagraha) for water in 1927.
7. Pratima Pardeshi, "The Women and the Counter Revolution". See also *Dr. Babasaheb Ambedkar: Writing and Speeches*, Vol. 3, pp. 429-37.
8. Suhas Palshikar, "Liberty, Equality and Fraternity in Ambedkar" in K.I. Vibhute (ed.), *Dr. Ambedkar and Empowerment: Constitutional Vicissitudes*, University of Pune, 1993, p. 40.
9. Sarojani Vaidya, "Dr Ambedkar's views on Women's Life". Paper presented in the seminar on "The Philosophical Legacy of Mahatma Phule and Dr Ambedkar", *Occasional Papers,* WRC, ICSSR, Mumbai, 1990.
10. See for details Jana Matson Everst, *Women and Social Change in India*, Heritage Publishers, New Delhi, 1979, p. 154.
11. As quoted by Gail Omvedt, "Hindu Code Common Code", *The Hindu,* 18 February 1988.
12. Ibid.
13. Changdeo B. Kharimode, *Dr. Ambedkar anni Hindu Code Bill* (in Marathi), Sugawa Publication, Pune, 1987, p. 61.
14. He made his speech at the conference of Dalit Mahila Federation in 1942 at Nagpur.
15. M.P. Mangudkar, *Dr. Ambedkar and Family Planning*, Suvarna Mangudkar, Pune, 1976.
16. Ibid., p. 6.

20 Dalit Emancipation through Education

K.S. CHALAM

The social demand for education during the last phase of the nineteenth century was an integral part of trade union movements. "Educate, agitate and organize" was the slogan of the Social Democratic Federation of H.M. Hyndman (1842-1921)[1] in England. He was largely concerned with parliamentary participation of the working class. Therefore, he and his fellow social democrats wanted that the working class should get necessary education so that they could be organized for achieving the legitimate demands of the day. During the same period, the British utilitarians, including Macaulay were instrumental in introducing liberal education in India through the Woods Despatch of 1854. It was this liberal education that brought western enlightenment in an Oriental society. It was this enlightenment that ignited the anti-Brahmin movement simultaneously in several princely states, including the Gaikwads of Baroda, Sahu Maharaj of Kolhapur, etc., and among "the Malis, drawn from within Maharashtra and also those who came from Andhra-the Kamathis".[2] Babasaheb Ambedkar is the direct spiritual heir of these two movements in Maharashtra. Naturally, the content of his ideology at least in the early part of his movement consisted of these elements, particularly the emphasis given by the princes as well as Mahatma Phule to education. In the written history of India we learn that it was Mahatma Phule after Sambuka and Ekalavya, who wanted the entry of non-Brahmins into the organized system of education. Phule gave a memorandum addressed to the Education Commission 1882, popularly known as the Hunter Commission, in which he indicated:

> There is little doubt that primary education among the masses in this Presidency has been very much neglected. ... I think primary education of the masses should be made compulsory up to a certain age, say at least 12 years. Under the promise of the Queen's Proclamation, I beg to urge that Mahars, Mangs and other lower classes, where their number is large enough, should have separate schools owing to caste prejudices.[3]

Phule and his wife Savitribai had already started schools for the untouchables at great risk of life and limb. This created a momentum in the educational development of Maharashtra, which Babasaheb wanted to strengthen and consolidate with the adoption of the slogan "educate, agitate and organize" through the Bahiskrit Hitakarini Sabha in 1924. Ambedkar clarified the objectives of the Sabha as:

> .... to bring about the uplift of outcastes, it is first necessary to awaken them. A community can progress only if it has developed a consciousness. As someone has put it, while the poor are certainly handicapped by their poverty, the real obstacle in their path is their inertia and their indifference! To overcome this inertia and indifference, it is necessary they should become charged with resentment of the injustice of their own condition. Without it, they cannot get rid of the factors that obstruct their progress.[4]

This appears to have been the broad consensus on which Ambedkar built his educational philosophy, which has been liberally adopted for the emancipation of the illiterate dalits in India.

Emancipation through Pedagogy of the Oppressed

Ambedkar's view about the need to educate the dalits is closely related to the ideology of the Brazilian educator Paulo Freire. Freire gave the justification for the pedagogy of the oppressed in the following words:

> How can the oppressed as divided, unauthentic beings participate in developing the pedagogy of their liberation? Only as they discover themselves to be 'hosts' of the oppressor can they contribute to the midwifery of their liberating pedagogy. As long as they live in the duality where to be is to be like, and to be like is to be like the oppressor, this contribution is impossible. The pedagogy of the oppressed is an instrument for their critical discovery that both they and their oppressors are manifestations of dehumanisation. Liberation is thus childbirth, and a painful one. The man who emerges is a new man, viable only as the oppressor-oppressed contradiction is superseded by humanisation of all men. Or to put it another way, the solution of this contradiction is born in the labour which brings this new man into the world: no longer oppressor or oppressed, but man in the process of achieving freedom.[5]

The pedagogy of the oppressed seeks to enter into a dialogue with people about their actions. The men who are engaged in the task of liberation or emancipation must begin to recognize themselves as oppressed and must be among the developers of this pedagogy. No education which is truly liberating can remain distant from the oppressed by treating them as unfortunates and by presenting for their emulation models from the oppressors. The oppressed must be their own example in their struggle for redemption or emancipation.

It is exactly in the same methodology that Ambedkar initiated his educational work among the wretched of the earth in India – the dalits. One can find a critical assessment of the situation made by Ambedkar as early as in 1924. But he put that ideology into action in 1927 at the Mahad water agitation, which is a watershed in the history of the dalit movement. Ambedkar made use of the occasion to educate the untouchable masses. He said:

> It is not as if drinking the water of the Chawdar Lake will make us immortal. We have survived well enough all these days without drinking it. We are not going to the Chawdar Lake merely to drink water. We are going to the lake to assert that we too are human beings like others. It must be clear that this meeting has been called to set up the norm of equality.[6]

More significant are his references to the French Revolution in the speech and the parallel he brought between the French society and the Indian caste system. He appealed to his listeners to see the significance of the Mahad meeting and the French National Assembly that met on 5 May 1789 at Versailles.

Ambedkar also mentioned the peaceful means through which the abolition of the caste system was possible. This was elaborated later in his unpublished writings and also in his last speech in Kathmandu in November 1956 on "Buddha and Marx". He said: "The Buddha's method was different. His method was to change the mind of man, to alter his disposition, so that whatever man does, he does it voluntarily without the use of force or compulsion. His central mean to alter the disposition of men was his Dhamma and the constant preaching of the Dhamma."[7] From the beginning, Ambedkar was of the opinion that the caste system and the associated evils including illiteracy were the creation of the wicked mind. Therefore, "the real remedy is to *destroy the belief*" [emphasis added] in the sanctity of Shastras".[8] The programme of action to destroy caste was also indicated in his advocacy of "annihilation of caste", which was largely a process of education. He extensively quoted his teacher and one of the greatest educationists of the twentieth century, John Dewy here: "A knowledge of the past and its heritage is of great significance when it enters into the present, but not otherwise. And, the mistake of making the records and remains of the past the main material of education is that it tends to make the past a rival of the present and the present a more or less futile imitation of the past."[9] One can see the relevance of these sentences today more than any time before in our educational pursuits.

Ambedkar as an Educationist

Ambedkar spent more than half of his life in the field of education as a student, scholar, teacher and builder of institutions. He served the education sector till 15 August 1936, the day on which he founded the Independent Labour Party, the first political party of the labourers in India, to contest general elections. In other words, out of his 65 years of eventful life, Ambedkar spent around 45 years in the service of education.

The people's education movement in this country was first started by Phule in the nineteenth century and Ambedkar was the direct heir to that movement. Therefore, the contributions of Ambedkar to the education sector are much more significant than his social and political contributions, considering that education will deliver long-lasting and permanent benefits to the community. It appears that Ambedkar's educational contributions have not attracted due attention from scholars and activists, though most of his followers still chant the slogan "educate, agitate and organize". If one is inclined to divide his movement into educational, social and political, the proportion of time, energy and intellect devoted by Ambedkar to education seems to be as significant as that given to the social and political aspects.

John Dewey's influence on Ambedkar appears to have been deep and permanent. Ambedkar claimed him as his mentor and quoted him in almost all his works relating to social and philosophical issues. Dewey was a pragmatist and humanist, a signatory to the first International Humanist Manifesto. He taught Ambedkar at Columbia University. Ambedkar seems to have realized the significance of democracy in human society due to his teacher's influence. Ambedkar quotes Dewey at several places in his works on social philosophy though he was also a student of Harold Laski in London.

Ambedkar's research till 1923 appear to be serious academic pursuits. His studies on currency and finance have been acclaimed as important contributions to the discipline of Economics during that period. Further, Ambedkar's methodology in approaching a problem is another significant contribution to the science. In all his serious writings, Ambedkar has adopted the deductive method, first approaching the issue from its historical context, explaining its theoretical underpinnings, and finally providing the necessary information and data in support of his arguments. The conclusions drawn by Ambedkar in these works are well supported by meticulous research. In this respect, his contributions as an academic researcher excel and are comparable to those of Dadabhai Nairoji and other first-generation economists of this country.

The little information available on Ambedkar as a teacher suggests that he was a popular teacher in Sydenham College of Commerce as Professor of Economics and also as a Professor of Jurisprudence in the Government Law College. Students from neighbouring colleges, it is said, used to attend his eloquent lecture sessions. He also worked as the Principal of Government Law College, Bombay. He used his practical experience as a teacher and administrator in discussing issues relating to education in the Bombay Legislative Assembly. He founded the Siddhartha College in Bombay in 1946 and Milind College in 1950 through the People's Education Society. He believed that without education the untouchables could make no progress. Education was important not only because it would help more and more of his followers to qualify for governmental jobs, but it was equally essential for gaining awareness of the social and political environment in which they functioned and which they had to fight.[10]

He advocated from the beginning of his public life for an ideal society that "should be mobile, should be full of channels for conveying a change taking place in one part to other parts. In an ideal society there should be many interests consciously communicated and shared". He knew that this conscious communication to share enlightened ideas was possible only through education. He also knew that the enlightened society should be based on liberty, equality and fraternity. He emphasized these principles in several of his public discourses and his evidences submitted before various committees formed by the colonial authorities to address these issues. More than that, he wanted to imbibe these values through a pedagogy that he devised to educate the masses.

Ambedkar's views on education seem to have remained invariable and were further strengthened in course of time as compared to his views on other issues wherein one can find some innovations. He was convinced that primary education is very important for the depressed classes as it provides the necessary background to enter into public life. He said: "We may forgo material benefits, of civilisation but we cannot forgo our right and opportunity to the fullest extent, as education is the greatest material benefit." Ambedkar was not parochial in arguing for more funds for primary education of the untouchables alone. He appealed to the government to provide more funds to develop primary education for all sections of the people. In his Legislative Council debates in the Bombay Assembly during 1927, Ambedkar made a historical appeal for grants for the education sector. Perhaps, he was the first economist in the country to calculate the costs and benefits of education. He has provided empirical examples to illustrate that investments made on education were much more beneficial than Back Bay Reclamation. Ambedkar said:

> I find that the increase in the number of pupils is certainly not commensurate with the increase of expenditure on education. If we take the statistics from 1916-17 to 1922-23, we find that the expenditure on education has increased by something like 100 per cent, while the increase in the number of pupils during the same period is only 29 per cent.... We have in this Presidency two departments, which, if I may say so, are working at cross-purposes. We have the Department of Education, the purpose of which is to mobilize the socialized people. We have, on the other hand, the Department of Excise, which is working, if I may say so, in the reverse direction. ... I plead that we should at least spend on education the same amount that we take from the people in the form of excise revenue. The amount of expenditure that we incur per individual in this Presidency on education is only 14 annas, but the amount of money that we recover in the form of excise revenue is Rs. 2-2-9 (Rs. 2.17). I think it is only fair that our educational expenditure should be so adjusted that we should spend on the education of the people as much as we take from them in the form of excise.[11]

This argument is still valid in terms of the excise duty contributed by the poor and the educational benefit that they receive from the government in return. In other words, no government should grudge in paying for the primary education of the people as they themselves are paying for their education through excise and other indirect taxes. Ambedkar pointed out that "the object of primary education is to see that every child that enters the portals of a primary school does leave it only at a stage when he becomes literate and continues to be literate throughout the rest of his life".[12] He also calculated the prevailing dropout rate at 82 per cent in primary education and lamented that if the same trend continued, society would lapse into illiteracy. The economist in Ambedkar argued:

> I therefore request the Honourable Education Minister to spend more money on primary education, if for nothing else at least for the purpose of seeing that what he spends bears some fruit ultimately. Sir, this argument is not very different from the argument that was urged from the official benches in the matter of Back Bay Reclamation. We were urged to spend money on Back Bay because we were told that if we do not spend more money on Back Bay, what we have spent would be an utter loss. I think, the same argument might be utilized in this case as well, and we can say that unless we spend a sufficient amount of money, to see that every child that enters schools reaches the fourth standard, what we have already spent upon him is of no purpose whatsoever.[13]

He also discussed educational finance and sources of finance of education. He criticized the government that a major portion of the expenditure on education, i.e., 31 to 36 per cent, was collected from the students by way of fees, which converted education into business.

Ambedkar's major contribution to the education sector in general and to the education of depressed classes in particular was his memorandum submitted to the Indian Statutory Commission in 1928 by the Bahishkrita Hitakarini Sabha. Quoting extensively from the report of the Board of Education and Hunter Commission, Ambedkar argued that Muslims were given their due share in the education sector by considering them as a minority. Similar benefits also needed to be extended to the depressed classes. He noted:

> I am not making this statement in any carping spirit nor grudge the efforts that government have made in the matter of the education of Mohammedans. I must here emphasize that this country is composed of different communities. All these communities are unequal in their status and progress. If they are to be brought to the

> level of equality, then, the only remedy is to adopt the principle of inequality and to give favoured treatment to those who are below the level. There are some I know who object to this and adhere to the principle of equality treatment. But I say Government has done well in applying the principle to the Mohammedans. For I honestly believe that equality of treatment of people who are unequal is simply another name for indifferentism and neglect. My only complaint is that Government has not yet thought fit to apply this principle to the backward classes. Economically speaking or socially speaking, backward classes are handicapped. I, therefore, think that the principle of favoured treatment must be adopted in their case.[14]

In the context of the recent controversy on reservations, it is necessary to make the anti-reservationists read these statements made by Ambedkar for its logical and rational argument developed in favour of equality of opportunity.

The education department is not a department, which can be treated on the basis of quid pro quo. Education ought to be cheapened in all possible ways to the greatest possible extent. I urge this plea, because I feel that we are arriving at a stage when the lower strata of society are just getting into high schools, middle schools and colleges and the policy of this department ought to be to make higher education cheaper to lower classes as it can be possibly made.

Ambedkar also commented on university education, including its administrative structure. He indicated that the objective of university education was to train students to enable them to distinguish between fact and opinion. The student, he said, should

(a) be accustomed to distinguish issues and to separate questions each on its own merits and without an eye on their bearing on some cherished theory;
(b) learn to state fairly the position to whose practical conclusions the learner is most stoutly opposed;
(c) be able to examine a suggested idea and see what came of it, before accepting or rejecting it, and
(d) develop an original thinking with the ability to weigh evidence, evaluate it and put his own value on authorities.[15]

In Ambedkar's view, a university is a corporation of scholars and a place of learning in the pursuit of advancement and diffusion of knowledge. In this context, he criticized the Bombay University, which did not fit into the above description of a university at that time. In his Assembly interventions during the Bombay University Amendment Act and through his written evidence before the University Reforms Committee in 1925, Ambedkar fully utilized the opportunity to express his ideas on higher education. He indicated that the primary function of a university was not merely to conduct examinations; it was an institution to provide opportunities to all capable people to develop their faculties.

Ambedkar argued for communal representation on the senate to control university affairs equitably. His idea of pooling the teaching resources of city colleges to avoid duplication and to improve efficiency is still valid. In most of our metropolitan cities dozens of colleges are offering similar courses and employing teachers with the same qualifications. Ambedkar therefore argued that if those resources were pooled, specialization in teaching could take place, which might ultimately benefit the students. He was seriously opposed to the distinction between undergraduate teaching and postgraduate teaching. He said:

> It is in the best interests of the university that the most distinguished of its professors should take part in the teaching of the undergraduates from the beginning of their university career. It is only by coming into contact with the junior students that a teacher can direct their minds to his own conception of his subject, and train them in his own methods, and hence obtain the double advantage of selecting the best men for research, and getting the best work out of them.[16]

This idea has freshness in its approach, especially in the context of the recent emphasis and orientation provided to college and university teachers. Ambedkar also proposed inter-collegiate teaching. He argued that teachers in the university should go to the affiliated colleges to teach and thus obtain experience. He was perhaps the first educationist who wanted power to be given to the academic council in matters of academic affairs in the university. He emphasized that a teaching university should really function as a teachers university in the sense that teachers hold all academic and administrative posts. However, he did not agree with the introduction of the post of rector as the functions of the vice-chancellor and that of the rector overlapped. In his evidence before the University Reforms Committee, Ambedkar gave a broad perspective plan for the development of university education. He emphasized that universities should be established in those places where the concentration of colleges was taking place. He proposed ten universities in 1926 in the country, including one at Karachi. Ambedkar was first to insist that the present development of the university departments on the lines of schools when Bombay University was being planned. In order to control the affiliated colleges, Ambedkar suggested that all seats in the colleges be processed through the university and the university should be involved in the payment of grants-in-aid to the colleges. Several other ideas of Ambedkar are quite relevant today to make the university system effective and accountable.

As an educationist, Ambedkar practised what he preached. He started the people's education movement by starting several colleges and educational institutions through the People's Education Society. Several groups of institutions were started in all fields of education at all levels under the auspices of this Society. As an educational historian, Ambedkar pointed out that the first scheme for untouchables was started in 1855 in Ahmednagar and the first application from an untouchable was received in June 1956 at Dharwar. He criticized the British for their discriminatory policy of providing education to the upper classes of society, including Brahmins. He argued that unless sufficient places in public employment were provided, the depressed classes did not have an incentive to get educated. Therefore, he proposed that scholarships and hostels be provided for the untouchable students, so as to encourage them to educate. Even in his Independent Labour Party manifesto, Ambedkar mentioned free and compulsory primary education. Perhaps it is the only party to date, which emphasized education in its election manifesto. Article 45 of the Indian Constitution, under the Directive

Principles, is the contribution of Ambedkar. It provides free and compulsory education to all, but our rulers are still negligent in fulfilling this obligation.[17]

Education as Investment

Ambedkar was perhaps the first Indian economist to capture the economic importance of education. During the Bombay Legislative Council budget debates on grants for education, he compared investment in education with that of the Back Bay Reclamation, with a futuristic orientation. In his written evidence before the Indian Statutory Commission on the State of Education of the Depressed Classes in Bombay Presidency, he strongly pleaded for the extension of the Hunter Commission recommendations regarding the education of the Mohammedans to the depressed classes. He argued that it was useless to make provision for higher education of the depressed classes unless steps were taken to ensure the growth of primary education.

In his memorandum on 'Grievances of the Scheduled Castes' submitted to the Governor-General on 29 October 1942, Ambedkar made a distinction between liberal arts and science and technology courses. He pointed out that education in arts and law cannot be of much value to the scheduled castes, either to the graduates themselves or to the people. It has not been of very high value, even to Hindus. What will help the *scheduled castes is education of an advanced type in science and technology* (emphasis added). But it is obvious that education in science and technology is beyond the means of the scheduled castes and this is why so many of them send their children to take up courses in arts and law.[18]

Without technical education, he said, their economic condition would not improve. The situation, however, has not improved even after independence, as indicated by the enrolment figures of scheduled castes in professional and technical courses, which remained less than 10 per cent of the total enrolment.[19]

Ambedkar was very emphatic about incorporating Articles 45 and 46 in the Constitution that provide for educational opportunities to weaker sections. Article 46 states that "the state shall promote with special care to the educational and economic interest of the weaker sections of the people and in particular of the scheduled castes and tribes and shall protect them from social injustice and all forms of social exploitation". The coefficient of equality estimated for scheduled castes and tribes at various levels of education during the 1980s by the Education Department of Government of India shows that it has not reached 50 per cent at higher education and it remained a distant dream even at the primary level.[20] This is because of the capitalist mode of socio-economic organization in India, according to Jagdish Bhagwati, who says:

> I do not believe that within the 'capitalist' mode of socio-economic organization, it is possible to eradicate significantly the inequalities arising in these ways. ... The inequalities arising from more intensive or higher quality education by the better off parents are again relatively intractable. Special quotas in the better schools for the poorer classes would help; but nothing really can be done to eliminate the advantage conferred on the children of the better off by private tuitions.[21]

It is in this context that one needs to understand the significance of Ambedkar's contributions for the educational development of socially and educationally deprived sections in particular and the ignorant masses of the country in general. Special strategies are to be devised, therefore, to make the scheduled castes and tribes fully utilize the constitutional provisions.[22]

The Future of the Ambedkar Project

Ambedkar was basically concerned about the educational development of the weaker sections as a means of achieving the goals of democracy in economic, political and social life. Ambedkar's life and mission itself is a case history of how education can shape a leader and the destiny of the people, whom he represented. His relentless struggle to bring education to the illiterate masses is now bearing fruits. However, these educational opportunities that are now limited to islands of interest groups leading to internal differentiation. This is what is expected from the limited progress made by dalits during the post-independence period. This happens with every social group. The Brahmins, for instance, did not enter the mainstream all at once throughout the country. But there is a systematic and rational approach in their collective action to reach their perceived goals. This is sadly absent among the dalits. It may be due to a lack of understanding of the educational project of Ambedkar or failure to apply his principles to the contemporary situation. It may also be construed as a neglect of developing institutional structures to carry on the work of Ambedkar. Except the caste associations created in the name of Ambedkar, no creative activity or educational programme was undertaken by the dalits during the post-Ambedkar period. There may be one or two exceptions here and there. Further, it is also due to the failure of the intellectual sections of the dalits to translate his project into action. It is much easier today with more than 5 lakh graduates and post-graduates studying in universities and colleges compared to around 1.5 lakh students in all educational institutions combined in 1891.[23]

The system could produce an Ambedkar with a low base of 1.5 lakh literate populations. And with a literate population of more than 5 crores today, one could expect a total transformation, if not emancipation of dalits.

Therefore, something is wrong with the scheme of things that has taken place during the last two decades, particularly after the advent of the new economic policy. Dalits are finding it extremely difficult to enter into the emerging modern sectors of employment, while more people are entering into the agriculture sector. Ambedkar had an answer for both these developments. He said: "Strange though it may seem, industrialization of India is the soundest remedy for the agricultural problems of India. Industrialization is a natural and powerful remedy and is to be preferred to such ill-conceived projects as we have considered above."[24] This is happening in India today without the concern of the dalits as they are now unqualified and alienated. One solution appears to be expanding the educational base of the dalits, particularly into the vocational and technical streams. This alone is not sufficient. This will create opportunities for individuals and not for the emancipation of dalits as a collectivity. This requires the original Ambedkar educational project of popular and mass based people's education movement. This is to be based on the philosophical underpinnings of his movement, starting with the annihilation of caste to Buddha and his Dhamma, incorporating the radical programmes of Mahatma Phule.

Notes

1. J.D. Bernal, *Science in History,* vol. 4, MIT Press, Cambridge, 1969, p. 1151.
2. M.S. Gore, "Social Movements and the Paradigm of Functional Analysis", in Ghanshyam Shah (ed.), *Social Transformation in India,* vol. I, Rawat, 1977, p. 98.
3. Government of Maharashtra, *Collected Works of Mahatma Jotirao Phule,* vol. II, Bombay, 1991, p. 122.
4. M.S. Gore, *The Social Context of an Ideology*, Sage, Delhi, 1993, p. 84.
5. Ibid.
6. Paulo Freire, *Pedagogy of the Oppressed,* Penguin, 1978, p. 25.
7. Arjun Dangle (ed.), *Poisoned Bread,* Orient Longman, Bombay, 1992, p. 225, from Dr. Ambedkar's Speech at Mahad.
8. Vasant Moon (ed.), *Dr. Babasaheb Ambedkar: Writings and Speeches*, vol. 3, Government. of Maharashtra, 1987, p. 461.
9. Ibid., vol. 1, 1979, pp. 22 and 68.
10. Ibid., p. 79 quoted from John Dewey.
11. M.S. Gore, op. cit., p. 209.
12. Vasant Moon (ed.), op. cit., vol. II, pp. 39-40.
13. Ibid.
14. Ibid.
15. Ibid., p. 42.
16. Ibid., pp. 296-297.
17. Ibid.
18. Ibid., p. 40.
19. Vasant Moon (ed.), op. cit., vol. 10, pp. 426-427.

20. K.S. Chalam, *Education and Weaker Sections*, Inter-India, 1988, pp. 130-131.

21. Government of India, *Progress of Education of Scheduled Castes and Scheduled Tribes, 1979-80,* Delhi, 1988.

22. N. Jagadish Bhagwati, *Wealth and Poverty*, Oxford, Delhi, 1985, pp. 201-202.

23. K.S. Chalam, *Educational Policy for Human Resources Development*, Rawat, 1993, ch. 26.

24. K.S. Chalam, *Education and Weaker Sections*, pp. 126-130.

Contributors

Y.S. Alone, Assistant Professor, School of Arts and Aesthetics, Jawaharlal Nehru University, New Delhi.

G. Aloysius, former Professor, Third World Academy, Jamia Millia Islamia, University, New Delhi.

Aryama, Lecturer, SGTB Khalsa College, New Delhi and a visiting faculty at Indian Institute of Dalit Studies, New Delhi.

K.S. Chalam, former Professor and Director of Academic Staff College, Andhra University, Visakhapatnam and currently member of Union Public Service Commission, New Delhi.

A. Gajendran, Research Scholar, Columbia University, USA

Gopal Guru, Professor, Centre for Political Studies, Jawaharlal Nehru University, New Delhi.

G. Haragopal, Professor of Political Science, Central University, Hyderabad.

Kancha Ilaiah, Professor, Department of Political Science, Osmania University, Hyderabad.

P.G. Jogdand, Professor of Sociology, Department of Sociology, University of Bombay, Mumbai.

Narender Kumar, Lecturer in Political Science, Motilal Nehru College, New Delhi.

Bhalchandra Mungekar, Member, Planning Commission, Government of India, New Delhi.

G. Nancharaiah, Professor of Economics and former Vice Chancellor, Babasaheb Ambedkar University, Lucknow.

Gail Omvedt, Director, School of Social Justice, University of Pune, Pune and former Professor, Department of Sociology, University of Pune.

Sudha Pai, Professor, Centre for Political Studies, Jawaharlal Nehru University, New Delhi.

Valerian Rodrigues, Professor, Centre for Political Studies, Jawaharlal Nehru University, New Delhi.

Ghanshyam Shah, former Professor, Centre for Social and Community Health, Jawaharlal Nehru University, New Delhi.

Sukumar, Assistant Professor, Department of Political Science, University of Delhi, Delhi.

Sukhadeo Thorat, Chairman, University Grants Commission, New Delhi.

Eleanor Zelliot, former Laird Professor of History, Carleton College, North Field, Minnesota (USA).

Index